The Steinbeck Question

The Steinbeck Question:
New Essays in Criticism

edited by
Donald R. Noble

The Whitston Publishing Company
Troy, New York
1993

Copyright 1993
Donald R. Noble

Library of Congress Catalog Card Number 91-75026

ISBN 0-87875-424-5

Printed in the United States of America

This book is for my daughters,
Julia Fern Noble
and
Jenny Claire Elizabeth Noble

Contents

Contributor's Notes

Michael G. Barry, SUNY-Buffalo, writes on political fiction of the 1940s, especially Robert Penn Warren.

Jackson J. Benson, San Diego State University, is the author of *Hemingway: The Writer's Art of Self-Defense* (1969), *The True Adventures of John Steinbeck, Writer: A Biography* (1984), and *Looking for Steinbeck's Ghost* (1988). He is the editor or co-editor of books on Hemingway, Steinbeck and Malamud and has published widely in journals and collections of essays.

Alan Brown, Livingston University (Livingston, Alabama), has published on Hemingway, Eliot and Ellison, among others.

Jeremy G. Butler, The University of Alabama (Department of Broadcast and Film Communication), is the editor of *Star Texts*: *Image and Performance in Film and Television*. He has published essays in such journals as *Jump Cut, Cinema Journal, Journal of Popular Film and Television, Journal of Film and Video* and *Film Reader*.

Sylvia J. Cook, University of Missouri-St. Louis, is the author of *From Tobacco Road to Route 66: The Southern Poor White in Fiction* (1976) and *Erskine Caldwell and the Fiction of Poverty*: *The Flesh and the Spirit* (1991), as well as numerous shorter pieces on the literature of the 1930s.

John Ditsky, University of Windsor, Ontario, is the author of *Essays on "East of Eden"* (1977), *The Onstage Christ: Studies in the Persistence of a Theme* (1980) and others. He has published volumes of poetry, scores of articles and hundreds of reviews in the field of modern American fiction.

Charles L. Etheridge, Jr., McMurry College (Abiline, Texas) writes on Steinbeck and literary naturalism.

Mimi Reisel Gladstein, University of Texas at El Paso, is the author of *The Ayn Rand Companion* (1984) and *The Indestructible Woman in Faulkner, Hemingway, and Steinbeck* (1986). She has published many shorter pieces on Steinbeck, Rand, Faulkner and others.

Charlotte Byrd Hadella, Arkansas State University, has published articles on Steinbeck and on William Gass.

Paul J. Hintz is a graduate student at Hamline University in St. Paul, Minnesota.

Robert S. Hughes, Jr., University of Hawaii at Manoa, is the author of *Beyond the Red Pony: A Reader's Companion to Steinbeck's Complete Short Fiction* (1987) and *John Steinbeck: A Study of the Short Fiction* (1988). He is also the author of many articles, notes and reviews on Steinbeck.

Michael J. Meyer, Concordia College (Wisconsin), writes on the moral dilemma of Americans in the fiction of John Steinbeck.

Robert E. Morsberger, California State Polytechnic University (Pomona), is the editor of Steinbeck's *Viva Zapata: The Original Screenplay* for the Viking Press (1975) and the author or editor of some nine other books on subjects as varied as Lew Wallace, Elizabethan stage swordplay and James Thurber. He has published some twenty articles on Steinbeck and scores of essays and reviews on a wide range of topics.

Donald R. Noble, the University of Alabama, is the editor of *A Century Hence or, A Romance of 1941* (1977), *Hemingway: A Revaluation* (1983), and *The Rising South*, with Joab L. Thomas (1976), and the author of numerous shorter pieces on twentieth century fiction.

Louis D. Owens, University of New Mexico, is the author of *John Steinbeck's Re-Vision of America* (1985), *The Grapes of Wrath: Trouble in the Promised Land* (1989), and the co-author of *American Indian Novelists: An Annotated Critical Bibliography* (1985). He has also published many articles and chapters of books on Steinbeck and fiction by Native Americans.

Dennis Prindle teaches at Ohio Wesleyan University and writes on American Fiction.

H. R. Stoneback, SUNY-The College at New Paltz, is the editor of *Selected Stories of Faulkner* (Beijing, China, 1985) and the author of many articles and essays on Hemingway, Faulkner, Durrell, Perse, Conrad and others.

John H. Timmerman, Calvin College, Grand Rapids, Michigan, is the author of *John Steinbeck's Fiction: The Aesthetics of the Road Taken* (1986) and *The Dramatic Landscape of Steinbeck's Short Stories* (1990). He is the author or editor of several other books on such subjects as fantasy literature and Frederick Manfred.

Introduction

I

In many important ways, the literary career of John Steinbeck was a straightforward and enviable one. Steinbeck found his vocation early, even before he took courses in fiction writing at Stanford University. After a respectably long, but not excruciating apprenticeship, Steinbeck had his first novel, *Cup of Gold*, published in 1929 and had the first of many best-sellers with *Tortilla Flat* in 1935. By the end of the 1930s Steinbeck had gone beyond being the author of best-sellers such as *In Dubious Battle* (1936) and become, in fact, a national figure. With the publication of *The Grapes of Wrath* in 1939 and the success of the movie in 1940, Steinbeck was a celebrity, one of those authors, like Hemingway or Fitzgerald, who are recognized wherever they go and are asked for their opinions on any subject, literary or not.

The Grapes of Wrath also brought the Pulitzer Prize and in 1962, Steinbeck received the Nobel Prize for Literature, most directly for *The Winter of Our Discontent* (1961) but, as is always the case, in fact for his lifetime achievement, especially the "social protest" fiction of the Depression decade.

The oeuvre is a large one. As Steinbeck fans know, there are some twenty-six volumes of fiction and nonfiction and they are all in print. Steinbeck also produced a quantity of journalism, some film scripts, several plays and a mass of correspondence. His work has been translated into dozens of languages and is read all over the globe today, selling annually several hundreds of thousands of copies.

What then is "The Question"? The Steinbeck question, as with all problems of this sort, is actually a collection of issues, mysteries and conundrums. For example, when, in an average year, his contemporaries and fellow Nobel Laureates, Faulkner and Hemingway, are each treated in perhaps 120 or 130 scholarly books and articles, why is Steinbeck the subject of only fifteen or twenty? Why is it that the work of this enormously popular author is disappearing from the pages of anthologies even faster than the work of Hemingway, Faulkner, Fitzgerald and other major figures of the traditional canon? Why has Steinbeck not received the intense academic scrutiny awarded his peers?

Why is it that Steinbeck, so clearly identified with social issues and causes in half a dozen books from *In Dubious Battle*, through *Of Mice and Men* and *The Grapes of Wrath* and beyond, is not the darling of the liberal academic community, now tenured into place? Why is it that Steinbeck, who worked closely with "Wild Bill" Donovan of the OSS (later the CIA) and who produced a large body of work especially for the Second World War "effort," a body of work some think to be virtual patriotic propaganda, including *The Moon Is Down, Bombs Away, Lifeboat* and *Once There Was a War*, is also not the darling of the academic right? This is further surprising when one considers that Steinbeck was on rather good terms with Lyndon B. Johnson and supported the American involvement in Vietnam.

These issues make Steinbeck seem to be the Lawrence Welk of American literature, the popular writer only millions of "regular people" like. Yet the Pulitzer and the Nobel, along with such prizes as the O. Henry Award for short fiction and the Drama Critics Circle Award make it clear that where judgments of quality were made, Steinbeck emerged a winner.

The very size of Steinbeck's oeuvre may be responsible for some problems. For example, have some works been, as it were, lost? Steinbeck's masterpiece, *The Grapes of Wrath*, may be the cause, overshadowing other work such as *The Moon is Down* or various of the short stories in *The Long Valley* or *The Pastures of Heaven*. Are there works of Steinbeck's which have *never* received a long look? What about lesser known works such as *Bombs Away, Cup of Gold, Lifeboat* or the film script for *Viva Zapata!*?

Are there works which have been examined and dismissed as failures of one sort or another which need to be looked at in a new way, having perhaps been misunderstood until now? *Burning Bright*, one of Steinbeck's hybrid play/novels, along with *The Moon is Down* and *Of Mice and Men*, has long been held in low esteem. Does it deserve better? Have we been reading it correctly?

For those pieces which are not, by nearly unanimous agreement, literary successes, pieces such as *Travels With Charlie*, might another look tell us *why* they fail, if they fail? And might not another look at the career *in toto* help us to understand why the work after World War II is not as high in quality as the work of the 1930s?

As with any established writer who has been the subject of critical discussion, there are elements in the work which were not on peoples' minds in earlier years, but are now uppermost. The representation of women is such an element, and considerable examination of this subject is useful and appropriate.

The volume at hand will not solve all these problems, will not answer all these questions, but attempts to make a start. These essays, all new and written for this volume, are by senior, established scholars in the field of Steinbeck studies and by newcomers. The essays are of course by writers young and old, by men and women, by critics from all geographical regions of the country. Some of the essays are sweeping in their scope, others focussed. Some are narrowly thematic, while others attempt to illuminate larger questions of Steinbeck's relation to the general culture, to music, to film, to previous literature. Taken together, this volume represents and attempts to answer as many parts as possible of the conundrum that is The Steinbeck Question.

II

In his lead essay to this volume, Jackson J. Benson, author of the standard Steinbeck biography, offers a few explanations for the state of Steinbeck's reputation. Westerners, he suggests, are often ignored by the Eastern intellectual establishment. Huge sales also undermine a writer's credibility as an *artiste*. Steinbeck, Benson reminds us, was too far left for the Hearst papers and for the publications of Henry Luce, but not far enough to please the true leftist press, socialist or communist. Having written comedy, and written it very well indeed in books like *Tortilla Flat*, Steinbeck opened himself up to not being taken seriously. Sometimes Steinbeck was accused of being sentimental, sometimes he was accused of writing propaganda. Taken collectively, it is enough to make one weep. Benson does a fine job of articulating the problem.

Dennis Prindle suggests that we may have misread Steinbeck right from his first novel, *Cup of Gold*. We have been so intent on seeing Steinbeck as a naturalist that we have missed his love of medieval literature, especially Arthurian legend, and overlooked his uses of allegory, romance and fable, especially in *Cup of Gold* but also in *To a God Unknown* and *Tortilla Flat*, and even in *In Dubious Battle* and *The Grapes of Wrath*.

Robert S. Hughes, who has devoted an enormous amount of attention to the Steinbeck short stories, offers an evaluation—which stories are his best—and an explanation as to why. Not surprisingly, Hughes rates "The Chrysanthemums," along with "Flight," "The Gift," "The Promise," and "How Mr. Hogan Robbed a Bank" at the top. What will surprise readers, however, is Steinbeck's indebtedness to his fiction-writing teacher at Stanford, Edith Mirrielees. Ms. Mirrielees gave students a basic rule to follow in writing a short story. Hughes argues, when Steinbeck followed the rule, his stories worked; when he didn't, they turned out flawed. Along the way, Hughes offers some fine explication of Steinbeck's best.

Continuing the discussion of Steinbeck's short fiction, Charlotte Hadella focusses on Steinbeck's cloistered women. She reminds the reader that Steinbeck meant to reproduce a kind of Garden of Eden in his fictional California Valley and that in order to achieve a sinless state, woman, the initiator of the original sin, must be chastised, purified, and controlled. Hadella discusses "The Harness," "Johnny Bear," "The Chrysanthemums," and other stories, demonstrating the dismal results, for men and women, of the arbitrary entrapment and isolation of the female.

Paul Hintz continues the discussion of the role of the female, focussing on *The Sea of Cortez* and *Cannery Row*. Hintz reminds us that the voice in each work is male and that the implied reader is male as well. The female is largely missing; even though there was one on board The Western Flyer, his wife, Carol, she is not mentioned. There are women in *Cannery Row*, but they are given little voice or, as in the case of the corpse Doc comes upon, no voice at all.

Mimi Gladstein has also noticed the absence of females in Steinbeck's work, but approaches the issue from another angle. She rejects the argument that Steinbeck's work contains few self-actualized, educated, independent women because his life contained few. Gladstein brings to our attention some of the many women of worth and achievement Steinbeck knew well. Steinbeck had an educated mother, several sisters, an important mentor at Stanford, Edith Mirrielees, an intelligent and forceful first wife, Carol, and a large number of female friends and acquaintances who were editors, writers, educators, and physicians. His agent, Elizabeth Otis, was friend and confidante. These women are notable for their absence from his fiction, where one often finds sentimental females or prostitutes. Gladstein offers a few answers as to why Steinbeck portrayed so few serious women in his fiction. He didn't understand women very well, he claimed. He also stated, in a letter to a woman friend, that women had been forced into predictable patterns of behavior, by men, and so were not useful to him as subjects. Steinbeck's fictional women don't represent the real women in his life, Gladstein concludes, and suggests that more serious biographical study of his life might one day yield more answers.

Along with Ma Joad and Dora the madame, the mysterious woman in "The Snake" is one of Steinbeck's most often discussed. Michael J. Meyer suggests that we might do better to make Doc the object of our study. Doc is an Adam figure, and his own ethical duality is at least partly revealed to him and the reader.

Michael G. Barry offers a new look at the most discussed Steinbeck work, The Grapes of Wrath. Previously, he believes, we have tended to see the novel as a study in polarities—rugged individualism vs. socialism, organism vs. mechanism, good vs. evil. Barry shows how Steinbeck is actually advocating "mediation." The Joad must, and do, accommodate to mechanism; they achieve a oneness with their Hudson. The Joads learn the uses of planning, abstraction and deferred gratification, all politically useful skills.

Sylvia J. Cook takes as her subject Steinbeck's poor people; indeed, the poor make up most of the cast of four novels, Tortilla Flat, Cannery Row, In Dubious Battle, and The Grapes of Wrath. In her essay, Cook discusses not only the differences between the poor of different novels, but also the distinctions among the poor in each novel. The poor were, without doubt, one of Steinbeck's major subjects and he recognized and demonstrated their multi-faceted nature. They could be simple and cunning, saintly and devious, violent, decadent, kind and generous, and no one knew them better than Steinbeck.

H. R. Stoneback, a professional folksinger and scholar, explores the relationship between Woody Guthrie and John Steinbeck, two men often connected in the public mind with the Dust Bowl and the Okies of the great Depression. First Stoneback discusses acutely the use to which Steinbeck put song in his novels, praising Steinbeck's deft inclusion of gospel and folk in *The Grapes of Wrath* and *In Dubious Battle*. He then concentrates on Guthrie and his career, asserting, surprisingly, that Guthrie may owe a lot more to Steinbeck than Steinbeck owes to Guthrie.

Of Steinbeck's many volumes of nonfiction, two travel books are the subject of Louis Owens' essay. *The Sea of Cortez* (1941) is regarded as an artistic success, though it was not a popular work. *Travels With Charlie* (1960) was a popular success, but is not highly regarded as a work of art. Owens examines the two works and suggests that in *The Sea of Cortez*, Steinbeck pursued what might be called an inductive method, revelling in the excitement of discovery. In *Travels*, the older, somewhat discouraged Steinbeck set out on his journey with preconceived ideas of what he would find, and, alas, he found it.

Although one may not think instantly of John Steinbeck when discussing writers of the Second World War, one certainly should. As Robert E. Morsberger shows us, Steinbeck wrote a novel, a play, three movies, two complete volumes of nonfiction, and parts of two more books, all concerned with the war. He was asked by William J. Donovan of the Office of Strategic Services to write the book that became *The Moon is Down*, and his contributions to the war effort, as a writer, lasted through *Bombs Away, Lifeboat, Once There Was a War*, and several other projects. Morsberger not only reminds us of the amount of Steinbeck's war writing, but examines the works in some detail, revealing Steinbeck's attitudes towards war, democracy, fascism, racism, and a number of other topics. Steinbeck and the Second World War is an area which will surely receive more study in the future.

Allan Brown devotes his essay to *Bombs Away*, but sees it differently. Where Morsberger believes *Bombs Away* to be a respectable, well-crafted book, Brown uses it as a means of explaining what he sees as the decline in Steinbeck's talents as the forties succeeded the thirties. Brown argues that Steinbeck learned, to his detriment, that he could write quickly and with minimum struggle by using the characters, devices, and themes he already had at his command. While Steinbeck did so in the service of his country, Brown says, it was at a considerable cost to his artistic integrity.

John Ditsky takes up the cause of the most-maligned Steinbeck work. *Burning Bright*, he insists, has never been judged on its own terms. To value it properly, we must understand that Steinbeck was attempting a variety of Epic Theater, as practised by Bertoldt Brecht. It is a mistake to find the piece failing in verisimilitude, as Steinbeck had consciously left realism behind. One honors this work most and understands it best, Ditsky insists, when one *emphasizes* its artifices, not when one tries to bring the piece back into line realistically by glossing them over.

Jeremy G. Butler discusses the movie production of *Viva Zapata!* made from Steinbeck's original screenplay and directed by Elia Kazan. Butler highlights the ironic relationship between the revolutionary content of the movie and Kazan's own cooperation with the House UnAmerican Activities Committee, and talks about the problems faced by revolutionaries in the film who succeed and are then faced with the corrupting influence of the power they have achieved. Butler places the film squarely in the context of the 1950s, that period in which traditional liberalism was beset by the powerful anticommunism of a nervous nation.

Charles L. Etheridge, Jr. takes up the subject of Steinbeck's naturalism, usually an issue when discussing *The Grapes of Wrath*, and instead studies the ways in which, as we understand better the complications and sophistication of Steinbeck's naturalism, our judgment of *East of Eden* also changes. It too is naturalistic, Etheridge says, but in the more subtle way we now understand Steinbeck to have meant.

The final essay in this volume is by John H. Timmerman, who takes up the issue of Steinbeck's reading and its influence upon his fiction. Over the years, a number of commentators have faulted Steinbeck for excessive "borrowings." Early in his career, Timmerman concedes, Steinbeck imitated other, successful writers. Later, however, any borrowings are thoroughly reworked, and Steinbeck makes any echoes or influences his own.

John Steinbeck:
The Favorite Author We Love to Hate

Jackson J. Benson

Pauline Pearson, who has worked with the John Steinbeck Library in Salinas, taping interviews with old-timers and locating historical sites, tells of the time when she took a group of Steinbeck enthusiasts on a tour of local points of interest. The bus stopped at the cemetery, and Pauline led a dozen people to the family plot and John's marker, where she began to give a talk about the author's death and burial. After a few minutes, right in the middle of her presentation, the sprinklers suddenly came on all around the group, getting everyone wet. Some groundskeeper was apparently registering his protest that John Steinbeck should be revered in this way by outsiders.

This small incident represents very well the mixed reaction that one of our most popular authors still evokes from people. John Steinbeck has made for himself a very special place in the hearts of many around the world—people seem to relate to him in a way, very personally and very emotionally, that they don't relate to other writers. He was a writer who not only created memorable stories, but he really cared about people, particularly the dispossessed and the persecuted.

This was a quality that the writer apparently had from childhood. Herbert Hinrichs, one of the very few people left in Salinas who remembers Steinbeck as a boy, recalls,

> If John could talk you into doing something, he delighted in that, especially if it got you into trouble. You wouldn't think John could show compassion at all. He was surly. He never laughed but he was always there to help somebody. He was always standing up for

> this one boy that the other kids picked on. One day, I
> asked him why. He said, "When you're down, some-
> one's got to help you." That was John. I've never for-
> gotten that.[1]

It is the genuineness of this caring, that he demonstrated throughout his life and in all of his work, that I think is the secret of his enduring appeal.

Some measure of this appeal can be seen in the thousands who come to the Steinbeck Library every year. Unfortunately, there is not much to see. The library has not had the money to expand, and so the first editions, manuscripts, letters and possessions of the writer must be displayed in a small room off of the main lobby, the bulk of the material stored in a basement vault. But people come from every state in the union and nearly every country in the world to stand and look in that small room, some with tears in their eyes.[2]

Visitors have included Ministers and members of parliament from several nations. Once, the librarians tell me, they observed a limousine which cruised around and around the block passing each time the front of the library. At last the automobile stopped, and a chauffeur got out and came into the library. The Ambassador from Japan, he said, would like to know if they could tell him anything about Steinbeck. Could they visit the house where he was born?[3]

The writer's appeal has been nearly world-wide and it has been strong. A book dealer in Denmark wrote to him to report that "a woman rowed in an open boat over eight miles to bring two chickens to my store to exchange for one of your paperback books" ("Our Man" 43). Once when he was in Paris, he had a visit at his hotel from an old French farmer who had travelled all night on the train in order to have the writer sample his wine (Benson 601). But the foreigners most attracted to Steinbeck have been the Japanese. One always wonders, however, how well an author's work can be translated into the language of a culture so very different from ours. Once when Elaine, Steinbeck's widow, was in Nagasaki, she asked an English-speaking bookstore clerk if he had any of her husband's books. "Oh yes," he said, "I have *Angry Raisins*."

Several hundreds of thousands of Steinbeck's books are sold every year (neither Viking nor the Steinbeck family will give out precise figures, but it has been estimated that *The Grapes of Wrath* sells two hundred thousand alone), and various books by him are required reading in high school and college classrooms across the country. But even more to the point, during the years I was working on the biography, I had so many people—from plumbers to librarians to electrical engineers—come up to me and tell me how much they enjoyed Steinbeck's work, that while I have no statistics to support it, my impression is that Steinbeck is nearly everyone's favorite author. And when he is loved, he is loved passionately.

Several years ago the National Endowment for the Humanities put out a list of the most important books a high school graduate should read. Citizens, including groups of well-known intellectuals and high school teachers attending NEH summer seminars, made out lists of the ten books they would recommend. These were compiled, the works ranked, and a list of thirty books then published by the National Endowment. The only twentieth-century writer to make the top ten was Steinbeck, whose *Grapes of Wrath* was ranked eighth (after Shakespeare, American historical documents, Mark Twain, the Bible, Homer, Dickens, and Plato) (Bencivenga n.p.).

I think it is significant that the other American writer singled out in the top ten is Mark Twain, since Twain and Steinbeck were both writers of the people, rather than writers that wrote to please the academy, and both have survived despite a great deal of snobbish disparagement over the years. Among literary scholars and critics generally, there is no doubt that Steinbeck's reputation is low, although not as low as it was in the 1960s. After I wrote my biography, it received a huge number of reviews, testimony to Steinbeck's continuing appeal, although many of the reviewers used the excuse of my book to express their disdain for the novelist. In *Newsweek*, for example, Walter Clemons wrote, "Fifteen years after his death, nearly all Steinbeck's books are in print [inaccurate—all of them are]; but until someone can make a stronger case for him, he will probably survive best as a classic young-adult author" (80). I suppose that Clemons felt he was assigning Steinbeck to the Siberia of teenage fiction, but I can't help but recall that was precisely what happened to the fiction of another Clemens—Samuel Longhorne—whose major works were for decades consigned to children's literature (although they were also often banned as presenting a corrupting influence).

Snobbishness is, of course, the curse of the literary and academic worlds, and Steinbeck has become, just as Thomas

Wolfe was for years, the goat of those who find satisfaction in playing the role of the cool, detached intellectual. I remember several years ago writing to a professor in the Midwest for some information about someone who knew Steinbeck. He replied that he would be glad to give me the information, but he was surprised to hear that anyone other than an undergraduate would be interested in Steinbeck's work.

A couple of years ago, a young high school teacher, Irvin Peckham, wrote a little essay for the *English Journal* called "Thank you, John" in which he mourned the fact that although he had an M.A. in English literature, he had never read a word of Steinbeck. Worse, he was taught by his professors to despise him:

> "Steinbeck? Are you kidding?" I said when someone asked whether I was including his novels in one of the cast-off courses I had inherited at Live Oak High School. Never mind that the course was called California Literature and that Live Oak was thirty miles north of Salinas, Steinbeck Country. "Who reads Steinbeck?" I said.
>
> Although I had been cloned in academia, I at least had the intelligence to discard the avocado green anthology of California Literature. Nosing around a dusty corner of the bookroom, I discovered a few copies of *Cannery Row*. I took one home, and I have been a Steinbeck addict since. He has added an immeasurable richness to my life and to the lives of my students, and that richness will spread.
>
> Back when we had money for new texts, I sneaked other Steinbeck novels into the curriculum over the protests of a well-meaning assistant principal who worried about the dirty language in *Of Mice and Men*. In a department littered with singletons, my one section of California Literature swelled into six, all of them packed . . . Steinbeck is [largely responsible] because he has a way of reaching out of his books, grabbing my students by their shirts and shaking them until they cut the bullshit and think and talk and write about things that really matter—their pride, their fear of censure, their repressed violence, their sexual confusion and desire, their loneliness and desperate need for love. (31)

Irvin Peckham is not alone in his experience. Your chances of reading Steinbeck in an English class in a major university are very low and in the Ivy League, practically zero. For example, I just got a letter from a friend who recently received her Ph.D. from Yale in American literature after graduating from Wellesley as an English major who wrote to me that she would never have read Steinbeck except that her husband is a marine biologist. Astounded that she, a teacher of courses in American literature, had never read Steinbeck, her husband and his scientist friends shamed her into reading *Cannery Row*, and that in turn led her to read the rest of the novels. Steinbeck is still included in American literature anthologies, but he is represented so meagerly that one has the feeling that it is a kind of tokenism. And now that it is the fashion to include more women and ethnic writers—which is, I think, generally a good trend—Steinbeck, unfortunately, will probably be one of the first white males to be left out.

The problem for the anthologists is that in addition to his continuing popularity, he remains historically so important—he is *the* spokesman for the thirties, as well as having written perceptively about other periods in our recent history. One measure of the mixed feelings held by anthologists toward Steinbeck can be seen in the explanatory material provided by Blair, Hornberger, Miller, and Stewart who edited the Scott, Foresman *The Literary History of the United States* (I quote here from the abstraction of interchapter material published as *American Literature: A Brief History*). Their comments are largely condescending, particularly toward the later work:

> Steinbeck . . . maintained his popularity, although most critics found his work after *The Grapes of Wrath* inferior and uneven. Some surprise was expressed when he was awarded the Nobel Prize in 1962. The public, however, followed him faithfully through *East of Eden* (1952), *Sweet Thursday* (1954), *The Winter of Our Discontent* (1961), and a number of lesser pieces, widely circulated in paperback. (259)

(Note that some of the author's best work is not included on this list: *Cannery Row* [1945], *The Pearl* [1947], and *The Log from the Sea of Cortez* [1951].)

At the same time as they heap scorn on his later work and consign him to cheap paperback popularity, the anthology editors turn to Steinbeck in order to describe the spirit of the post-WWII period:

> The development of technology in the last few
> decades, however, has unquestionably added to world-
> wide anxiety about the future. Can the instruments of
> death be destroyed or banned? Can the vast new sources
> of power be used to improve the human condition rather
> than to set the stage for a world-wide holocaust?
> These are questions which all Americans, and all
> thoughtful and informed men everywhere, continue to
> ask. Their effect upon the American psyche is well
> summed up by the central character in Steinbeck's *The
> Winter of Our Discontent*. (246)

The editors go on to quote a paragraph from the novel. Am I the
only one who sees a certain contradiction in all of this?

The main factor that seems to cause such mixed signals is
that scorn of Steinbeck is not so much a matter of discriminating
taste or the result of reasoned rejection, as it is a matter of fashion. Just as some people have to wear certain name brand T-
shirts or jeans with a label or logo prominently displayed on
breast or hip in order to assure their status, so, too, academics
have to assure their status by showing they know what's in and
what's out, what's hot and what's not. How did Steinbeck get on
the "out" list? I think it has been a combination of factors. First,
he is a Westerner, and Western writers have always had a hard
time impressing the Eastern establishment critics. Second, he
was a popular writer, and academics have always been suspicious (and perhaps jealous) of popularity. Third, he has written
comedies, and few writers of comedy are ever considered important. Fourth, he has been accused of being sentimental, which is
the worst of literary sins. And fifth, although he personally was
nearly apolitical in his approach to his work, it has frequently
been judged not on literary, but political grounds.

Steinbeck was a Western writer in a country that still, after
two hundred years, looks to the East coast for cultural guidance,
and with an Eastern literary establishment that looks to Europe
to set its fashions. One wonders what Mark Twain would say
about Jacques Derrida. Let me give you an example of this
prejudice in regard to Eastern treatment of a Westerner. I am
currently working on a critical biography of another author—
Wallace Stegner. He is an extremely accomplished author who
lives in California, who usually writes about the West, and who
has received just about every award and honor a writer can be
given except the Nobel Prize. Of the two novels which were
given major prizes, *Angle of Repose* for the Pulitzer and *The*

Spectator Bird for the National Book Award, neither was reviewed at the time of publication in the *New York Times Book Review*. Just a year ago at the age of 78, he published his eleventh novel, a marvelous one, called *Crossing to Safety*. It was reviewed by Doris Grumbach, who praised it inordinately, but the review was safely tucked away in the back pages—on page 14, as a matter of fact. Can you imagine a book by Updike, or Roth, or Mailer receiving that kind of treatment?

In writing about Steinbeck, two of our most prestigious critics, Edmund Wilson and Alfred Kazin, have both declared that it is impossible for any novelist writing out of and about California to produce great literature. The tradition is too short-lived and diverse and the culture too thin. You may not care for California, but such a statement would be stupid if applied to *any* state or region of the country. Regardless of its stupidity, the judgment has stuck and influences still the Eastern media and, in turn, academics all across the country.

In our book culture, one finds several obvious paradoxes. One is that unless a writer is discovered and trumpeted by the media, his career may, like Stegner's, languish. Appearing on the cover of *Time* and *Newsweek* did more for John Cheever's career than any number of literary awards. On the other hand, if you become a media darling, as Ernest Hemingway or Truman Capote were for many years, the literary establishment becomes irritated with you. The same thing is true of sales and popularity. If an author does not have at least one great popular success, he or she may well be ignored by reviewers and academics, but if he or she is constantly popular, the critics become suspicious of the writer's serious intentions. Steinbeck had the good luck, from a financial point of view, of having nearly every book he wrote, starting with his fourth, *Tortilla Flat* (1935), sell well, even though he never wrote fiction with an eye on potential sales and never used his serious work to try to make money. But as the quality of his work generally declined in his later years, he had the bad luck, in terms of his reputation, of continuing to hit the best-seller lists.

Even a book like *The Short Reign of Pippin IV*, which he wrote as a tongue-in-cheek experiment and which he thought would have almost no sales at all, was, much to his amazement—and amusement—chosen as a Book-of-the-Month Club selection. The popularity of such works led the critics to accuse him of writing junk to please a mass audience, and the author, feeling put-upon by a barrage of criticism, began to wish for more modest sales, particularly for works that in retrospect he realized had not achieved the artistic success he had aimed for. What argues against the idea of Steinbeck as a writer of potboilers is his seriousness of purpose, even in a light and funky—too funky, as it turned out—comedy such as *Sweet Thursday*, as well as his dedication throughout his life to the art of fiction. What is both amusing and a bit sad is that Steinbeck—who had comparatively little ego and almost no snobbishness—himself looked down on the sort of best-selling author that he was often taken to be.

In addition to the popularity which undermined his reputation, there was the extensive use of his books in junior high and high schools which suggested to elitist critics and academics that his work was simple-minded and fit only for younger, less sophisticated readers. As *The Grapes of Wrath* became more and more often a part of the high school curriculum, colleges and universities tended to shy away from it, partly for fear of repeating material already studied, but also because they came to believe that such adoptions demonstrated that the novel was not college-level material.

Another strike against the author's reputation is that we have a tendency to discount the work of anyone who writes comedy. Neil Simon, no matter how well he writes, will never be taken seriously—or *as* seriously as Tennessee Williams or Arthur Miller—by the literary establishment. Frequently discarded or overlooked, Steinbeck's comic trilogy—*Tortilla Flat*, *Cannery Row*, and *Sweet Thursday*—is not even considered as part of the canon by some critics. The scorn heaped upon *Cannery Row* at the time of its publication came largely, in my view, for political reasons and suggests why all the comedies have been viewed so negatively: in brief, the author was thought to be trivializing serious social problems.

While the fantasy-comedy of *Tortilla Flat*, an early work, was largely forgiven, the fantasy-comedy of *Cannery Row* aroused outrage—not too strong a word—among those who felt the author had abandoned his social responsibility. The book was called inconsequential; it "smells," one reviewer declared, "of fish and reeks with kindness" and was "as sentimental as a book can be" (*Commonweal*). "Sentimental" is the ultimate pejorative in modern literary criticism, tending automatically to disqualify anything tinged with it from further serious consideration. The term has stuck to Steinbeck, partly because his themes, even when they were recognized, seemed irrelevant to Eastern, urban critics, and partly because he was, in fact, sentimental at times.

As I said at the beginning, we value Steinbeck precisely because he was a kind and compassionate man who cared deeply for people in trouble. But this sense of caring can occasionally degrade his fiction when it lapses into mere tearful sadness. If there is one episode in *Cannery Row* that qualifies as sentimental, it is Chapter 10, concerning the mentally retarded boy, Frankie, who wants so desperately to please, but who cannot deal with society's rules. Designed to break the reader's heart with the injustice of Frankie's fate, the segment reflects two themes that are almost Steinbeck obsessions: society's failure to accept the handicapped on their own terms, and the intolerance and hypocrisy of respectability. Here, as occasionally elsewhere, the author's emotions have led him into artistic excess.

What saves this artist from constant excess is that his compassion is, in much of his writing, balanced and disciplined by a very objective view of the world and of man. Although not an expert, he wrote out of a more-than-casual knowledge of biology, anthropology, and astronomy, and a biological-ecological view of man's nature and place dominated his thinking. He saw mankind not at the center of creation, but as just another species, one, which, after the advent of nuclear weapons, he had little faith would survive its own "self-hatred," as he called man's propensity toward war, terrorism, and brutality. When, for example, he writes of the plight of Lennie and George in *Of Mice and Men*, he does so with a strange mixture of compassion and distance. There is no motivation for social reform behind the novelette at all—simply the presentation of a story, of a "Something That Happened," as he first called his manuscript. It was the social reformers who made this, a very deterministic picture of man's fate, a novel which calls for social action.

On this basis, one might be inclined to believe that for the most part, those who have felt that Steinbeck has "sentimentalized the folk," to use Richard Hofstadter's phrase, have brought their own sentimentality with them. As early as *In Dubious Battle*, Steinbeck showed that he had no illusions about the dispossessed whom he presents in that novel as sometimes careless, greedy, and easily manipulated. Although the tourists that flocked to Monterey after the publication of *Tortilla Flat* may have considered the *paisanos* as quaint or cute, that did not reflect the author's attitude, which was one of distanced respect for their dignity and for their best attributes in a grasping, materialistic society.

The paisanos, like the down-and-outers of *Cannery Row* and *Sweet Thursday*, are material not for the sociological study or political tract that the Marxists would have desired, but for fables which alter our perspective so that we might re-examine our values. What bothered the political-minded was that these works, dealing with the dispossessed in our society, were essentially apolitical. Accusing the author of sentimentality, leftists would have substituted their own brand: the melodrama of the proletarian novel with its noble workers and wicked bosses.

"Perspective" is a key word here, for Steinbeck's fiction invariably asks us to step out of our traditional way of looking at things to take another point of view. We might note that in *Cannery Row* Doc is given a microscope and in *Sweet Thursday*, a telescope, so that the whole range of seeing is thereby covered. The range is crucial, for what leads Steinbeck to object to politics, in the immediate, short-sighted sense, is its narrow view of the world. We should stop and look and consider as the scientist would, and we should approach life with the scientist's objectivity and distance. For Steinbeck, one can be detached in his observations on the one hand, while at the same time express compassion on the other. This combination, which has been often mistaken by negative critics of Steinbeck for sentimentality, is really quite the opposite when examined closely. Detachment and compassion together are major components of an overall attitude toward the universe—nature, including that speck of dust called "man"—which Steinbeck calls "acceptance."

To "accept," in the sense that Steinbeck employs it, is to stand aside from all those factors that limit our vision and confine our sympathies and to see people and events within the indefinite continuums of time and space. It is to be broadminded in the largest possible sense. Contrary to the behavior of the weepy-eyed, sentimental liberal, the person who practices acceptance is open-eyed and realistic—he or she not only casts aside preconceptions and prejudice, but also looks to see people and events clearly for what they actually are. Sentimentality, within Steinbeck's scheme, is simply another avoidance, another self-deception, another mode of categorizing so that we can feel righteous or superior. We would do well not to

approach Mac and the boys from the motives of the do-gooder or
naive bleeding heart, for we are likely, first, to be taken to the
cleaners and then, second, shocked by their independence and
ingratitude.

One of the great ironies of Steinbeck's career was that
although he was only mildly political in life and almost apolitical in his approach to writing, his work was very often judged
from a political point of view. From nearly the beginning of his
career, with the publication of *In Dubious Battle* in 1936, reactions to his work, condemning him in the most abusive terms,
have come from both the right and the left. For Steinbeck's
home region, an ultra-conservative rural area, the writer had
"betrayed his class" by deserting the upper-middle class Republi-
canism of his parents to embrace the plight of the despised and
dispossessed. One can only think that it has been greed that has
led a dozen very wealthy lettuce growers in the Salinas Valley to
resist tooth and nail, for over sixty years, anything that might
improve the lot of their workers, and greed that has led to
their abiding hatred of the author who told their workers' story.
Much of the public, throughout the author's career, automatically associated him with Communism, although he was
never a Marxist and never endorsed its doctrines. It is a sad
commentary on our society that anyone who takes the part of
the underdog, the powerless, and the persecuted should so often
be tarred with the blackest brush in our political vocabulary.

While throughout his career he was attacked by the conservative press—Randolph Hearst's newspaper chain, Colonel
McCormick's *Chicago Tribune*, Norman Chandler's *Los Angeles
Times*, and Henry Luce's *Time* magazine—he was also squeezed
on the other side by expressions of snobbish disdain by liberal intellectual journals, particularly the *New Republic* and *The New
York Times Book Review*. He was too liberal for the right and
not liberal enough for the left, and I think this had a profound
effect on his reputation, since throughout most of his career the
print media was essentially conservative, and disapproving, and
many of the most influential critics in the Eastern literary establishment were Marxists or sympathetic to Marxism, and disapproving.

The novels that caused the most political furor, *In Dubious Battle* and *The Grapes of Wrath*, were not written out of political motives and came out relatively early in the author's career, yet the political labels attached to him then followed him

for the rest of his life. For over thirty years *Time* expressed its antagonism for him as a "proletarian" writer (a code word for communist) and never gave him or his work a kind word until it wrote his obituary. It is hard to imagine the depth of hatred for Steinbeck held by someone on that magazine, presumably Henry Luce, which would feed on itself and fester for so long, so consistently. On the other hand, leftists, who tended to applaud his early writing and who tried to use Steinbeck for their own purposes in whatever way they could, scolded him when he turned away from the subject of farm labor.

For example, Stanley Edgar Hyman wrote that he began to lose interest in Steinbeck after the shift in "social commitment" as marked by *Of Mice and Men* versus *The Moon is Down*. That shift away from social commitment seemed to him confirmed by *Cannery Row*, which he found "merely an insipid watering down of Steinbeck's engaging earlier book *Tortilla Flat*." "I stopped reading him," he adds. Later, however, he was sent *The Winter of Our Discontent* for review but decided that it was "far too trivial and dishonest a book to waste space on." Then when he learned of the Nobel Prize, given in response to Steinbeck's recent publication of *Winter*, he found the choice and its occasion incredible. He reread the book and found it confirmed his earlier impression of it. "It is the purest soap opera, a work of almost inconceivable badness." When he discovered on the dust jacket that the book had been praised by Lewis Gannet and Saul Bellow, Hyman declared that "to assume their honesty I must disparage their intelligence" (113).

As if this were not nasty enough, liberal-radical attacks on Steinbeck in his late years were particularly acrimonious. During the early years of the Vietnam War he was only one of many writers and correspondents who tended to have hawkish views. Yet, the bitterest commentary was reserved for Steinbeck—the Marxists were particularly upset with him for acting what was, in their minds, a traitor. They had the gall first to make him a Marxist, which he never was, and then to accuse him of betraying that which they had made him out to be. Peter Collier, for example, compares him to Ezra Pound during WWII and thus presumably to Pound's fascism and giving of aid and comfort to the enemy. This is a very peculiar comparison when one considers that Steinbeck's "crime" was *support for* American troops fighting under difficult circumstances in a foreign war. Most of the time, Collier insists, Steinbeck sounds "like a naive political hireling mouthing platitudes." Steinbeck's betrayal comes down to this: "It is unaccountable that Steinbeck should not be able to see how similar these Vietnamese peasants are to the Joads" (61). Regardless of how one feels about the Vietnam War, its rights and wrongs, which were plentiful on both sides, it is difficult not to ask how many times the Joads set off a Claymore at a crowded bus stop or threw grenades into a restaurant filled with women and children. The aftermaths of two such incidents were witnessed by Steinbeck as a war correspondent—hospital wards filled with screaming children, many of whom were missing at least one limb.

Now that the author is dead, the political attacks on his books continue, coming now particularly from the New Right, the Moral Majority, and allied groups that have worked to ban or censor books that do not fit their political agenda. In addition to objections to realistic uses of language, to any depictions of sexuality, and to any questioning of the traditional role of women, they have also objected to any material that points out injustice and turmoil in American history.[4] Needless to say, John Steinbeck has been one of their favorite targets. While a number of challenges have been made on the basis of language, there is reason to believe that this is a smoke screen for attacking books that in the view of the New Right undermine faith in the free enterprise system.

Irvin Peckham, the high school teacher I quoted earlier, speaks of the fear of dirty language in *Of Mice and Men*, and both it and *The Grapes of Wrath* have been banned every year by school districts, from the classroom or the library, and by public libraries all across the country. But these are not the only Steinbeck books banned, and they are not banned just in the provinces by backwoods school boards. In 1980 *The Red Pony* was banned by a school district in New York because it was "a filthy, trashy sex novel."[5] Steinbeck has had the dubious distinction, usually having two books on the most-banned lists published annually by library and publisher associations, of probably being the most banned author in the nation.[6] In 1988 *Of Mice and Men* led the lists.[7] Of course, such wholesale negative reactions to his work would not be possible if his books were not so admired and frequently taught. Once again we are brought back to our thesis—that while John Steinbeck may be our most beloved author, he is also, by all evidence, the most hated.

In defending Steinbeck from what I believe to be prejudice

and misunderstanding, I don't mean to imply blanket approval for all his work or all of his ideas. Some of the things he wrote, particularly at the beginning and the end of his career, were failures or only partial successes. He took a lot of risks in his work, and as a result the quality of his fiction is very uneven. But whatever else one might say, one must note that he has written one book, *The Grapes of Wrath*, which seems destined to join *Moby Dick, The Scarlet Letter, The Adventures of Huckleberry Finn,* and *The Red Badge of Courage* as an American classic.

Frank Kermode, in his study *The Classic: Literary Images of Permanence and Change,* distinguishes two types of classic works of literature: the work that encapsulates an era and thus allow us to reenter it mentally and the work that states our basic humanity so well as to triumph over time and space (43-44, 130). It seems to me that *The Grapes of Wrath* performs both functions admirably. There is no doubt in my mind that Faulkner and Hemingway are two great American writers of prose fiction in our century. Yet, I cannot think of a work by either, taken alone, which has a chance to achieve the status that *The Grapes of Wrath* seems to be achieving. Almost exactly fifty years after its publication, Steinbeck's novel has demonstrated a remarkable staying power, transcending its original categorization as a propaganda novel or social document. No other novel of this century seems quite so typically American. No other American novel of our time seems so firmly planted on land while it reaches out, not for the American dream in a small sense, but the dream of our founders, a vision of liberty and justice for all.

Notes

[1] Ellen Uzelac. "Salinas Tries to Remember Its Once Least-Favorite Son." *The Sacramento Bee* 17 August 1988, final ed.: D6.

[2] John Gross, Director, Salinas Library, personal interview, 3 February 1989.

[3] Mary Gamble, Steinbeck Archivist, John Steinbeck Library, personal interview, 6 February 1989.

[4] Heather Dewar. "Decade of the Censors?" *The Commercial Appeal* (Memphis, Tennessee) 29 May 1983: G1.

[5] Maury Chauvet. "Bookstore Celebrates the Freedom to Read." *The Daily Aztec* (San Diego State University), (clipping) n/d: 1.

[6] See monthly *Newsletter on Intellectual Freedom*; and the yearbook *Banned Books Week 1981 [yearly to 1988]: Celebrating the Freedom to Read*

(Chicago: American Library Association, 1981-1988).
    [7] "Censorship Continues Unabated; Extremists Adopt Mainstream Tactics." *Newsletter on Intellectual Freedom*, November 1989: 193.

Works Cited

Bencivenga, Jim. "Must-Read List for High School." *The Christian Science Monitor* (clipping) n/d: n/p.

Benson, Jackson J. *The True Adventures of John Steinbeck, Writer*. New York: Viking Press, 1984.

Blair, Walter, Theodore Hornberger, James E. Miller, Jr., and Randall Stewart, eds. *American Literature: A Brief History*. Glenview, IL: Scott, Foresman and Company, 1974.

Clemons, Walter. "Cursed by Success." *Newsweek* 6 February 1984: 80.

Collier, Peter. "The Winter of John Steinbeck." *Ramparts* July 1967: 61.

Grumbach, Doris. "Crossing to Safety." *The New York Times Book Review* 20 September 1987: 14.

Hyman, Stanley Edgar. "John Steinbeck and the Nobel Prize." *Standards: A Chronicle of Books for Our Time*. New York: Horizon Press, 1966.

Kermode, Frank. *The Classic: Literary Images of Permanence and Change*. New York: Viking, 1975. I am in debt to Louis J. Budd's "Introduction" to *New Essays on "Adventures of Huckleberry Finn"* (New York: Cambridge University Press, 1985): 6, for this definition.

"Our Man in Helsinki." *The New Yorker* 9 November 1963: 43, 45.

Peckham, Irvin. "Thank You, John." *English Journal* 75.7 (1986): 31-32.

Review of *Cannery Row*. *Commonweal* 26 January 1945: 379-80.

The Pretexts of Romance:
Steinbeck's Allegorical Naturalism
from *Cup of Gold* to *Tortilla Flat*

Dennis Prindle

The rise of the new naturalist fiction between the wars has usually been seen as the ascendancy of an aggressive modernism over inherited tradition. Hemingway, Dos Passos, Farrell, Steinbeck—with their passion for the raw and immediate, these young authors once seemed a wholly new force in our literature, inimical to everything cooked and conventional, and a clear break with the traditions of an older generation. The critics did not inquire much into possible interactions between these writers and the more genteel traditions they displaced. In fact, the presumed estrangement between the two groups was accepted almost as a critical tenet about American literature generally. Henry James, tradition and the Eastern literary establishment all stood at one extreme, it seemed, while naturalism, keeping company with Western naifs and radicals like Twain, Norris, Jack London and Steinbeck, represented the ultimate repudiation of literary tradition and artifice at the other.

Philip Rahv termed the two camps Paleface and Redskin, the one making a fetish of tradition, the other constituting a cult of experience. Following Edmund Wilson and others, Rahv found this "dichotomy between experience and consciousness" a debilitating rift in our literature (Rahv 1). "The paleface," Rahv observed, "continually hankers after religious norms, tending toward a refined estrangement from reality. The redskin, on the other hand, accepts his environment, at times to the degree of fusion with it" (2). As to form, the corollary was that the genteel "paleface is drawn to allegory and the distillations of symbolism, whereas the other inclines to a gross, riotous naturalism" (Rahv 1-2). Inevitably, in this view, Steinbeck was the redskin, at first a regionalist identified with a particular environment, later a high priest of naturalism proclaiming the primacy of instinct and environment generally over the claims of tradition and culture.

So sensitive was this older view to Steinbeck's naturalism that today what seems so striking about this criticism is its blindness to the strong vein of allegory and fabulation in Steinbeck's work. As Peter Lisca and others demonstrated for the next generation of Steinbeck's critics, the rawness of the migrants' unself-conscious experience in *The Grapes of Wrath*, which Edmund Wilson compared to the movement of "a flock of lemmings on their way to throw themselves into the sea," is powerfully mediated by the pervasive role of Steinbeck's Exodus theme and other appropriations of biblical language and motifs (Wilson 42). Today, in fact, the Steinbeck question need not be whether his work collapsed toward one of the poles of naturalism or tradition, but whether he succeeded in repeatedly devising strategies to connect them. For while Steinbeck, especially in early novels, features the behavior of characters driven by instincts and necessities resistant to the traditional values of society, he does so in a framework of myth and symbol that asks us to locate that behavior in relation to older, still more traditional paradigms of culture, such as the quest for the Holy Grail or the patriarchal narratives of the Old Testament. Thus narrative form in Steinbeck's novels is tied to some of the most basic myths informing the dream of culture in the west, or what in America Rahv characterized as the paleface hankering after religious norms and spiritual value. Within this narrative form, however, Steinbeck's protagonists are free to answer to the imperatives of nature and environment, and thus to make us as readers reconsider our understanding of the traditional myths and cultural paradigms they reenact.

Modern fictions rendering problematic the romance of old myths and symbols, particularly those of Arthurian romance, did not begin with Steinbeck, of course. They are very much in the grain of the late nineteenth-century medievalism in America and, surprisingly enough, of naturalism itself. Like other writers coming of age in the first decades of this century, indeed like Zola and Frank Norris in the first generation of naturalists before him, Steinbeck began writing under the influence of a medieval revival that continued to appropriate the once genteel traditions of Arthurian romance and allegory, adapting them for new purposes well into the new century.[1] Reshaping those older traditions to the demands of an increasingly naturalistic vision was for Steinbeck a continuing and individual struggle. Yet it took place in a literary context. In what follows I am considering some ways in which both Arthurian romance and allegory—"the distillations of symbolism"—were repeatedly refashioned, rejected or re-appropriated in the early work of John Steinbeck.

The literary context for this reconsideration of Steinbeck's early novels can be briefly sketched here. Our understanding of the medieval revival in late nineteenth- and early twentieth-century American culture has become more complicated in recent years, and so, on the other side, has our thinking about Steinbeck and naturalist fiction. T. J. Jackson Lears' study, *No Place of Grace*, for example, finds that the genteel turn-of-the-century enthusiasm for the dream of culture in idealized medieval forms is but one part of a larger reaction to the strains of modern society, producing not just the genteel dissent of a self-conscious arts and crafts movement but a popular vogue for knighthood and codes of chivalry in everything from temperance societies to jingoist poetry and pulp fiction, including children's novels.

Meanwhile, the concept of literary naturalism as a mode resistant to literary convention has been challenged, both in general and specifically as a characterization of Steinbeck's work.[2] Today Steinbeck is more often recognized as a writer who combined a biological vision of his material with a penchant for the modes of romance and allegory that persisted throughout his career, from his first novel, the historical romance *Cup of Gold*, through repeated reworkings of the Arthurian legend, to the allegorical fable of *The Pearl* and his unsuccessful attempt at a modern morality play, *Burning Bright* (originally titled "Everyman"). Of Steinbeck's interest in biology much has been written. Less has been made of what we sometimes take to be his private penchant for allegory, fable and Arthurian romance.

In fact, Steinbeck's attachments to romance, allegory and fable go back as far as we can trace his development and antedate his biological naturalism. Steinbeck spoke freely of his first infatuation with the creative power of language as coming in an early encounter with Malory's *Morte d'Arthur*. At age nine he received a copy of *The Boy's King Arthur*, the sort of gift he was conditioned to associate with the public utilities of his culture. Dutifully, he says, he began to read. Then, "The magic happened."

> The Bible and Shakespeare and *Pilgrim's Progress* belonged to everyone. But this was mine—secretly mine. It was a cut version of the Caxton "Morte d'Arthur" of Thomas Malory. I loved the old spelling of the words —and the words no longer used. Perhaps a passionate love for the English language opened to me from this one book. I was delighted to find out paradoxes—that "cleave" means both to stick together and to cut apart. ... For a long time, I had a secret language. (Benson 20)

The cultural context of that moment is worth recalling. What Steinbeck was looking at was the last book in "The Boy's Library of Legend and Chivalry," Sidney Lanier's last project and an attempt to pass on the legacy of romance and chivalry to youth still untainted by the materialism of the Gilded Age. Retaining nearly all archaic words, with glosses and footnotes, *The Boy's King Arthur* was published in 1880, just as the medieval revival was about to take off in America, and achieved enormous popularity, especially after 1890, a decade after Lanier's death. Lanier's introduction, a rather apologetic summons to romance and the ideal of chivalry in a scientific age, deprecates the credulous, "skimble-skamble stuff" of Geoffrey of Monmouth, but singles out for praise the manly Layamon and "our own simple, valorous, wise, tender Sir Thomas Malory" (Lanier ix, xvi). Lanier's introduction was eventually dropped, but between 1889 and 1924 Scribners' re-issued the book at least ten times, often with N. C. Wyeth illustrations for the Christmas trade.[3] Clearly, Malory's appeal to Steinbeck's imagination was not unusual in that generation.

Later, as a student at Stanford in the early 1920s, Steinbeck's apprentice work showed how closely allied in imagination were the magic of archaic language (romance) and the power of a secret language (allegory). A strong vein of the allegorical and fabulous appears to have dominated his stories published at Stanford, stories designed to vex as much as amuse an undergraduate audience with arcane terms and tendentious allegory.[4] The story titles give some sense of this: "Fingers of Cloud: A Satire on College Protervity," for example, and "Adventures in Arcademy: A Journey into the Ridiculous," the latter featuring an obscure dreamscape of allegorical flora and fauna reflecting Stanford life. Another piece, entitled "The Nail," seems, as Jackson J. Benson reports, indebted to Donn Byrne's historical romance, *Brother Saul* (Benson 77). Here Steinbeck adopts the cadences of the King James Version in a fable reworking the Israelites' arrival in the Promised Land of Canaan as a grim and fanatical overthrow of a peaceable and pleasure-loving people. More importantly, Steinbeck's apprentice work here clearly anticipates the strategy of such later allegorical narratives as *To a God Unknown* and *The Grapes of Wrath* with their ironic revision of biblical narratives. Thus, to borrow terms from Maureen Quilligan's recent study of allegory, Steinbeck's fiction re-enacts and thus allegorically comments on more familiar narratives—what Quilligan terms the "pretexts" which allegory assumes—pre-eminently the Bible.[5]

Steinbeck quickly turned his back on this vein of fiction, which he came to associate with the self-conscious manner of both Cabell and Donn Byrne. "I think I have swept all the Cabellyo-Byrneish preciousness out for good," Steinbeck wrote in 1929 as he began his next novel (*SLL* 17). Such avowals have encouraged readers to look upon *Cup of Gold* as a false start for Steinbeck. Certainly the imagery of Steinbeck's opening paragraphs is not encouraging. "Night drew down like a black cowl, and Holy Winter sent his nuncio to Wales," does not augur well for the beginnings of a career that was to stake much on the effects of natural scenery freshly observed. Though the touches of the master are also there—in the "great work horses nervously stamp[ing] their feet" and the birds and goats restlessly moving to the rhythms of nature—Steinbeck's novel looks backward in several ways to the turn-of-the-century tradition of high romance and quasi-Arthurian adventure.

But Steinbeck's undertaking in this tradition also looks forward. For taking shape within *Cup of Gold* are the beginnings of what will be an enduring conflict in Steinbeck between tradition and experience, framed here with Arthurian romance on one side and a slyly ironic naturalism on the other. Built upon the legend of Henry Morgan, Steinbeck's novel traces the career of the seventeenth-century Welsh youth who actually rose from obscurity to achieve the fabulous plunder of Panama and eventual knighthood back in England. Yet Steinbeck's novel reveals Morgan's achievements as but the ironic shell of romance. Morgan, a lumpish man who drives men like machines and uses women as instruments of pleasure, is a ruthless dreamer with a childlike obsession which he actually carries into action. But his exploits are utterly divorced from the traditions of his native Wales that might once have given them mythic shape and meaning. The estrangement begins when the young Morgan hears the old dream-tossed poet, Merlin, in whom song has failed, try to rouse in the boy the bright vision of Arthur and what he terms the "ghosts of those good, brave, quarrelsome, inefficient men" whose spirits, he would like to believe, are still abroad. "I will plead with you for this dear Cambria," he begins, "where time is piled mountain high and crumbling, ancient days about its base" (*Cup of Gold* 17).

It is as though the old man were voicing that apologetic plea for chivalry and the often flawed idealism of romance from Lanier's introduction to *The Boy's King Arthur*. Merlin offers an old world of half-dreamed subjectivity—of myth, magic and tradition; the boy burns with an animal passion for a new world, real and substantial, offering wealth and pleasure. He leaves Wales, never to return, declining both Merlin's summons and the mysterious sexual awakening that baffles him in the haunting figure of the village girl, Elizabeth. Yet Morgan thinks in later years about the romantic absence of both figures in his life, magnifying and belying the loss of the village girl in progressively more banal, swaggering accounts of a virgin who gave herself to him, incurring the wrath of a powerful family that drove the hapless Morgan into exile to wander the world alone.

Wraith-like, the dream of romance eludes him, until at the height of his power, in the apparent fulfillment of his private grail quest, he sacks Panama, the fabled Cup of Gold of the Spanish empire, and captures the secret, forbidden object of all men's desiring, the Red Saint, Ysobel. The setting is a far cry from the Welsh village where this quest began. Morgan now makes and unmakes his world at will, a demented romance-world of nearly apocalyptic violence, rendered in the sometimes egregiously purple prose of a first novel. Yet the result here is fundamentally no different than when the quest began; Morgan can neither accept nor understand his feelings toward the object of his now murderous quest: "'You are like Elizabeth,' he said in the dull monotone of one dreaming. 'You are like, and yet there is no likeness. Perhaps you master the power she was just learning to handle. I think I love you, but I do not know. I am not sure'" (*Cup of Gold* 141). Least of all can Morgan accept or understand the idea that his obsession is not absolutely unique, setting him apart from all men. "You cannot understand my yearning," he tells the debonair Coeur de Gris; "It is as though I strived for some undreamed peace. This woman is the harbor of all my questing" (128). Ironically, in the end Morgan's safe harbor is mediocrity, a safe and shallow marriage to another Elizabeth, the wealthy daughter of a plantation owner, and a peaceful accommodation with the hypocrisy of Restoration England. Here the successful buccaneer can be officially condemned and secretly condoned, and eventually knighted for his very useful predation upon the Spanish. Claiming to have "lost my unnameable desires," Morgan returns as Lieutenant-Governor to Jamaica to prosecute, judge, and hang the now inconvenient remnant of the buccaneering brotherhood he helped to spawn. Yet in the end the old emptiness returns and he dies asking for Merlin and gazing upon the still-young apparition of Elizabeth.

Set in the seventeenth century, bounded on one side by the magical world of Wales and on the other by the cynical, urbane one of Restoration London, Steinbeck's novel is well situated to suggest the ironies of the deformed survivals of romance and medieval grail quests living on in the schizophrenic modern world. "Civilization will split up a character, and he who refuses to split goes under," Morgan tells former shipmates who cannot recognize in the judge who tells them they must hang the anarchic individual who once led them in exploits of unparalleled audacity. Morgan's accommodation is perhaps the last and greatest of the audacities he gets away with, but more fundamental is the fact that the hollowness which keeps him afloat at the end is the same quality that sets him on his quest in the first place. Outwardly the stuff of swashbuckling romance, Morgan's story is from first to last an empty and ironic re-enactment of a familiar narrative, Steinbeck's answer to those turn-of-the-century historical romances, with their dreaming heroes and high adventure. And in this sense those predictable narratives of extraordinary men mastering the world to the shape of their own heroic desiring contribute a kind of allegorical pretext which Steinbeck's narrative slyly comments upon.

Key to this commentary is the seeming rejection of the dreamy Merlin and the traditions of romance, a rejection which is neither decisive nor complete. As Steinbeck is never tired of pointing out, the modern author's dilemma is that the gods, heroes and kings that Boileau had said were necessary to literature were no longer available. Later, he might find their function displaced into other, less exotic figures, but at the start his comment on the dilemma is the anti-hero, Morgan. Morgan, Steinbeck's natural man, understandably leaves behind the exhausted forms of heroic tradition and romance, but his career is a virtual allegory of the dilemma of human ambition—the instinctive drive toward self-hood—divorced from the meanings traditionally available in romance itself. In the last scenes of the novel that allegory becomes explicit. As an old man who has purchased respectability and knighthood from the cynical court of Charles II, Morgan asks whether it has all been a dream: "We did go there, didn't we? . . . Sometimes I doubt whether this body ever went to Panama. I am sure this brain did not" (*Cup of Gold* 188-89). Morgan's past thoughts and deeds then come to his deathbed in the shape of faceless children, the ghostly inward vacancy of his fabled outward deeds. "Why did you do me," they ask, demanding some meaning or reason for their being (196). Elizabeth the village girl similarly asks why he left her. Morgan cannot answer, except to say, "I was motivated by a power that is slipping out of all the worlds" (197). Morgan is once again at sea, seeking again the thing he has missed in his life. His mind wanders through youthful memories of the Wales he abandoned, never really knew. We are at that point where Morgan asks after Merlin, "Where is Merlin? If I could only find him." "Merlin," replies the apparition of Elizabeth, "You should know of him. Merlin is herding dreams in Avalon" (198). And so, we now recognize, is Morgan, seeking in his now disembodied consciousness the dream of romance that his exploits have only parodied and belied. The divorce of tradition from experience, consciousness from action, the split that civilization will repeatedly demand of the "adjusted" individual in Steinbeck, is given its first important formulation here in allegorical form.

Steinbeck's next novel, *To a God Unknown* (1933), enlarges upon the theme of this dilemma through yet another course. Influenced by his association with Joseph Campbell, the comparative mythologist, Steinbeck now took as allegorical pretext not Arthurian romance but the Bible, especially the patriarchal books of the Old Testament. Thus in *To a God Unknown* Steinbeck's two worlds of culture and nature are now New England and California—the austere land of patriarchal tradition and the passionate world of Mexicans, mystics and a consuming relationship to the land. The connecting figure is the brooding and intensely spiritual Joseph Wayne, a latter day son of Jacob who leaves behind an exhausted farm in Vermont to find in the fertile Salinas Valley a new life, first for himself and then for his brothers who follow. Joseph abandons the religion of his fathers as he becomes absorbed in the amoral vitalism of nature, identifying and eventually achieving an ecstatic union with the land in the novel's bizarre conclusion. Joseph opens his veins in a blood sacrifice undertaken to save the drought-stricken land for his people. In the extravagant imagery of the novel's close, the dying man, blood springing from his veins, becomes both the dark land and the life-giving rain needed to end the drought which threatens his family and people.

In outline, then, the novel is a literal rendering, almost a parable of what Philip Rahv termed paleface religiosity transformed into a radical identification with the environment. Yet when Rahv spoke of the Paleface in America "hankering after religious norms" in refined estrangement from reality, while the Redskin escapes into a passionate identification with his environment, he was referring to two opposed responses to the world with but little literary commerce between them. Steinbeck in *To a God Unknown* actually places these responses into relationship. In *To a God Unknown*, then, Steinbeck shifts from the debilitating estrangement of tradition and experience in *Cup of Gold* to the possibility of their radical confusion.

Signalling this confusion and complicating the apparent transformation of Joseph Wayne in *To a God Unknown* is Steinbeck's use of allegory. For in its re-enactment of the Joseph-in-Egypt and other Old Testament narratives, the novel inevitably draws attention to its biblical pretexts. Having established this relation to its biblical pretexts, to use Quilligan's term again, Steinbeck opens the way for the reader to observe a great irony. Even after forsaking the religion of his fathers, Joseph remains the acknowledged leader and new patriarch of his family. His is a new covenant with the demands and deep mysteries of the land itself, but he is nonetheless the patriarch, the new Abraham of this new covenant. Religious tradition and patriarchal authority only *seem* to yield to a complete identification with an unmediated experience of nature.

In fact, in his self-created nature worship Joseph is reading

nature as though it were culture, shaping its neutral facticity to
the form of his own desire. Even as Joseph descends into the
lushly green Valley of Our Lady, where he will settle, Steinbeck
strongly hints with his architectural imagery at Joseph's need to
see nature as a primordial form of culture: "The endless green
halls and aisles and alcoves seemed to have meanings as obscure
and promising as the symbols of an ancient religion" (*To A
God* 7). Notwithstanding the otherness, felt as the curious fe-
maleness of the land, Joseph is soon satisfied that between this
new life and the old "there was no quarrel, for his father and this
new land were one" (7-8). Eventually, he senses the spirit of his
dead father in the ancient rock that has become the focus of his
own nature worship. Joseph may identify passionately with the
vitalism of nature, but he never ceases to feel the patriarch's
sense of responsibility for what happens in his world and guilt
when he fails to control it. "I was appointed to care for the land,
and I have failed," he concludes, when the more or less predictable drought, as the older natives all expect, blights his land.
Sacrificing himself upon his rock, then, Joseph allegorically re-
enacts the spiritual paradigm of the old patriarchal religion. Escaping his brooding subjectivity into nature, he becomes at the
same time both another Isaac and another Abraham, convinced
of the mysterious need to sacrifice to nature, which has become
the father in the stone.

Steinbeck here has adopted the strategy of the allegorical
narrative to comment on the potential confusion, or perhaps the
underlying identity, of the fundamental imperatives of culture
and nature, the generative powers of mythology on the one
hand and biology on the other. In fundamental ways this
method persists in Steinbeck's later work. Steinbeck continues
to focus his narrative on the drama of raw experience lived close
to the survival level where the demands of culture and nature,
tradition and experience converge, in poverty, hardship, or agri-
cultural subsistence as in *To a God Unknown*. Yet this is not
simply a reductive naturalism. For beyond this naturalist narrative where instinct, obsession and necessity keep collapsing the
differences between culture and nature, human and animal, we
become aware of the allegory, the fable, or the romance detach-
ing meanings from immediate experience that connect it to biblical or other mythic pretexts.

In his next work, *Tortilla Flat*, Steinbeck was at great pains
to ensure that readers would recognize and respond to the me-

dieval pretexts for this episodic narrative of the simple, appeti-
tive lives of Monterey's paisanos. Steinbeck, in fact, was count-
ing on his reader's finding here the surprising re-creation not
only of Arthurian legend and chivalry but of the outrageously
arbitrary moralizing of medieval narrative in the manner,
Steinbeck suggested, of the *Gesta Romanorum* (*SLL* 97). Steinbeck even seems to be essaying in this novel the possibility that
the tension between culture and nature might include a creative,
a life-enhancing, which is to say a fundamentally comic, confusion. The comedy, however, depends on seeing that certain
conventions of genteel culture become functional, indeed have
survival value in the lives, as Steinbeck puts it, of a "people who
merge successfully with their habitat. In men this is called
philosophy, and it is a fine thing."6 What Steinbeck terms a
"courtesy beyond politeness," for example, functions repeatedly
for the paisanos as a gentle evasion and prevarication, especially
when dealing with females, authority, and conventional
morality. As I have been arguing, such sly appropriations of
literary tradition should not surprise us, may be found in fact
going all the way back to the Stanford stories. Unfortunately,
what readers—reviewers at any rate—found in *Tortilla Flat* was
a charming quaintness, and readability too. The novel succeeded, but the literary experiment had failed.

But also found in *Tortilla Flat* is another, less comic appropriation of romance, the motif of the talisman that binds together Steinbeck's Round Table, the male *comitatus* whose
collective life is the central vision of the book.7 That talisman is
the house which Danny inherits, symbol of the dream of
fellowship and a life of ease. Initially Danny's house draws the
other landless, propertyless paisanos forth from that marginal or
liminal condition between nature and culture where Steinbeck's
narratives often begin. No longer do Danny's friends sleep and
dream alone beneath the pines at the edge of town. Allegorically, of course, it is a re-creation of the Round Table in an
age of private property. It is the forbidden, or perhaps self-
defeating, dream of culture, a life beyond the struggle and
predation dictated by nature.

Later, the dream of culture and the organic community
may appear naive or hopeless, a fragile vision embraced in less
explicitly mythic forms: living off the fat of the land, as they call
it in *Of Mice and Men*, or having a nice house in an orange
grove with the nuclear family still "unbroke" as Ma Joad would

say. Yet at a deeper level there persists in these works the mythic pretext of the grail quest, or the restless exodus toward a promised land. Steinbeck's simultaneous appropriation of and argument with the pretexts of myth and romance—what by then he was calling "teleological thinking"—can thus continue. We find it in the bitter inversions of certain biblical motifs in *The Grapes of Wrath*. The disposal of Rose of Sharon's baby, for example, allegorically re-interprets in bleak, naturalistic terms the miraculous deliverance from oppression and a watery grave of the baby Moses. And the Ark-like vehicle that delivers the Joads from the ravages of a drought is abandoned first by a Noah who wanders away, then by the family facing their inevitable break-up in a flood.

More central to Steinbeck's vision in the period of *The Grapes of Wrath*, however, is the mediation between tradition and experience, attempted in that novel in the figure of Jim Casy. Casy's words and deeds point toward something difficult to find in the earlier Steinbeck: the possibility of a usable, naturalistic translation of such traditional categories as sin, and a non-teleological equivalent of such myths as the Exodus story and the messianic narratives of the New Testament. Formally, Jim Casy's self-sacrifice and Christ-like death may follow the pattern of Joseph Wayne in *To a God Unknown* or Jim Nolan in *In Dubious Battle*—figures with immortal longings and a messianic intensity in their willingness to die for their people. But those earlier deaths are qualified by irony and some recognition that these men die as much to satisfy some terrible inner compulsion as to meet the needs of the people they serve. With Jim Casy the irony has abated: the death is unsought. The deep-down tension between naturalism and the yearnings of romance has noticeably slackened. Certainly in his next work, *Cannery Row*, Steinbeck not only mellows much of the old tension between culture and nature but virtually dispenses with pretexts of myth and romance altogether. There his hero, Doc, combines the culture of an acute sensitivity to art and music with the readiness to accept experience on its own, often amoral terms. For the time being, at least in this recuperative post-war novel, Steinbeck's long quarrel with the grand obsessions and betrayals of the old myths seems to have been stilled.

But in the early work, from *Cup of Gold* to *Tortilla Flat*, reflections of the turn-of-the-century medievalism that Steinbeck picked up mainly through Malory can be found, I believe, in a significant and creative tension with Steinbeck's naturalism. Perhaps more significantly, we find that Steinbeck in mediating this tension developed and retained the allegorical habit. In *The Grapes of Wrath* Steinbeck, who spoke of having five layers in that novel, proves particularly adroit in establishing a complex relation between the narrative and the Biblical pretexts of both the New Testament and Exodus narratives. This allegorical naturalism, as I would call it, may prove a flaw in his weakest work, but it helps Steinbeck at his best to evade the trap of naturalism as Rahv and others analyzed it. For with it Steinbeck can invite and equip his reader to do what allegory has always required and what his characters are notoriously unwilling or unable to do— to evaluate their experience in relation to traditions and ideas quite beyond the demands of their own environment.

Notes

[1] In this respect Steinbeck's first novel, *Cup of Gold*, with its Arthurian *topoi* (its grail quest, its Celtic characters in the Welsh Henry Morgan and his *magnus manque*, Merlin), follows in the tradition of Zola and Norris, both of whom began their literary careers with chivalric romances in imitation of Sir Walter Scott. More generally, Steinbeck's struggle with the warring spirits of naturalism and romance is prefigured in Norris's own early infatuation and later redefinition, in more robust, naturalistic forms, of the once genteel traditions of knighthood, chivalric romance and allegory.

[2] See, for example, the revised treatment of Steinbeck and literary naturalism in Warren French's second edition of *John Steinbeck* (Boston: Twayne Publishers, 1975). Challenges of Edwin Cady and others to the hitherto accepted use of the term naturalism are discussed.

[3] Publication of *The Boy's King Arthur* would have more or less kept pace with the thirty-odd other editions or abridgements of Malory appearing in those years (as compared to perhaps a half-dozen for the 25 years preceding 1889). Judging from the publishing history, popular interest in Malory and the medieval chivalric romance began falling off in the mid-twenties.

[4] One of these undergraduate pieces, never published at Stanford, was subsequently reworked and published by Steinbeck. This was his mock saint's legend, "Saint Katy the Virgin," a clever appropriation of the simple language and credulous temper of hagiography to frame an outrageous tale of an evil-tempered pig exorcised, tamed, converted and finally canonized at the initiative of the pious simpleton, Brother Paul. Though published in 1938 as part of *The Long Valley*, this carefully studied send-up of piety and the sophistry of theology (allowing the pig to be declared a virgin by intention) marks the work as an early experiment with droll medievalism in the vein of Cabell.

[5] This definition of the allegorical narrative derives from Maureen

Quilligan, *The Language of Allegory* (Ithaca: Cornell University Press, 1979). The allegorical narrative opens itself to additional interpretation by revealing relationship to what Quilligan calls the "pretexts" of allegory, the sources which stand outside the allegorical narrative and which "the narrative comments upon by reenacting" (97-98). Chapter 3, "The Pretext" develops the idea at length.

[6] From Steinbeck's Foreword to the Modern Library edition, n.p.

[7] By this time (1934-35) Steinbeck's phalanx theory of "group man" as a distinct organism, with needs quite different from and largely unknown to the individual, had transformed his conception of the hero, which itself had been mightily influenced by Joseph Campbell's views of collective human needs as revealed by comparative mythology. Campbell's association with Steinbeck and the Monterey circle is discussed in Jackson J. Benson, *The True Adventures of John Steinbeck, Writer* (New York: Viking Press, 1984) 223.

Works Cited

Benson, Jackson J. *The True Adventures of John Steinbeck, Writer*. New York: Viking Press, 1984.

Lears, T. J. Jackson. *No Place of Grace: Anti-modernism and the Transformation of American Culture, 1880-1920*. New York: Pantheon Books, 1981.

Lisca, Peter. "*The Grapes of Wrath* as Fiction." *PMLA* 57 (1957): 269-309.

Malory, Sir Thomas. *The Boy's King Arthur*. Ed. Sidney Lanier. New York: Scribner's, 1880.

—. *The Boy's King Arthur*. Ed. Sidney Lanier, illus. N.C. Wyeth. New York: Scribner's, 1923.

Quilligan, Maureen. *The Language of Allegory: Defining the Genre*. Ithaca: Cornell University Press, 1979.

Rahv, Philip. "Paleface and Redskin." *Image and Idea: Twenty Essays on Literary Themes*. New York: New Directions, 1957. 1-6.

Steinbeck, Elaine, and Robert Wallsten, eds. *Steinbeck: A Life in Letters*. New York: Viking Press, 1975.

Steinbeck, John. *Cup of Gold*. New York: Bantam Books, 1970.

—. *To a God Unknown*. New York: Penguin Books, 1987.

—. *Tortilla Flat*. New York: Penguin Books, 1987.

Tebbel, John. *Between Covers: The Rise and Transformation of Book Publishing in America*. New York: Oxford University Press, 1987.

Wilson, Edmund. "The Boys in the Back Room." *Classics and Commercials: A Literary Chronicle of the Forties*. New York: Random House, 1962. 19-56.

Steinbeck and the Art of Story Writing

Robert S. Hughes Jr.

I

Most people agree that John Steinbeck won his greatest fame as a novelist. Yet his achievement in the short story is also impressive. I intend to deal with two questions about his work in this latter genre. These two questions are: First, which are Steinbeck's best short stories? And second, why are they his best? My premise in judging Steinbeck's short fiction is this: when Steinbeck followed the basic rule of story writing taught by Edith Mirrielees at Stanford, he wrote his best short stories. When he failed to follow this rule, his stories turned out flawed. Those pieces that are Steinbeck's best, I will argue, include "The Chrysanthemums," "Flight," "The Gift," "The Promise," and "How Mr. Hogan Robbed a Bank." I will also explain how Mirrielees' basic rule helped Steinbeck to achieve excellence in these five stories.

II

In 1973, in an undergraduate English course, I read my first John Steinbeck short story. My English professor had instructed us to buy a Bantam paperback entitled *50 Great Short Stories*, which editor Milton Crane said represented the best "stories by English, American and Continental writers of the past hundred years." To make his selection of the fifty best stories, Crane had consulted some five hundred professors of English at colleges and universities across the country, who, in turn, recommended some of the then most famous names in short fiction.

To mention a few: from the British Isles, D. H. Lawrence, Katherine Mansfield, and James Joyce; from America, Ernest Hemingway, Shirley Jackson, and Edgar Allan Poe; and from the Continent, Anton Chekhov, Anatole France, Guy de Maupassant, and Alexander Pushkin. Among these masters in short fiction appeared the name, John Steinbeck, represented by "The Chrysanthemums."

Some years later I learned why it was not surprising that "The Chrysanthemums" had been reprinted in *50 Great Short Stories*; editors of such collections have made "The Chrysanthemums" Steinbeck's most frequently anthologized story. During the 1950s, 60s, and 70s, "The Chrysanthemums" was chosen nearly twice as often as its nearest rival, "The Leader of the People." And in anthologies published in the 1980s, eight of the eleven I checked containing Steinbeck's work—an overwhelming majority—also reprinted "The Chrysanthemums."[1]

These statistics suggest that during the last four decades, no Steinbeck tale has been more widely read than "The Chrysanthemums." Almost without exception, Steinbeck critics have offered unreserved praise for this masterpiece. Brian Barbour lauds the story as Steinbeck's "most artistically successful" (122). Jackson J. Benson and Louis Owens consider it his "finest" (Benson 276; Owens 113). And Mordecai Marcus simply calls it "one of the world's great short stories" (54).

Given its popularity and critical praise, "The Chrysanthemums" provides a good starting point to answer our first question: which are Steinbeck's best short stories? Before turning to "The Chrysanthemums," however, we should examine Edith Mirrielees' idea of the "central core," which corresponds to what Steinbeck remembered as the "basic rule" that helped to shape his career as a story writer. Then we can also answer our second question: what makes Steinbeck's best short stories his best?

III

Long before he wrote "The Chrysanthemums" in 1934,

Steinbeck had been developing his skills as a story teller. Even as a boy in the first decade of this century he sometimes gathered his childhood friends in the basement of the Steinbecks' Salinas home to tell them stories of "spooks, sprites, and other invisible beings." As one friend, Max Wagner, recalls, "Storytelling was natural for [John] . . . not only spooky stuff but other kinds too. And he made them all up" (Valjean 33). Of course, as Jackson J. Benson tells us, the young Steinbeck also grew up listening to and reading tales that fired his imagination, especially the *Morte d'Arthur* (20). By adolescence, he had begun writing his own tales late nights in his attic bedroom. As Steinbeck once recalled:

> I used to sit in that little room upstairs . . . and write
> little stories. . . and send them out to magazines under a
> false name. . . and I never put a return address on them
> . . . I wonder what I was thinking of? I was scared to
> death to get a rejection slip and more to get an accep-
> tance. (Valjean 43)

Though he had been spinning yarns since his childhood days, not until Steinbeck enrolled at Stanford did he receive training in story writing. According to Robert DeMott, in 1924 Steinbeck took Edith Mirrielees' "Short Story Writing" class and "later remembered [it] as one of the best [courses] he ever took" (DeMott xxiii). Since Mirrielees' course was a favorite of Steinbeck, and since it probably represents his only formal training in story writing, what he learned in her class takes on special significance. Fortunately, we have some clue as to what Steinbeck learned from Mirrielees. He discusses Mirrielees' class explicitly in some of his letters; and Mirrielees, soon after Steinbeck left Stanford, published a textbook very likely based on the methods she used in her course. This textbook went through at least four editions from 1929 to 1962. I might also add that it appeared under three different titles.

Throughout his career, Steinbeck remembered very clearly what his favorite Stanford teacher had taught him. In a 1962 letter to Mirrielees, which became the preface to the final edition of her textbook, Steinbeck said:

> The basic rule you gave us was simple and heartbreak-
> ing. A story to be effective had to convey something
> from writer to reader, and the power of its offering was
> the measure of its excellence. Outside of that, you said,
> there were no rules. (Hughes 136-137)

That "something" conveyed from writer to reader—
which Steinbeck remembered so clearly—is what Mirrielees calls
the "central core" of the short story. "From the writer's stand-
point," says Mirrielees, "the central core . . . is identical with
[what] he is really trying to say." In using this organic metaphor,
Mirrielees implies the importance of oneness and unity. In fact,
she argues that the writer must say only one thing and say it
briefly. Mirrielees concludes that every part of the story must do
its share toward revealing the central core (Mirrielees 8).

In his most successful short fiction, Steinbeck develops his
narratives in just this way—with every word doing its share toward revealing a central core. This central core is often manifested in a single passage or scene enabling the reader to perceive
the story's meaning. In "The Chrysanthemums" two brief sentences near the story's conclusion provide such a passage.

IV

To set the scene, "The Chrysanthemums" opens one foggy
December morning on the Allens' Salinas Valley ranch. Elisa
Allen works vigorously in her garden. She is a lean, strong, and
handsome woman of thirty-five, who grows the biggest and
brightest chrysanthemums in the Salinas Valley. Behind Elisa
stands her "neat white farm house with red geraniums close-
banked around it." Soon Elisa's husband, Henry Allen, appears.
While Elisa tends her garden and keeps the farm house immac-
ulate, Henry runs the ranch, a foothill spread of apple orchards
and beef cattle. Henry invites Elisa out to dinner that evening,
to celebrate the nice profit he's just made on thirty head of cattle.
Elisa accepts his invitation and continues to garden.

So far, the scene looks idyllic. The Allen ranch appears to
run smoothly and happily. A traditional wife and husband each
work contentedly at their chores, reflecting their separate, but
equal, marital roles. Yet Steinbeck hints that these roles are far
too confining for Elisa. In clipping the old year's chrysanthemum stalks with scissors, she is "over-eager, over-powerful."
The stalks seem "too small and easy for her energy." And on
closer inspection we see that Elisa's "neat white farm house"
looks excessively clean, with "hard-swept" floors, "hard-polished"
windows, and a clean mud-mat on the front steps." Elisa appar-

ently sweeps and scrubs and polishes with strength far beyond what is needed for the job. In terms of sexual stereotypes, one might say that she demonstrates a strength normally associated with men. In fact, Steinbeck even dresses her like a man, with "heavy leather gloves," "clod-hopper shoes," and "a man's black hat." *And* Steinbeck describes her not with an adjective normally applied to women, such as "pretty," but with one commonly used for men: "handsome" (*Valley* 10).

Any thought we might have had that Elisa is a traditional farm wife contented with her role as homemaker and gardener cannot survive close scrutiny of the story. Soon it becomes clear that Elisa longs for a wider sphere of activity than that of her house and garden. In imagining another world than the one she knows, she fancies herself entering traditionally male domains and becoming a rival of men. For example, to the itinerant pot mender who calls on the Allen ranch she boasts, "You might be surprised to have a rival some time . . . I could show you what a woman might do." When he responds that his life of roaming from town to town in a horse-drawn wagon wouldn't be right for a woman, Elisa shows her teeth and retorts, "How do you know? How can you tell?" (*Valley* 19).

It is the itinerant pot mender, the tinker, who finally reveals how dissatisfied Elisa is. When his old covered wagon wobbles up the drive in front of her garden, she at first acts coolly toward him. However, once he feigns interest in her chrysanthemums, Elisa suddenly warms. Her breast swells passionately and she tears off her hat and shakes "out her dark pretty hair." In an obviously erotic gesture, she reaches trembling, on hands and knees, to touch his soiled trousers' leg. When the tinker trumps up a story about a lady on his route who wants some chrysanthemums, Elisa lovingly prepares several sprouts in a new red flower pot. Even after the tinker disappears with her sprouts, Elisa remains aroused and excited.

The crucial scene which reveals the "central core" in "The Chrysanthemums" comes near the story's end. Elisa and Henry drive in their car toward Salinas for dinner, following in the path of the tinker's covered wagon. Elisa, still buoyant from her encounter with him, suddenly notices something wrong. Here are two sentences from the story:

> "Far ahead in the road Elisa saw a dark speck. She knew." (*Valley* 22)

This "dark speck," of course, is the remains of Elisa's chrysanthemum sprouts the tinker has thoughtlessly tossed from the red flower pot. Elisa whispers sadly to herself, "He might have thrown them off the road. That wouldn't have been much trouble, not very much. But he kept the pot . . . He had to keep the pot. That's why he couldn't get them off the road" (22).

Why are the discarded chrysanthemum sprouts, this "dark speck," crucial to the story's meaning? These sprouts are the most important variant of the story's dominant symbol. This chrysanthemum symbol appears in several different forms: as seeds, buds, sprouts, stems, and as the giant blooms Elisa produces, some "ten inches across" (*Valley* 11). Given the dearth of creative outlets for her on the Allen ranch, the chrysanthemums Elisa grows become more than a pleasant hobby; they represent her vocation, perhaps even the very essence of herself. Like Elisa, chrysanthemums are handsome and sturdy, yet also like her, they are fragile and perishable too.

Considering Elisa's great personal investment in her flowers, it is no wonder that she can be manipulated through them. The tinker exploits this opportunity and brings about the story's catastrophe. By tossing away Elisa's chrysanthemum sprouts and keeping only her new red flower pot, the tinker's actions amount to a symbolic seduction or, more aptly, a "deflowering." When Elisa learns upon seeing the "dark speck" in the road that she has meant virtually nothing to the tinker, she crumbles inside. Though, up to now, she fancied herself strong and attractive, and a rival of men, she suddenly transforms into a sobbing, disappointed old woman—her charms lost, her confidence collapsed.

The "central core" of "The Chrysanthemums," to recall Mirrielees' basic rule, becomes readily apparent when Elisa sees the "dark speck" in the road. Then we perceive clearly what we've been intuiting all along, that Elisa's existence is desperation and frustration and thwarted desires. When we finally recognize this "central core," all other narrative elements in the story, even the seemingly vagrant, suddenly click into place. Then we can see, as Edith Mirrielees tells us, that "every part does its share" toward conveying the story's meaning from writer to reader. Nowhere does Steinbeck achieve this better.

V

While most critics call "The Chrysanthemums" Steinbeck's short story masterpiece, four other stories approach this one in excellence. These are "Flight," two *Red Pony* tales, "The Gift" and "The Promise," and the later, "How Mr. Hogan Robbed a Bank." In each of these stories, Steinbeck is at his best in revealing a "central core."

To my mind, Steinbeck's most successful story next to "The Chrysanthemums" is "Flight." As in the former tale, the "central core" in "Flight" is manifested in a single scene. This scene requires only a brief introduction. After knifing a man in Monterey, nineteen-year-old Pepé Torres flees his pursuers in the rugged Santa Lucia Mountains along the California coast, near Big Sur. While trying to avoid his pursuers, Pepé loses his food and water and rifle; even his horse is shot out from under him. He crawls onward like an animal as bullets ricochet nearby. Chased through granite canyons and over redwood slopes, the wounded and dying Pepé finally ascends to the top of a ridge peak and rises to his feet. As he rises, we reach the crucial scene.

> [He] arose slowly, swaying to his feet, and stood erect.
> Far below he could see the dark brush where he had
> slept. He braced his feet and stood there, black against
> the morning sky. (*Valley* 70)

Though he is shot and tumbles to his death, Pepé's dying act of rising to silhouette himself against the sky embodies the "central core" of the story. Peter Lisca explains the meaning of this act: "[M]an, even when stripped of all civilized accoutrements . . . is still something more than an animal" (99-100). Peter Lisca's remarks suggest that Pepé retains at least some vestige of his humanity. He greets his death in the open, standing on his feet, rather than cowering behind a rock. And Pepé's final gesture, rising to embrace his demise, reverses the dehumanizing process of his flight.

Steinbeck, in fact, provides Pepé as a type of every-man and -woman on the universal journey through life—from youth to middle and old age and finally to death. When Pepé first enters the Santa Lucia Mountains, the trail is lush and green with the spring-like freshness of youth. But as he ascends the trail the landscape grows "more rough and terrible and dry"

(*Valley* 57), evoking the advent of middle and old age. Finally, when Pepé nears his death, the trail turns "waterless and desolate." His trek ends where "granite teeth [stand] out against the sky" (69). These "granite teeth" are the "Jaws of Death" (to borrow Louis Owens' term) which swallow Pepé, making him one again with nature (Owens 29).

In sum, Pepé begins his flight healthy and alert and ends it enfeebled and unconscious. He loses all his possessions, and departs this world empty-handed. His brief journey, thus, is only a foreshortened version of the journey we all take. And although in the end we may lose our youth and even appear animal-like, we nonetheless can retain our humanity.

VI

Rivaling "Flight" and "The Chrysanthemums" as one of Steinbeck's greatest achievements in short fiction, *The Red Pony* has received almost universal praise. Even Arthur Mizener, who viciously attacked Steinbeck, credits *The Red Pony* with "an integrity, a responsibility to experience and a consequent unity of surface and symbol [that Steinbeck never again achieved] (4). Keeping in mind the idea of the "central core" taught to Steinbeck by Edith Mirrielees, I judge two of these four *Red Pony* stories to be of the highest quality: "The Gift" and "The Promise." In a moment, I will explain why I believe the other two stories fail to achieve this highest level.

In "The Gift" Steinbeck recounts what happens when Jody Tiflin's father, Carl, and ranchhand Billy Buck, give the boy a pony, which Jody names Gabilan. Before Gabilan can be halter trained, Billy Buck leaves him in the rain and the pony catches pneumonia. Jody watches helplessly as Gabilan slips closer and closer to death. The "central core" of the story is suggested by the last scene, when one morning the dying Gabilan wanders from the Tiflins' barn into the open fields. Jody finds him too late. Here's how Steinbeck concludes:

> Jody "saw a high circle of black buzzards, and the slowly revolving circle dropped lower and lower . . . When he arrived, it was all over. The first buzzard sat on the pony's head and its beak had just risen dripping with dark eye fluid. . . . (*Valley* 237)

Jody then plunges into the buzzards, grabbing the offending one by its wing and pulling it down. As Jody watches the bird in its death-struggle, the boy receives a kind of revelation. This is how Steinbeck concludes the scene:

> The [buzzard's] red fearless eyes . . . looked at [Jody], impersonal and unafraid and detached. (*Valley* 238)

The "central core" in "The Gift," suggested by the buzzard's "red fearless eyes," seems to be the inevitability of death and the indifference of nature. The fact that Jody would like his pony to live matters little. And the boy's attempt to strike back at death—symbolized by the buzzard—proves futile. Only new life, as Jody learns in the later story, "The Promise," can compensate for death.

Winner of the O. Henry prize in 1938, "The Promise" is one of Steinbeck's finest short stories. To replace the pony Jody has painfully lost, Carl Tiflin promises his son a new-born colt if Jody will work off the cost of breeding the mare and care for her during gestation. This experience affords Jody new insights into the two extremes of mortal existence—death and procreation. The boy watches as the wild black stallion, Sundog, mates with the Tiflins' mare, Nellie. And he waits nervously like an expectant father as Nellie becomes due.

It is at the moment of the colt's birth that Jody once again sees the darker side of life. As Nellie struggles in labor, ranch-hand Billy Buck realizes her foal is turned the wrong way. He must make an instant decision. Only one of the two animals' lives can be spared. Billy chooses the colt. He crushes the mare's skull, cuts open her belly, and delivers the slick, black pony. He lays the wet bundle at Jody's feet, and the boy becomes perplexed with conflicting emotions—birth joy and death guilt.

> [Jody] ached from his throat to his stomach. His legs were stiff and heavy. He tried to be glad because of the colt, but the bloody face, and the haunted tired eyes of Billy Buck hung in the air ahead of him. (*Valley* 279)

The "central core" of "The Promise" is revealed in these lines, especially the cowhand's "bloody face" and "haunted tired eyes." Although in this scene Billy Buck evidences deep and troubled emotion, and thus hardly resembles the indifferent forces of nature in the earlier story, "The Gift," the ranchhand nonetheless acts at nature's behest. He simultaneously gives life and takes life away. A healthy colt is born at the cost of the mare. In this way, Steinbeck suggests the interrelatedness of the two opposites and enemies—death and life.

VII

Though I do not consider the second and fourth *Red Pony* stories, "The Great Mountains" and "The Leader of the People," to be Steinbeck's best, these two tales carry forward the themes of life and death introduced in the stories I just discussed.

In "The Great Mountains," Jody once again confronts the specter of death, this time in the person of the old Indian, Gitano, who comes to the Tiflin ranch to die. Carl Tiflin turns the Indian away, saying the ranch can't afford to feed a man too old to work. Carl even cruelly compares Gitano to the Tiflins' nearly lame horse, Easter, which Jody's father says ought to be shot. Nonetheless, Jody is taken by the old Indian and especially by his gleaming rapier. When the rebuffed Gitano quietly disappears from the Tiflin ranch the next morning riding old Easter into the great mountains, Jody notices a strange sight upon the brooding slopes.

> In a moment [Jody] thought he could see a black speck crawling up the farthest ridge. [He] thought of the rapier and of Gitano. And he thought of the great mountains. A longing caressed him, and it was so sharp that he wanted to cry to get it out of his breast . . . [He] was full of a nameless sorrow. (*Valley* 256)

The "black speck" moving slowly up the mountain ridge and Jody's reaction to it comprise the crucial scene of the story, the scene which we might expect would reveal the "central core," the one thing Steinbeck tried to convey to the reader. However, the "central core" of "The Great Mountains" is not one thing, as Steinbeck's teacher Edith Mirrielees taught him it should be, but many things: the ominous nature of the great mountains, the mystery of the old Indian and his rapier, the questing impulse he represents, and finally his impending death and that of the Tiflins' horse, Easter. Perhaps Steinbeck tried to pack too many ideas and too many symbols into "The Great

Mountains." Though the final "black speck" scene arouses curiosity, it does not fully integrate these various elements in the story.

The last *Red Pony* tale, "The Leader of the People," has proven to be the most controversial. Though this piece shares the same setting and many of the same characters with the other *Red Pony* stories, in "The Leader of the People" Jody's initiation into the mysteries of life and death is rivaled by an entirely new theme. The controversy over the story involves this new theme, the grandfather's recollections of "westering"—of crossing the prairie in a wagon train to the American west.

The problem with the grandfather's tales is that they portray him and the "westering" impulse in two entirely different lights. Consequently, the reader is never quite sure in which light the old man and the "westering" experience should be viewed. Indeed, the grandfather's recollections can be divided into two categories, those purveying oral history to his grandson, Jody, and those illustrating Steinbeck's theory of group behavior. This theory of group behavior, called the "Group Man" or "Phalanx," maintains that a group is greater than the sum of its units, and actually controls their behavior toward its own ends. During the 1930s, Steinbeck was much enamored of this theory; and, consequently, it turns up in several of his works from this period, including "The Leader of the People."

The grandfather's first recollections in the story, those purveying oral history, include Indian raids on the wagon train, prairie feasts when the old man ate "five pounds of buffalo meat every night" (*Valley* 293), and contrasting times of famine when hunters failed to shoot even a coyote. In these first reminiscences, the grandfather, as wagon train leader, appears heroic and courageous. In his later recollections, however, he transforms from a Natty Bumppo-like pathfinder to a mere figurehead. He likens the wagon train to a phalanx or "big crawling beast."

> "[I]f I hadn't been there," he says, "someone else would
> have been the head. The thing had to have a head."
> (*Valley* 302)

Thus, in these last reminiscences, the old timer becomes a mouthpiece for Steinbeck's "Group-Man" theory, rather than a frontier hero, as he was before. Because of this abrupt shift in the grandfather's recollections, "The Leader of the People" contains a "central core" expressing two different messages, and it is unclear which we should take more seriously.

VIII

Published in 1956, twenty years after "The Leader of the People," Steinbeck's "How Mr. Hogan Robbed a Bank" is one of his most delightful tales. Mr. Hogan is a middle-aged grocery clerk who lives in the mid-1950s among the aspiring middle class. The Hogans' house on Maple Street looks identical to another house on the same street, and no doubt like many others in the same neighborhood. Mr. Hogan, as a husband, father, and sole-provider of his family, resembles every other husband, father, and sole-provider in town, except for one crucial difference. While his neighbors succumb to the blinding routines of everyday life, Mr. Hogan keeps his eyes open. He retains the ability to see things as they are. As the narrator tells us,

> Mr. Hogan was a man who noticed things, and when it came to robbing a bank, this trait stood him in good stead. (*Portable* 632)

This sentence reveals the story's "central core": Mr. Hogan's ability to "notice things" keeps him from falling into a rut and gives him an advantage over his less perceptive neighbors.

The story also illustrates the hypocrisy of people who publicly endorse the values of hard work, religion, and the American way of life, yet who don't live by these values. Some examples: Although Mr. Hogan belongs to the Knight Templar's Lodge, a chivalric order, he nonetheless robs a bank. And though Mr. Hogan's wife, Joan, is nominally religious, she divines messages in her tea cup and tells fortunes with tarot cards. And then there are the Hogans' children who enter the William Randolph Hearst "I Love America" contest hoping to win a trip to Washington, D. C. Though neither child plagiarizes—as happens in *Winter of Our Discontent*, the 1961 novel that grew from the story—Steinbeck no doubt attached the Hearst name to this "I Love America" contest because of the newspaper tycoon's reputation as an empire builder. Hearst was a powerful figure in America. Mr. Hogan's modest income and frugal ways, in contrast, fail to raise him above the daily grind of a grocery clerk.

Thus, in this short story, nearly the last of his career, Steinbeck hints at a moral and spiritual bankruptcy spreading in America. "How Mr. Hogan Robbed a Bank" evokes the anesthetized 1950s—with its smiling conformity, apparent prosperity, yet festering inequality and rage. These conditions exploded into the cultural revolution of the 1960s, which Steinbeck seems to have prophesied in this story. Thus Steinbeck, like his protagonist Mr. Hogan, "was a man who noticed things, and . . . this trait stood him in good stead" (*Portable* 632).

IX

John Steinbeck was taught well in short story writing. His Stanford University teacher, Edith Mirrielees, instructed him in a basic rule that he remembered to the end of his career. Following this rule, the successes Steinbeck enjoyed in short fiction were many. He won the O. Henry Memorial Award four times and his stories were included in such prestigious collections as the *50 Great Short Stories* volume, in which I first encountered his masterpiece, "The Chrysanthemums." In praise of the author, Mary Rohrberger has said: "In the end [Steinbeck's] reputation may rest on the short stories. As a novelist he is competent; as a short story writer, he can be superb" (178). Though I would argue that, at his best, Steinbeck is both a superb novelist and story writer, when considering the author's fame we seldom think of his short stories first. Yet, I can only concur with André Gide who once said that Steinbeck wrote "nothing more perfect, more accomplished, than certain of [his] short stories" (Watt 42).

Note

[1] See *Short Story Index: 1900-1978* (New York: H. W. Wilson, 1979) and *Chicorel Index to Short Stories in Anthologies and Collections*, 1st. ed., Ed. Marietta Chicorel, (New York: Chicorel Library Pub. Corp., 1974).

Works Cited

Barbour, Brian. "Steinbeck as a Short Story Writer." *A Study Guide to Steinbeck's "The Long Valley."* Ed. Tetsumaro Hayashi (Ann Arbor: Pierian Press, 1976) 122.

Benson, Jackson J. *The True Adventures of John Steinbeck, Writer*. New York: Viking Press, 1984.

DeMott, Robert J. *Steinbeck's Reading: A Catalogue of Books Owned and Borrowed*. New York: Garland Publishing, 1984.

Hughes, R. S. *John Steinbeck: A Study of the Short Fiction*. Boston: Twayne Publishers, 1989.

Lisca, Peter. *The Wide World of John Steinbeck*. New Brunswick, NJ: Rutgers University Press, 1958.

Marcus, Mordecai. "The Lost Dream of Sex and Childbirth in 'The Chrysanthemums.'" *Modern Fiction Studies II* (Spring 1965): 54.

Mirrielees, Edith. *Writing the Short Story*. Garden City, NJ: Doubleday, 1929.

Mizener, Arthur. "Does a Moral Vision of the Thirties Deserve a Nobel Prize?" *New York Times Book Review* 9 December 1962: 4.

Owens, Louis. *John Steinbeck's Re-Vision of America*. Athens, GA: University of Georgia Press, 1985.

Rohrberger, Mary. In *The American Short Story, 1900-1945: A Critical History*. Ed. Philip Sterick. Boston: Twayne Publishers, 1984.

Steinbeck, John. *The Long Valley*. New York: Viking Press, 1938.

—. *The Portable Steinbeck*. New York: Viking Press, 1971.

Valjean, Nelson. *John Steinbeck, The Errant Knight: An Intimate Biography of His California Years*. San Francisco: Chronical, 1975.

Watt, F. W. *Steinbeck*. Edinburg: Oliver and Boyd, 1962.

Steinbeck's Cloistered Women

Charlotte Hadella

John Steinbeck, in pursuing his depiction of America as a New World Garden of Eden, created an idyllic, pastoral setting for most of the stories in *The Pastures of Heaven* and *The Long Valley*. In a letter to Mavis McIntosh, Steinbeck identified the setting for the stories in the first collection as a valley about twelve miles from Monterey called Corral de Tierra (*SLL* 42). To George Albee, Steinbeck announced his intention to represent "the valley of the world" in the second collection of stories (*SLL* 73). Commenting upon Steinbeck's preference for setting stories in "small confined valleys," Jackson J. Benson notes that "the California coastal valley seems to suggest to [Steinbeck] a dramatic climax to the American Eden myth, a last chance for paradise at the end of the frontier" (Benson 13). And, as Louis Owens asserts in *John Steinbeck's Re-Vision of America*, the California valley setting dictates that the stories "will take place in a fallen world and that the quest for the illusive and illusory Eden will be of central thematic significance" (*Re-Vision* 100).

Consistent with the theme of restoring Eden to its prelapsarian state, a theme which informs so many of Steinbeck's valley stories, the women in the valley of the world are often guarded, fenced, repressed. Since an attempt to regain Eden motivates Steinbeck's characters, Woman, as the initiator of the original Fall, must be chastised, purified, and controlled. Consequently in *The Pastures of Heaven*, Shark Wicks becomes pathologically obsessed with the virginity of his daughter Alice; and Helen Van Deventer inflicts upon herself a life of sterile martyrdom while jealously guarding the chastity of her mentally disturbed daughter, Hilda. In *The Long Valley*, an even larger cast of cloistered women appears: Elisa Allen in her fenced-in chrysanthemum garden; Mary Teller behind her locked bed-room door; Emma Randall, bedridden for weeks every year in response to her husband's annual escape from sexual repression; the Hawkins sisters of Loma, separated from the community by their high thick hedge of cypress.

Though this emphasis upon female purity plays a major role in a number of Steinbeck's garden stories, in "The Harness," the fixation with chastity resonates with a nineteenth-century tone. Emma, as the woman of the house, is regarded as "the keeper of the faith" and depicted as someone totally lacking in sensuality. The very slightness of her stature intimates that Emma is not a complete human being. Steinbeck writes: ". . . people generally agreed that it was hard to see how such a little skin-and-bones woman could go on living, particularly when she was sick most of the time. She weighed eighty-seven pounds. At forty-five, her face was as wrinkled and brown as that of an old, old woman, but her dark eyes were feverish with a determination to live" (*Valley* 109-10). As Peter Lisca describes Emma, she is "frigid and prematurely aged" (191). Furthermore, Emma's restraining influence keeps her husband's sensual, erotic nature in harness. When he breaks out of the harness, he can always rely upon her to chastise him. Through this ritual, Peter then feels that his sins are expiated.

Emma Randall cannot interact with her spouse as a sexual being because both she and Peter believe that the spiritual em-bodiment of the family resides in the female, and therefore her purity is of primary importance. According to Owens, Emma "attempts to deny the reality of human imperfection or change . . . Peter is cut off from warm human contact with his wife by her very nature and from the rest of the world by the illusion his wife forces him to maintain" (*Re-Vision* 116). The narrative structure of the story further emphasizes this theme of moral restraint. "The Harness" is dominated by an omniscient narra-tive voice that describes the Randalls and the pattern of their life together. Just as Emma dominates Peter, the narrator dominates the story by telling the reader how to judge the characters and how to interpret events. The ranch is "an ideal balance of bottom and upland," and the house "was as neat and restrained as its owners. The immediate yard was fenced, and in the garden, under Emma's direction, Peter raised button dahlias and immortelles, carnations and pinks" (*Valley* 110). Everyone in the valley respects Peter, but there is some force in him "held caged" (*Valley* 109). By the end of the story, Steinbeck reveals that Peter lives a double life. In the valley, he is a devoted husband burdened with an unhealthy wife. But, periodically, Peter flees from the valley and indulges in one week of drunkenness and whoring in San Francisco.

Brian Barbour criticizes the mechanical symbolism of this story as a structuring device (119). But Joseph Fontenrose sees the story as an interesting pattern of characterization with the marriage as an important element in character development. He views Emma as the restraining force that Peter needs and wants in order to be an upright citizen (Fontenrose 49). And certainly Steinbeck does not intend to show Emma as a fully developed character. She represents an unhealthy moral prudery, so lacking in carnal substance that she withers away and expires. Peter, on the other hand, is not a wild, lustful maniac who has to be harnessed, but simply a normal human being with a "profound need for sensation, color and warmth" (Owens, *Re-Vision* 117), a need he exhibits by planting the whole farm with sweet peas after Emma dies. When the sweet peas bloom into "forty-five acres of color, forty-five acres of perfume," Peter sits on his porch, inhales deeply, and opens his shirt "as though he wanted to get the perfume down to his skin" (*Valley* 123). But Peter's release from Emma's mortality, a burst of freedom symbolized by the flowering acres, is as transient as the blooming sweet peas. Perhaps this is why Peter tells Ed, "I'll hate to see the petals drop off . . . I'll be sorry when the smell stops," even though Ed reminds him that he will make a lot of money when the seeds are harvested (124).

Only symbolically, then, and only for a season, is Peter able to blend his sensuality with his everyday life. After Emma's death, Peter strips himself of the brace that she made him wear (the symbol of marital restraint), confesses about "busting loose" once a year in San Francisco, and proclaims that he can now live the way he wants to live at home because Emma can no longer make him feel guilty (*Valley* 117). The irony of the story is that Peter never really changes. He does remove the harness, and he gambles on his farm crop one year by planting sweet peas, but by the end of the story he reverts to his pattern of one week of debauchery and fifty-one weeks of respectability. Emma's dominance over him does not end with her death, and Peter still relies upon "the angel of the house" to keep guard over his soul, impose punishment, and offer retribution. As Peter explains to Ed Chappell, "She [Emma] didn't die dead . . . She won't let me do things. She's worried me all year about those peas" (127). Admitting to Ed, in the last scene of the story, that he has been slovenly drunk and has spent the evening with prostitutes, Peter claims that this behavior is all right because he can "fix it" when he gets home by putting in the electric lights which Emma had always wanted (127). Thus Steinbeck illustrates, through Peter's refusal to deal with the complexity of his own human nature, how blind faith in the virtue of Woman limits humanity.

Similarly, in "Johnny Bear," another story in *The Long Valley*, Steinbeck demonstrates how the inhabitants of an entire community depend upon two women, Amy and Emalin Hawkins, to generate a sufficient supply of moral virtue for the salvation of the whole town. Alex Hartnell explains to the narrator that "the Hawkins women, they're symbols. They're what we tell our kids when we want to—well, to describe good people" (*Valley* 153). Later in the story, after the narrator has seen the Hawkins sisters on their way to church, he concludes: "It was easy to see. A community would feel kind of—safe, having women like that about. A place like Loma with its fogs, with its great swamp like a hideous sin, needed, really needed, the Hawkins women. A few years there might do things to a man's mind if these women weren't there to balance matters" (156). That the community depends upon the virtue of Amy and Emalin for its moral sustenance is obvious to an outsider like the narrator. It is he who assigns the label "community conscience" to the Hawkins sisters in response to Alex's insistence that "They [Amy and Emalin] can't do anything bad. It wouldn't be good for any of us if the Hawkins sisters weren't the Hawkins sisters" (161).

Consistent with the sisters' role as the untouchable moral exemplars of Loma is the physical appearance of their home: "Little of the house could be seen, for a high thick hedge of cypress surrounded it" (*Valley* 154). Yet, the narrator speculates that "there must be a small garden inside the square too" (154). Pointing to these elements of the story as Steinbeck's depiction of "man's futile attempts to wall out reality in order to maintain an illusion of moral perfection" (*Re-Vision* 118), Owens writes: "The Hawkins sisters' aristocratic house, carefully walled in by a seemingly impenetrable cypress hedge, is the small town's unfallen garden, and the sisters bear the weight of this burden much as Peter Randall bore the harness of Emma's illusion" (118). But eventually Amy Hawkins can no longer bear up under her assignment as keeper of the perfect Eden. She succumbs to a natural human drive for affection and sexual fulfillment by taking one of her Chinese sharecroppers as a lover. Then, when she discovers that she is pregnant, she commits suicide. Alex Hartnell's violent attempt to prevent Johnny Bear from revealing Amy's secret to the clientele at the Buffalo Bar underscores the man's desperate need to cling to the illusion of Woman as virtue incarnate.

In Chapter III of *The Pastures of Heaven*, Edward Wicks, or "Shark," as he is called by his neighbors, also dwells excessively on female purity; in fact, his obsession with his daughter's chastity almost destroys him. Early in the story Steinbeck establishes Shark's obsessive nature by describing his fascination for an imaginary bank account. When Alice is born, however, Shark is so awed by her beauty that his desire to protect her supercedes the "first joy of his life," manipulating his illusory bank account (*Pastures* 22). And when Alice reaches puberty, Shark "came to regard the possible defloration of his daughter as both loss and disfigurement. From that time on he was uncomfortable and suspicious when any man or boy was near the farm" (28). By having Shark transfer his illusive pursuit of wealth to his crazed protection of his daughter's chastity, Steinbeck cleverly blends the myth of the American Dream with the myth of returning to Eden before the fall.

The flower imagery that Steinbeck attaches to the women of this story characterizes them as passive beings whose fates depend upon their caretaker. When Shark married Katherine, "she had the firm freshness of a new weed" (*Pastures* 24); but after becoming Mrs. Wicks, Katherine "lost her vigor and her freshness as a flower does once it has received pollen" (26-27). Wicks shrank from the idea of Alice's marrying: "She was a precious thing, to be watched and preserved. To him it was not a moral problem, but an aesthetic one. Once she was deflorated, she would no longer be the precious thing he treasured so" (29).

Significantly, the opening paragraph of the chapter draws our attention immediately to Shark's garden and to the women of the family as its natural inhabitants: "Behind the house there was a peach orchard and a large vegetable garden. While Edward Wicks took care of the peaches, his wife and beautiful daughter cultivated the garden and got the peas and string beans and early

strawberries ready to be sold in Monterey" (*Pastures* 21). But
Steinbeck also indicates that this garden has been tainted—
poisoned by Shark's delusion and his failure to recognize his
wife (and, by extension, his daughter) as a human being. We
learn that Shark never talked to Katherine as if she were
human, "never spoke of his hopes or thoughts or failures, of his
paper wealth nor of the peach crop" (25). He also has little regard
for his wife's domain; the Wickses' house is described as "the
only unbeautiful thing on the farm" (25). We are told that Shark
tends his orchards diligently, but "could see no reason for wast-
ing good water around the house" (25). As a result, "the only
place on the farm where grass and flowers would not grow was
the hard-packed dirt around the house, dirt made sterile and
unfriendly by emptied tubs of soapy water" (25). With this
description, Steinbeck offers a subliminal representation of the
Wickses' family life: that the fertile soil of Shark's property has
been reduced to sterile dirt in the spot where the family actually
lives is no accident.

Shark also has little regard for his daughter as a human
being; she is merely a beautiful vessel which he wishes to preserve intact, untouched and unchanged. Steinbeck's emphasis
upon the girl's vacuity strengthens her symbolic role in the
story. Alice, the beautiful but "incredibly stupid, dull and backward" girl, functions as a flesh and blood representation of her
father's demented ambition—the compilation and preservation
of attractive numbers in his ledger, registering thousands of dollars to his account but representing a vacuum. The events of the
story also link "empty" Alice to the "empty" ledger: when Shark
mistakenly believes that Alice has been violated by Jimmie
Munroe, his rash response to the news leads to the dismantling
of his financial illusion. Shark's inability to post his bond for
release from jail, where he is held for allegedly trying to kill
Jimmie, broadcasts to the whole town that his wealth was only a
fantasy.

Only after Shark's public humiliation, when Katherine
comforts him, does he seem to relate to his wife as a human being: "He looked at Katherine and saw how beautiful she was in
this moment, and as he looked, her genius passed into him"
(*Pastures* 45). Mimi Gladstein comments that in this scene
Katherine "is the embodiment of the Earth Mother . . . she
reaches the apex of her strength"; but, significantly, "when
Shark's vitality has been restored, he forgets about Katherine"

(94-95). Fortunately, Shark's shattered illusions lead to the family's escape from their poisoned garden. The story ends with Shark promising Katherine that he will sell the ranch. As Owens concludes, Wicks "is much better off after he has been exposed, for at the end of the story he has a strong, supportive wife and an opportunity to make real money by real application of his talents and to win real self-esteem" (*Re-Vision* 81).

Another character's illusive longing to be other than herself is an important theme in "The Chrysanthemums," the first story in *The Long Valley*. Elisa Allen's imaginative creation of another self, and the ultimate destruction of her alter ego by a masculine force, demonstrate Steinbeck's sensitivity to the female's struggle for autonomy in the early part of the twentieth century. The opening paragraphs of "The Chrysanthemums" introduce the idea of illusion: "The yellow stubble fields seemed to be bathed in pale cold sunshine, but there was no sunshine in the valley now in December" (*Valley* 3). In addition to the illusion of sunshine, Steinbeck permeates the scene with images of repression and isolation: "the high grey-flannel fog of winter closed off the Salinas Valley from the sky and from all the rest of the world. On every side it sat like a lid on the mountains and made of the great valley a closed pot" (3). The reference to the pot foreshadows the entrance of the pot-mender, who may help Elisa free herself from repression. The phallic imagery of the flaming "sharp and positive yellow leaves" (3) of the willow scrub along the river indicates that the repression in this story is sexual.

After commenting upon the whole valley, Steinbeck then fixes our attention upon the Allen ranch and Elisa. As soon as he has introduced Elisa by name, but before he provides a physical description of her, the author has her look "down across the yard" where Henry is talking to two men: "The three of them stood by the tractor shed, each man with one foot on the side of the little Fordson. They smoked cigarettes and studied the machine as they talked" (*Valley* 4). Thus, our first view of Henry is through Elisa's eyes, and the only specific detail offered is that he is with other men. Elisa is described as "lean and strong," but looking "blocked and heavy" in her "gardening costume" consisting of "a man's black hat" and "clod-hopper shoes" (4). The word *costume* here signifies role-playing, just as a later description of Elisa underscores an alteration of character when she puts on the dress that is the "symbol of her prettiness" (15).

Steinbeck clearly depicts Elisa as a woman who is curious about the world around her and searching for ways to expand her role in the world. William Miller says that Elisa is "seeking a satisfactory identity, a complex of roles which would be fulfilling on at least three levels: the conventional, the sexual, and the 'romantic'" (4).

To emphasize the complexities of Elisa's character, the author also establishes a narrative pattern of describing Elisa's actions fairly objectively with selective omniscient commentary, but allowing the reader to see the other characters through Elisa's eyes. Twice more, before Henry approaches his wife, she glances toward the tractor shed. In commenting upon this scene, Marilyn Mitchell notes that the men's world is "a sphere of money, tobacco, and machines from which she [Elisa] is deliberately excluded" (32). Elisa is absorbed in her work, however, by the time Henry speaks to her. She has taken off her gloves, "and put her strong fingers down into the forest of new green chrysanthemum sprouts that were growing around the old roots" (*Valley* 5). Henry tells Elisa that he has sold some cattle; then he comments upon the "strong new crop" of chrysanthemums that she is planting (5). Her response is to straighten her back, pull on her glove, and answer with smugness on her face and in her tone, "Yes. They'll be strong this coming year" (5). Several times throughout the story both the narrator and Henry, as well as Elisa herself, refer to Elisa as strong. With the repetition of this word, Steinbeck presents Elisa's chrysanthemums as extensions of the woman. Several critics have suggested that the flowers represent the children that Elisa has been unable to conceive. Her work in the garden that day, focusing on the nurture of new plants which will eventually mature and flower, and the androgenous nature of her appearance, point to Elisa's function as a dual parent figure tending her progeny.

Certainly, in the first encounter between husband and wife, Steinbeck intimates several important details of character and theme. He identifies Elisa closely with the soil as well as with her chrysanthemums; he emphasizes the concept of new growth and the idea that there is a waiting period involved in the process. He illustrates the separate spheres of men and women, Elisa's desire to belong to both worlds, and Henry's inability to understand his wife's predilection for a more challenging existence. Henry leans over the fence that protects the flower garden, but he does not come inside; Elisa straightens her back, pulls on her gloves, and puts on an air of smugness as if in defense of her domain. The scene continues with a discussion of Elisa's gifts, and a comment by Henry: "I wish you'd work out in the orchard" (*Valley* 5). Elisa takes his offer seriously and mentions her "planting hands," but Henry turns his praise back to the flowers to direct his wife back to her proper sphere. This interchange between the characters supports Elizabeth McMahan's comment that Henry and Elisa respect each other's capabilities, but their marriage "is not a warm mutual confidence of things shared" (455).

Steinbeck again reminds us of the separate worlds of men and women when he has Henry jokingly ask Elisa if she would like to go to the fights after they have dinner in Salinas. She says "no" to the fights and gets back to the work of transplanting her chrysanthemum sets while Henry goes off to another farm chore. Thus the stage is set for the entrance of the tinker, the vehicle for the change which is foreshadowed in the second paragraph when "a light wind blew up from the southwest so that farmers were mildly hopeful of a good rain before long" (*Valley* 3). The scene that takes place between Elisa and the pot-mender as he manipulates her sympathy by pretending to be interested in her garden is the passage of this story most often discussed by critics. F. W. Watt claims that "the encounter arouses a disconcerting and not necessarily baseless illusion of mystery and adventure" (43). Owens agrees with Miller that the tinker's exotic life symbolizes "a kind of escape for Elisa from the barrenness of the farm" (*Re-Vision* 112). And McMahan comments that what the tinker has that Henry lacks is "an aura of freedom, unpredictability, perhaps adventure, maybe even poetry, which his gypsy life produces" (456).

Steinbeck, manipulating the narration of this scene so that we view the stranger from Elisa's perspective, writes: "A squeak of wheels and plod of hoofs came from the road. Elisa *looked* up" (*Valley* 6).[1] This is followed by a description of the wagon, the man, and the words painted on the canvas. Then, Elisa "*watched* to see the crazy, loose-jointed wagon pass by" (7). Instead, the wagon pulls up to the fence; the man speaks, and "Elisa *saw* that he was a very big man" (8) (italics mine). Whatever the tinker is in reality, from Elisa's romantically deluded perspective, he is a romantic figure. The description of Elisa's conversation with the stranger parallels her conversation with Henry, but introduces important reversals. The man, instead of just leaning over the fence, "drew a big finger down the chicken wire and made it sing" (8). Elisa takes off her gloves, and finally takes off her hat and lets her hair fall down. In the discussion of planting hands, Elisa is intense and describes in detail what she means by the term. In the discussion of the tinker's work, Elisa takes over the conversation with a passionate, erotic description of what she thinks his life must be like. And instead of straightening her back, Elisa kneels, reaches toward the stranger, and crouches like a "fawning dog" (12).

The man fails to respond to Elisa's fervent mood and focuses, instead, on the practical matter of his next meal. Feeling ashamed of her passionate outburst, Elisa goes back to the house to find some work for the pot-mender. While watching him work, she returns to the theme of separation between the working world of men and the sheltered world of women: "I wish women could do such things," she says, referring to living in a wagon (*Valley* 13). But perhaps Elisa's longing to step out of her culturally defined role is motivated by a feeling that she has failed to do the most important job in her narrowly defined world—she has failed to produce children. The details of this scene support Miller's claim that the male role means more to Elisa than a sense of equality. Elisa's romantic illusions are what make the tinker seem so poetic: "few mortal husbands or tinkers could live up to her dream" (Miller 6).

In "The Chrysanthemums," just as the wind does not really bring rain because the valley is still in "a time of quiet and waiting," and the "fog and rain do not go together," so the potmender as embodiment of Elisa's romantic dreams does not really bring fulfillment. By giving the tinker some of her young, tender chrysanthemum plants to take to someone he knows "down the road a piece" (*Valley* 10), Elisa feels as if she is sending part of herself on a romantic journey beyond her enclosed garden. As the man rides away, Elisa whispers to herself "Good-bye—good-bye . . . That's a bright direction. There's a glowing there" (10). Immediately following this, Elisa's bathing scene further demonstrates that she feels more complete and strong after the encounter with the stranger. Her preparations for the evening denote a sensuous self-awareness and "militant femininity" (Miller 6-8).

Elisa's sense of release from repression, however, is short-lived. She cannot respond positively to Henry's awkward recognition of her sexual awakening, his comment that she looks strong enough to break a calf over her knee. Elisa exclaims, "Henry! Don't talk like that. You didn't know what you said" (*Valley* 16). Gerald Noonan contends that "the tinker didn't know either, but Elisa was willing to supply the romantic context with him. Nothing is either good or bad, or romantically fulfilling—whether it's sleeping in a rickety wagon (the tinker), or attending prizefights, and drinking wine (Henry)—but thinking makes it so" (Miller 8). That Steinbeck wants his readers to think about how Henry falls short of Elisa's romantic ideal is evident. Moreover, whether Henry could ever be capable of satisfying Elisa were she to supply the romantic context and direct her passions toward him is not a simple matter to discern since we really only see Henry through Elisa's eyes.

Later that evening, when the couple goes into town, Elisa sees her plants lying in the road where the deceitful pot-mender has dumped them. She realizes that her new feelings had been based on illusions; she suffers from a broken promise, and the intensity of her disappointment is clear if the chrysanthemums represent her outlet for maternal instincts (Owens, *Re-Vision* 110-113). However, when Elisa is at her lowest point emotionally, Steinbeck writes: "She swung full around toward her husband so she could not see the little covered wagon and the mismatched team as the car passed them" (*Valley* 17). Elisa has a strong reality to turn to, however unromantic or unexciting that reality might be. But even though Elisa tries to console herself with the promise of wine with dinner, at the end of the story "she was crying weakly—like an old woman" (18). Elisa's dilemma at the end of "The Chrysanthemums" is unresolved. Finding satisfaction in her marriage and life on the farm will mean sacrificing illusive dreams and compromising her view of herself as strong and talented enough to compete with men in a man's world.

Elisa is not helpless, however; even though, in the end, she thinks of herself as a weak, old woman, the powerful imagery of the strong, new crop of chrysanthemums waiting for rain still dominates the story. Perhaps Elisa's disappointment is her pruning—the clipping back of the romantic "shoots" of her imagination before they bud so that her energy can feed a strong reality and produce large, healthy blooms. Nevertheless, the answer to personal dissatisfaction is not in the story of "The Chrysanthemums." Steinbeck merely points his readers to possible solutions while emphasizing the difficulties of a happy marriage. That Elisa is crying is not a positive sign, and it is doubtful that Henry could understand her pain were she able to tell him about it. Elisa's symbolic adventure beyond her cloistral garden has ended in rejection and disappointment.

Two more of Steinbeck's short works offer equally dismal perspectives on the topic of female entrapment: the Helen Van Deventer story in Chapter V of *The Pastures of Heaven,* and "The White Quail," from *The Long Valley* anthology. The dominant male figure, however, is absent from these two works which feature women who cloister themselves in the illusion that the preservation of virginity equals the preservation of innocence. The plot of each story centers upon actions devoted to or resulting from the repression of female sexuality; and in both stories, Steinbeck shows ironically that a quest for purity leads to unnatural relationships and impure actions.

Helen Van Deventer, Steinbeck tells us, shrouds herself in sorrow from the time she is fifteen years old. She mourns her kitten's death until her father dies six months later; then her "mourning continued uninterrupted" (*Pastures* 64). Life, it seems, obliges Helen's hunger for tragedy, and her husband dies in a hunting accident three months after the wedding. Helen does not weep for her loss; instead, she "closed off the drawing room with its [hunting] trophies. Thereafter the room was holy to the spirit of Hubert" (65). Six months later, Helen has a baby girl, Hilda, "a pretty, doll-like baby, with her mother's great eyes" (65). Hilda's destructive, angry temperment, however, is the antithesis of Helen's controlled, restrained personality, and the mother's calmness only serves to fuel the child's anger. Steinbeck explains that Helen's attempts to soothe and pet her daughter "usually succeeded in increasing the temper" (65).

When Hilda is six years old, her doctor tells Helen "the thing she had suspected for a long time," that the child is mentally ill (*Pastures* 65). With Helen's response to this announcement, Steinbeck prepares us for the subsequent development of Hilda's personality as a violent, distorted externalization of the mother's repressed self: Helen immediately blames herself for Hilda's illness by claiming "I didn't have the strength to bear a perfect child" (66). Then she rejects all of the doctor's suggestions for professional help insisting that she will keep Hilda with her always, and "no one else must interfere" (66). Helen emphasizes that she wants to involve no other doctors because she "shouldn't ever be sure of another man" (66).

Consequently, Helen Van Deventer isolates herself from productive interaction with others; she worships daily at the shrine of her dead husband, and nurtures a violent, mentally disturbed child who symbolizes the mother's own repressed emotional and sexual self. Throughout the story, Steinbeck quietly draws attention to the symbolic role of Helen's daughter. Hilda, for example, suffers from visions and dreams of "terrible creatures of the night, with claws and teeth," and "ugly little men" who "pinched her and gritted their teeth in her ear" (*Pastures* 67). Such visions function as parallel, but contrasting, manifestations of Helen's ritual hour in Hubert's trophy room during which she "practiced a dream that was pleasure to her" (76). By staring at the mounted trophies—controlled, subdued versions of Hilda's nightmare creatures—Helen evokes Hubert's presence: "She almost saw him before her. In her mind she went over the shape of his hands, the narrowness of his hips and the length and straightness of his legs. After a while she remembered how he said things, where his accents fell, and the way his face seemed to glow and redden when he was excited" (76-77). Though the daughter's fantasy is a nightmare, and the mother's fantasy is a "pleasure," Helen appears to have control over the phenomena of dreams. Just as she sits at Hilda's bedside all night to banish the nightmare creatures, Helen also practices banishing the creature of her own dreams: "She built up his [Hubert's] image until it possessed the room and filled it with the surging vitality of the great hunter. Then, when she had completed the dream, she smashed it" (77).

When Helen suspects that Hilda has made contact with the world beyond her garden because the child proudly shows her a wrist watch which she claims was a gift from an old man, the mother is horrified. Steinbeck writes: Helen "crept into the garden, found a trowel and buried the watch deep in the earth. That week she had a high iron fence built around the garden and Hilda was never permitted to go out alone after that" (*Pastures* 68). Helen's burying the watch and installing the fence underscore her delusive drive to stop the progress of time, resist change, and return to an innocent Eden. When Hilda reaches puberty, she becomes even more difficult to restrain. The girl runs away for four days, is found by the police, and then tells her mother that she "was married to a young gypsy man," and that she was "going to have a little baby" (68). Even though the doctor affirms Helen's suspicion that Hilda is lying about the gypsy man, Helen decides to move to a new place. She builds the log cabin and retreats even further from life by taking Hilda to Christmas Canyon. The name of the place evokes Christian associations of new life, a chance for salvation—Helen's apparent reasons for moving; but Steinbeck undercuts these positive expectations with Helen's insistence that the yard appear as "an old garden" (71) and with Bert Munroe's comment that Christmas Canyon is "not a place to farm" (73). With these details, Steinbeck points to Helen's quest for an illusion of Eden, a quest that renders her life sterile. By isolating Hilda in an enclosed garden to protect her virginity, Helen acts out the inner dream of repressing her own sexual urges and denying herself the fulfillment of physical and emotional desires.

But retreating further into an illusion of paradise does not placate Hilda; in a screaming rage, she declares, "I won't ever like it here, ever," and then "she plucked a garden stick from the ground and struck her mother across the breast with it" (*Pastures* 72). Nor does the retreat to paradise eliminate Helen's unarticulated need to overcome her morbid self-repression. On the first night in Christmas Canyon, Helen plans to "welcome her dream" of Hubert "into its new home," but while she is walking in the garden, she experiences a sense of release from her tragic history; she feels as if she is "looking forward to something," and "all of a sudden Helen realized that she didn't want to think of Hubert any more" (79-80). Apparently while Helen is experiencing this sensation of release, Hilda is also plotting her own escape from repression. When the two meet at dinner, "all traces of the afternoon's rage were gone from Hilda's face; she looked happy, and very satisfied with herself" (80). Helen comments upon her daughter's pleasant demeanor and Hilda announces her plan to "run away and get married" (81). Ironically, Helen muses that her daughter's story is just another of "the little dramas Hilda thought out and told. And they were so real to her, poor child" (82). Then the mother engages in her own fantasy and imagines that the figure of her dead husband is present in the new house. She discovers, however, that "when her mind dropped his hands they disappeared" (81), and she was free from Hubert's presence for the first time since his death. The expectancy she had experienced earlier returns to her as she opens the windows, drinks in the night air, and enjoys the sounds of life which "came from the garden and from the hill beyond the garden" (82-83). While the mother is experiencing this emotional, spiritual release, Hilda is sawing through one of the oaken bars on her bedroom window and escaping from the house. By representing these scenes as simultaneous occurrences, Steinbeck emphasizes Hilda's symbolic role as a physical representation of her mother's spiritual state.

When Helen shoots Hilda in the garden, she is killing, symbolically, that part of herself which has rebelled against her naturally morbid, sterile personality and has almost escaped the boundaries of her control. Steinbeck allows Hilda's doctor, as he affirms the coroner's verdict of suicide, to articulate, unknowingly, the allegorical interpretation of the story: he concludes that a girl like Hilda "might have committed suicide or murder, depending on the circumstances" (*Pastures* 84). However, only the reader knows "the circumstances,"—that Hilda has committed neither murder nor suicide, but that her mother has, in a sense, committed both acts simultaneously. As Melanie Mortlock notes in her allegorical reading of *Pastures*: "With the murder of her daughter, Helen feeds her voracious appetite for self-pity and Old Testament guilt. Because she has fancied herself to be a victim, she inevitably becomes a victimizer, and creates the situation she wants and needs to believe in, the one which permits her '"the strength to endure"' (11). By shooting Hilda, she is capable of whatever measure is required to maintain her delicious martyrdom and to purge her cloistral garden from the temptation of happiness.

On the other hand, in "The White Quail," Steinbeck employs symbolic murder as opposed to actual murder to demonstrate the negative results of a woman's obsession with chastity in a mock-Eden (Owens, "Steinbeck's *Pastures*" 206). From an omniscient narrative voice, the first two paragraphs of "The White Quail" establish the garden as a central symbol of the story. By the end of paragraph three, the narrative voice has fused with Mary Teller's voice and the controlling image of the garden has fused with Mary as well. In a mock dialectical questioning of herself about finding a husband, Mary says, "She didn't think so much, 'Would this man like such a garden?' but, 'Would the garden like such a man?' For the garden was herself, and after all she had to marry some one she liked" (*Valley* 22).

That Mary likes her prospective husband is not positively established in the first section of the story, however. The fourth paragraph begins with "When she met Harry Teller, the garden seemed to like him" (*Valley* 22). And then she remembers that she "let him kiss her," but when he became too ardent and expressed his lust with "You make me kind of—hungry," (and one naturally goes to a garden for food when hungry) she became annoyed and "sent him home" (23). Mary's confusion about the nature of commitment that marriage requires is evident from the beginning of the story. Her only concept of commitment is of her commitment to herself as an individual apart from everyone and everything. At one with her perfect, sterile garden, Mary is unable to participate in a union with another person. Marriage is simply a means to an end for her, and that end is a total isolation. In Mary Teller, Steinbeck underscores the irony of distorted vision that sees the union of a marriage as a means of achieving isolation.

Thus Steinbeck presents Mary Teller in "The White Quail" as a character whose perceptions are warped. Marilyn Mitchell, commenting on the opening paragraphs of the story, notes: "Steinbeck introduces the reader to the narrow world of Mary Teller's garden through a dormer window composed of leaded, diamond-shaped panes. The convex curvature of the window and the fragmentation of its space indicate that the vision of the person within, Mary Teller, is distorted" (28). Later in the story, Steinbeck employs this same technique to emphasize Mary's distorted perception of her marriage by reversing her position and having her outside in her garden looking into her living room and imagining that she sees herself sitting there with her husband. The scene, to her, is "like a picture, like a set of a play that was about to start" (*Valley* 27).

But Mary's perceptions are warped and she is only deceiving herself to think that she will create something that "won't ever change" (*Valley* 24), whether it be a garden or a marriage. Louis Owens views Mary's garden "as a barrier between herself and all contact with the world outside . . . an attempt to construct an unfallen Eden in a fallen world, a neurotic projection of Mary's self" (*Re-Vision* 113). Arthur Simpson, in discussing Mary's garden as a form of artistic withdrawal, says that it represents "static perfection" (12). And Brian Barbour comments that although a garden basically symbolizes fertility, Steinbeck uses it ironically "to deny change . . . and as a manifestation of Mary's sexual inhibition . . . She keeps her garden, as she keeps herself, untrammelled" (117).

Yet Steinbeck does not hold Mary totally responsible for

the sterile, static condition of her life and her marriage. In Part II of "The White Quail," Harry becomes a willing partner in the illusive quest for a perfect Eden, a quest that destroys the couple's chances for a rewarding relationship. His admiration as she supervises the creation of the garden pleases Mary so much that she extends the following invitation: "You can plant some of the things you like in the garden, if you want" (*Valley* 23). Harry declines immediately what, in the context of the story's symbolism, is his only opportunity to consummate the marriage. And Mary, of course, "loved him for that" (24). But once her garden is completed just the way she wants it, with no contributions from Harry except his awe, Mary expresses a moment of misgiving when she says, "In a way I'm sad that it's done," which is followed by, "But mostly I'm glad. We won't ever change it, will we Harry? If a bush dies, we'll put another one just like it in the same place" (24). Mary's inclusion of Harry as a keeper of the perfect Eden indicates her perception of his willingness to preserve the garden, forever untouched, unchanged—in other words, his willingness to preserve her virginity.

Stanley Renner, who describes Mary Teller as "ethereal, unearthly, fleshless," contends that the devotion she inspires from Harry is "suggestive of divine adoration rather than earthly love" ("Birds of a Feather" 37). Renner also acknowledges that Harry is a partner in Mary's self-idealization which is "set in the larger cultural idealization of womanhood itself" (36). Harry's comments at the end of Part II certainly support his role as worshipper of purity. He admits his fear of violating Mary (the garden) and he calls her "untouchable" (25). She responds with "You let me do it. You made it my garden" (25). Renner observes that in "the pointless heart-shaped pool" which is the centerpiece of the garden, "Steinbeck has deftly symbolized the romantic ideal that lies at the heart of it all, a spiritualized, sexless, and thus, in several senses, pointless love" ("Sexual Idealism" 79).

Part III of the story features the description of the couple killing slugs and snails together in the garden, the introduction of the threatening cat, and Mary's speech proclaiming her fuchsias as a fortress from the "rough and tangled" world that wants to get into her garden (*Valley* 26). Critics agree that Harry's sexual needs are identified with the stalking cat which is mentioned in Part III, preparing the reader for the information in Part IV that Mary always locked her bedroom door and that

"Harry always tried the door silently" (30). Mary muses that it "seemed to make him ashamed when he turned the knob and found the door locked," but her response is to turn out the light in her bedroom and look out the window "at her garden in the half moonlight" (30). In this way Steinbeck shows Mary retreating further into her unnatural world of illusory perception as Harry becomes less able to suppress his natural sexual urges.

Though Renner is correct in noting that the final two sections of the story "move toward a striking climax that dramatizes the explosive potential of the unconscious stresses building up in the marriage" ("Sexual Idealism" 83, 85), his contentions that Harry kills the quail unintentionally, and that this act shows Harry finally succumbing to his sexual urges in spite of Mary's protests, seem contradictory. It is more logical to assume that in a world as symbolically contrived as the world of the Tellers' marriage, Steinbeck allows Harry to kill the white quail intentionally. Harry's violence against the symbol of Mary's chastity, "an essence boiled down to utter purity" (*Valley* 33), is a symbolic action by a character who is incapable of real action. It is also important to note that the cat does not even enter the picture in this scene. Mary's hysterical reaction may have scared him away from her garden forever; or Harry may simply have *become* the cat, symbolically.

Steinbeck includes a subtle detail in Part V of the story to underline Mary's ability to dominate Harry so thoroughly that he is only capable of symbolic violence. Just after she sees the white quail, Mary experiences a series of memories that she associates with the kind of pleasure that she feels at that moment. One of those memories is simply a statement someone once made about her—"She's like a gentian, so quiet"—a statement which filled her with "an ecstasy" like the ecstasy in seeing the white quail (*Valley* 33). A gentian is a medicinal plant that destroys bacteria, and Mary, like a gentian, has sterilized her marriage completely, so completely that Harry is incapable of contaminating it even if he refuses to poison the cat.

The narrative shift from Mary's point of view to Harry's point of view at the end of the story emphasizes the total lack of understanding between man and wife. She cannot perceive of the despair that causes him to kill the quail. But the fact that the cat does not even appear in this scene indicates that Harry's violence against the quail and his remorse afterward are not simply eruptions of violent sexual urges but expressions of the altered environment of the marriage. Harry has become the cat, the Old Harry in Mary's Eden, the sexual threat, the potential "fall" that cannot be exorcised; but on a realistic level, he and Mary cannot interact as marriage partners unless he resorts to violence and forcefully invades her cloistral chamber.

Steinbeck suggests that the self-induced isolation practiced by both Helen Van Deventer and Mary Teller results from concepts of womanhood espoused by an American society which quests for an illusory Eden. He also demonstrates that such sterile self-repression affects not only the females, but inspires violent reactions from the men who attempt to interact with them. Helen's stoicism, for instance, elicits this response from Dr. Phillips: "the obvious and needless endurance of the woman always put him in a fury," and he admits the temptation "to smash her placid resistance" (*Pastures* 66). The doctor even tells Helen, "I think I'm a mild man, but right now I want to beat your face with my fists" (70). Harry, on the other hand, never confronts Mary openly with his hostility; instead he deliberately kills the white quail that she begs him to rescue, and then he cries aloud to an empty room, "Oh, Lord, I'm so lonely!" (*Valley* 37). Though Steinbeck does not portray these two women as particularly admirable characters, he does illustrate that each woman suffers from self-delusion as many of his valley characters do. Ultimately, cloistering women to prevent the human race from falling into sin proves to be a major cause for unhappiness in Steinbeck's disturbed "valley of the world."

Note

[1] The italics here are my addition.

Works Cited

Barbour, Brian. "Steinbeck as a Short Story Writer." *A Study Guide to Steinbeck's "The Long Valley."* Ed. Tetsumuro Hayashi. Ann Arbor, MI: Pierian Press, 1976.

Benson, Jackson J. "Environment as Meaning: John Steinbeck and the Great Central Valley." *Steinbeck Quarterly* 10.1 (1977).

Fontenrose, Joseph. "The Harness." *A Study Guide to Steinbeck's "The Long Valley."* Ed. Tetsumuro Hayashi. Ann Arbor, MI: Pierian Press, 1976.

Gladstein, Mimi Reisel. *The Indestructible Woman in Faulkner, Hemingway, and Steinbeck.* Ann Arbor, MI: UMI Research, 1986.

Lisca, Peter. *John Steinbeck: Nature and Myth*. New York: T. Y. Crowell, 1978.

McMahan, Elizabeth E. "'The Chrysanthemums': A Study of a Woman's Sexuality." *Modern Fiction Studies* 14 (Winter 1968-69).

Miller, William. "Sexual and Spiritual Ambiguity in 'The Chrysanthemums.'" *A Study Guide to Steinbeck's "The Long Valley."* Ed. Tetsumuro Hayashi. Ann Arbor, MI: Pierian Press, 1976.

Mitchell, Marilyn. "Steinbeck's Strong Women: Feminine Identity in the Short Stories." *Steinbeck's Women: Essays in Criticism*. Ed. Tetsumuro Hayashi. Muncie, IN: Ball State University Press, 1979.

Owens, Louis. "John Steinbeck's *The Pastures of Heaven*: Illusions of Eden." *Arizona Quarterly* 41.3 (1985).

—. *John Steinbeck's Re-Vision of America*. Athens, GA: University of Georgia Press, 1985.

Renner, Stanley. "Mary Teller and Sue Bridehead: Birds of a Feather in 'The White Quail' and *Jude the Obscure*." *Steinbeck Quarterly* 18 (1985).

—. "Sexual Idealism and Violence in 'The White Quail.'" *Steinbeck Quarterly* 17 (1984).

Simpson, Arthur. "'The White Quail': A Portrait of an Artist." *A Study Guide to Steinbeck's "The Long Valley."* Ed. Tetsumuro Hayashi. Ann Arbor, MI: Pierian Press, 1976.

Steinbeck: A Life in Letters. Eds. Elaine Steinbeck and Robert Wallstein. New York: Viking Press, 1975.

Steinbeck, John. *The Long Valley*. New York: Viking Press, 1986.

—. *The Pastures of Heaven*. New York: Penguin Books, 1982.

Watt, F. W. *Steinbeck*. New York: Chip's Bookshop, 1962.

The Silent Woman and the Male Voice
in Steinbeck's *Cannery Row*

Paul Hintz

It is a commonplace in criticism of Steinbeck's work that the non-fiction collaboration with Ed Ricketts, *Sea of Cortez*, serves as a kind of gloss on Steinbeck's fiction, that it is a more direct (and so more "real") exposition of the philosophy underlying his novels of the 30s and 40s. Put another way, it is argued that *Sea of Cortez* "tells" us what the fiction, especially *Cannery Row*, attempts to "show" us (Timmerman 17, Alexander 140).

This paper will follow that critical strategy only in form, by focusing on *Cannery Row (CR)*, and using *Sea of Cortez (SC)* as source for additional examples. The operating assumption is different, however. The usual assumption is wrong on two counts: first, it obscures the real issues involved in narrative representation of experience, by applying abstract categories of "non-fiction" and "fiction"—categories which on examination raise as many questions as they answer. This paper attempts to specify some of those questions as they relate to Steinbeck's works. Second, the commonplace view avoids addressing the issue of the implied author/reader "contract." Such a contract exists as a subtext in all of Steinbeck's work, and is a contract which contains substantially the same "language" in both *Sea of Cortez* and *Cannery Row*. This paper suggests some of the terms of that contract.

It is the premise here, then, that these two works are not best understood in a hierarchical relation—the usual implication of the "*Sea of Cortez* is real account of life, *Cannery Row* is fictionalized re-creation" argument. Such an implication is a concept that makes *Sea of Cortez* the subject to *Cannery Row* the verb. Rather, both works are parallel narrative solutions to Steinbeck's version of a stock dilemma in literature: the Male Consciousness confronting the Other—first in Nature, then in Society, then in Woman, and exercising power over that Other by the process of naming it.

MOTHER NATURE

"Cannery Row in Monterey in California is a poem" is the beginning of *Cannery Row*. The introduction to *Sea of Cortez* begins with:

> The design of a book is the pattern of a reality con-
> trolled and shaped by the mind of the writer. This is
> completely understood about poetry or fiction, but it is
> too seldom realized about books of fact. (1)

Both works are in fact shaped by the contradictions in this relation of Word to World. It is the thesis of this paper that because Steinbeck's concept of the Word fits within a tradition of thought and practice in Western civilization, it re-creates the problem it is an attempt to solve. That problem is a paradox: the process of naming estranges the mind from the thing named, at the same time that it makes knowledge of the thing possible. The paradox is initially presented in *Cannery Row* in that, while Steinbeck says Cannery Row "is" a poem, he claims to be letting the stories "crawl in." In *Sea of Cortez*, the contradiction lies between the authors' assertion that they are "going open" into the experience to record it "as is," and things they leave unsaid. This paper's conclusion is that Steinbeck's solution to this dilemma, this paradox, is faithful to the tradition in that it effectively robs the Other of its (and most crucially *her*) voice—creating a worldview comprised of a lonely, voiced Subject, surrounded by silent Objects.

Both works hinge on silent women. In the case of *Sea of Cortez*, it is the mystery of the seventh passenger. The opening chapters name six participants in the collecting expedition: Steinbeck and Ricketts, the "we" of the narrative, never named for us in the actual narrative, but listed on the title page; Tony, the owner and skipper of the *Western Flyer*, the boat chartered for the trip; Tex, the mechanic; Sparky Enea and Tiny Colletti, the crewmen. So the list is given, so every commentator on the book lists the crew. But what of this: "It is amazing how much food seven people need to exist for six weeks" (*SC* 10). The riddle is answered in Thomas Kiernan's biography: Steinbeck's first wife, Carol, insisted on coming along on the trip in hopes of using the enforced time together to repair their failing marriage. The attempt was a failure (Kiernan 246-48). Apparently the "going open" and acceptance of what "is," which are the putative guiding principles of the narrative, are principles conditioned by unspoken limits. There is an additional irony here in an oblique comment by the Authors late in *SC*:

> We find after reading many scientific and semi-scientific accounts of exploration that we have two strong prejudices: the first of these arises where there is a woman aboard—the wife of one of the members of the party. She is never called by her name or referred to as an equal. In the account she emerges as "the ship mate," the "skipper," the "pal." She is nearly always a stringy blonde with leathery skin who is included in all photographs to give them "interest." (237)

Since Carol Steinbeck never is acknowledged in *SC*, and the Authors are at pains to describe their lack of success in picture taking, no record survives to judge how relevant this stereotype is to their own work. No record but the silence itself.

The silent woman appears in different forms in *Cannery Row*. Most central is the corpse found by Doc in the tidepool. More on this below. Also present are such characters as Mrs. Malloy, Mrs. Talbot and Mrs. Frost, whose talk is divorced from reality (Mrs. Malloy's demand for curtains for the windowless boiler, Mrs. Talbot's tea parties with cats) or overwhelmed by inarticulate tears (Mrs. Malloy and Mrs. Frost, both in response to their husbands). The only woman given voice in the novel, with approval (the approval of the Implied Author organized for us through a two-step device: we are given to understand that Mack is a character we should sympathize and agree with, and he expresses approval of her), is Dora, the madame of the Bear Flag Restaurant whorehouse.

Fontenrose's discussion of *Cannery Row* has as its central point that

> The principal mythical theme of *Cannery Row* is the Logos, the Word made flesh. It is not a myth in the

> traditional meaning of the term; rather, it is a doctrine,
> religious and philosophical, Christian and pagan,
> which was used to interpret myth. . . . (102)

He goes on to discuss the various levels on which Steinbeck presents this theme: first in the prefactory statement (the "is a poem") and one of the intercalary chapters (the "Word is"), next in the way each of the leading characters creates order out of chaos, a process that begins with naming: Mack the Palace Flophouse and Grill, and the naming of a space for each of the boys; Dora the whorehouse; Doc his lab, and his collecting work as a process of naming; and the Author, whose

> word has shaped the novel's Cannery Row; and this
> demiurge is a biologist who collects stories and puts
> them in his book as he collects marine animals and puts
> them into a bottle of sea water. . . . (Fontenrose 103)

But Fontenrose does not address two points: first, that use of naming is Steinbeck's attempt to mystify the real basis of inter-relationship on Cannery Row; and, second, his discussion of the Word/words as providing the motor to drive the plot raises but does not resolve the issue that the narrative need to have "something happen" "caused by" something else in the story is in ironic contradiciton to the stated non-teleological theme.

Fontenrose, though he does not identify with precision why Steinbeck's ideology fails in *Cannery Row*, is right to see in Steinbeck's metaphor of the tidepool an inadequate analysis of human society. The inadequacy is two-fold: first, it is a too-superficial presentation of the biological-reductionist position, a position that has been argued from the days of Herbert Spencer's Social Darwinism to E. O. Wilson's sociobiology; second, it shares the flawed premise of all such arguments, a willed overlooking of the essentially metaphorical use of language. Any reductionist argument depends on language, and a level of comprehension which is not allowed for within the argument itself. Reductionist arguments compound the problem all narratives have: the name of the thing is not the thing itself. Steinbeck describes the Thing becoming the Word and back to the Thing again. The reductionist argument presents a picture which denies its frame.

Much of the discussion of *Cannery Row*'s structure has centered on whether or not any structure exists. The focus is typically on the intercalary-chapters device. Lisca argues that lack of structure is the greatest weakness of CR while Benton argues the novel has a structure which duplicates its theme: a scientific examination of "what-is" (Benton 134).   His analysis of CR as statement of ecology overlooks an intriguing if side-light aspect: the root meaning of "ecology" itself: from the Greek words for "household" and "word" . . . a play Steinbeck himself, with his lifelong interest in etymologies (evidenced by his letters, research on Malory, etc.) would have appreciated. Benton's argument identifies the structure of the book as paralleling the theme (or in the terms Levant borrows from Warren and Wellek and applies as thesis to Steinbeck's work as a whole: the successful fusion of structure and materials). In other words, the idea of a world made up of commensal relationships is shown us in *Cannery Row* by both the way the relationships among people are described, and the non-causal way the chapters themselves are ordered.

The real basis of inter-relationship in CR is the power to sell.   Lee Chong sells commodities, as, according to Steinbeck, does Dora. As does Doc. Mack controls, by virtue of his leadership role, the selling of the labor-power commodity possessed by the Boys (as when he decides, for the group, not to work a few days in the canneries to raise money for the party, or when he commits them to go frog-hunting). It is this power over the exchange of commodities that confers the power to name. It is the condition of being a commodity, an object, that condemns to silence. Therefore Dora is presented as a sympathetic and intelligent character, whose word helps set the second party in motion. Unlike Mrs. Malloy, Mrs. Talbot or Mrs. Frost, whose speech is ridiculed, unlike the silent, absent, unnamed wife of the "captain" in the frog-hunting episode, Dora has the right to speak— because she speaks with a Male voice.

In contrast to the extensive discussion over CR's structure, debate over the structure of SC has been in the main nonexistent, apparently because its shape as simple travelog is taken as not worth examination. That most discussions of SC could be in unwitting error as to the passenger list demonstrates the consensus judgment to take SC at face value. The following summary of the tangled use of autobiographical material in both books is intended as pertinent to this point.

Ironically, both *Cannery Row* and *Sea of Cortez* have as a theme the question of telling the truth.

THE MOTHER TONGUE

Both books blur the border between non-fiction and fiction by making mixed use of materials.

First, both share material explicitly: the appearance in both of Sparky Enea and Tiny Colletti; the inclusion of the good-versus-successful dialogue point-for-point and almost word-for-word; the inclusion of the walk-through-the-south anecdote, in which the issue of Do People Want To Hear The Truth is raised; various traits and habits of Ed Rickett ascribed to Doc in *CR*.

Second, both are held in tension between an avowed "tell-it-like-it-was" stance and traditional genre-forms which shape the narrative.

Third, both contain most of the Steinbeck Repertory Company of Characters. *Sea of Cortez*, which has the Doc, the Mechanic, the Paisanos, the colorful small boys at the port, the foil for intellectual barbs (the skipper) and the author hidden in the Doc (here through the "we" device) is missing only the Mother and the Whore. Perhaps that's why it is labelled a work of non-fiction.

If, *within* both *Sea of Cortez* and *Cannery Row*, devices are employed to present the Self/Other relationship, those devices in turn betray Steinbeck's attempt to define that relationship as it exists between Author and Reader.

One aspect of the role of the author is the appearance of the Author as a literary figure/voice. The Alexander essay, in its discussion of the Pastoral voice as looking down on characters/events being narrated, is suggestive here. In both *SC* and *CR* the author assumes a greater knowledge than the characters being narrated about possess. This leads to another level: the Author as Narrator, i.e., as being *inside* the narrative. In *SC* this is part of the premise; the "we" speaking is Steinbeck/Ricketts. In *CR* the matter of the Author being inside is raised by the inclusion of the various "mixed materials" listed above, and by the "fixed toilet" reference, an "inside" joke that raises as well the second part of the question: Who is the Reader?

In *Sea of Cortez*, the overall use of "we" as the narrative voice is a device that has two purposes: it de-personalizes the Author, adding weight to the self-immersed-in-Nature argument of the book, and it seduces the Reader into directly being "at-one" with the Author. Who that "one" is becomes a little clearer through the device used in *Cannery Row*.

Cannery Row is dotted with direct appeals to "you" the Reader. The most important occurs early on, in the description of Lee Chong's store, where it is reported that any commodity "you" cannot buy there, can be bought at Dora's whorehouse, clarifying the "you," the Implied Reader, as male (*CR* 115).

CR presents the Author/Reader axis with several complications. As already suggested, "Ricketts" is inside the narrative as Doc. And "Steinbeck" is inside as well, as an unacknowledged (save for the plumbing repairs reference) presence. And the book itself—addressed to "you"—is dedicated to Ricketts.

Other devices reinforce the basic identification of both Author and Reader with a male focal point. For example, in the scene on the beach with the two soldiers and the two women, the women's bodies are described in some detail, the men's not at all (*CR* 196-98).

Besides adopting the pastoral voice/viewpoint, both books depend for their structure on the pastoral theme of a person or persons of higher class journeying into the lower class world close to Nature. In the case of *Sea of Cortez*, this journey explicitly forms the reason for the book, and the beginning and end of the trip provide the beginning and end points for the narrative. The use of the theme in *Cannery Row*, effectively argued by Stanley Alexander, occurs on several levels. First, identifying Doc as the upper-class representative who has descended to the lower world, Alexander points to a two-step journey: into the social world of Cannery Row, and then, further down, into the animal world of the tidepool. Of course, it is at the bottom-point of this descent that Doc encounters the Silent Other, the "beautiful" corpse, an encounter paralleled in *SC* by the Silent Indians who visit the boat.

What is insufficiently pointed out by Alexander, and missed by Fontenrose in his Word-creates-Order dynamic, is the lack of a return to a higher world. That return is, in a muted way, present in *Sea of Cortez* (although the references earlier on to the world "back-home" with the impending war, unsolved Depression, etc. make clear that this return is not a triumph) but it is wholly absent in *Cannery Row*. Indeed, the implicit tragedy of *Cannery Row*'s ending is in keeping with its themes of death and violence, and its unacknowledged adoption of a males-only view of the Self.

This view involves two equations. In the first, Man=Nature=Animal. In the second, Woman=Civilization=Death.

Since over and over the world of *Cannery Row* shows that
Animal=Death, that intersection leads by transposition to Man=
Woman. The tension required to sustain a denial of this is
released and shown in *Cannery Row* by a pattern of violence:

- three suicides, one "on-stage,"
- a language of "murder" used to describe the
  feeding of animals in the tidepool,
- domestic violence as a way of life. The Gays,
  Frankie's "uncles,"
- the violence of the two parties.

Since the first is (rhetorically) shown to us as being a failure, and
the second as a success, and on the surface the activities involved are little different, the value of the second must be found
elsewhere than the action itself. Fontenrose and Levant find it
in the use of words and communication to establish bonds, that
since the first party was a preemptive effort by Mack and the
Boys, while the second was a cooperative effort by all on Cannery
Row, the first was bad and the second good. Another way of arguing the issue is found by those critics who see *Cannery Row* as
a Love-versus-Loneliness debate, with the winner of the debate
being Loneliness, but the number of points awarded to Love
varying according to the critic. (See Levant for the argument fa-
voring Loneliness; Marks is the strongest advocate of the Love
view.)

     It is relatively easy to agree with the idea that Loneliness is
a theme. References to loneliness can be found throughout the
book. What is at issue is the cause of the Loneliness. The only
time Love is mentioned in the book is in describing the feelings
of Mack and the Boys for Darling the dog (in a passage which is a
parody of the standard courtship process) and when Frankie the
retarded boy declares "I love you" to Doc. Doc runs away, just as,
in the earlier episode when Frankie spills the tray and runs into
the basement to hide, it is said by the Author (of Doc) that there
was "nothing he could do." This doing nothing, and the running away, take the issue of Loneliness' cause out of the narrative itself (that is, its contents) and place it in the realm of the
Author's fixed ideas (betrayed by the rhetorical devices of telling
us Doc could do nothing, and telling us nothing about how to
feel about his running away). This denial of the possibility of
effective and affective relationships between people is in keeping

with the book's underlying people-as-objects/commodities view.

Even more "telling" is the central episode of the book, the discovery by Doc of the "beautiful" corpse in the tidepool. Steinbeck goes to some lengths to describe the face as "peaceful" and "beautiful"—the entire scene is rendered to have the Reader identify with Doc's feelings of horrified fascination. Then along comes a guy who tells him there's a bounty for corpses and asks whether it was "rotten or eat up." Of course it's eaten up. It's a corpse, in salt water, wedged in rocks along the shoreline. Steinbeck isn't interested in showing us the "what-is" of corpses in sea-water. He is interested in setting up the end of the book, when the mesmerized contemplation of "death and the maiden" is given us in Doc's silence and the snakes' dusty eyes.

FATHER TIME

At the beginning of this paper the opening line of *Cannery Row* was quoted: "Cannery Row in Monterey in California is a poem. . . ." If the aesthetic center of the book (Alexander 146) is the corpse in the tidepool, and the mythos of the book is the Word (Fontenrose 102), both come together in the psychological and narrative-focus center of the book: the poem-within-the-poem, the quoted section from "Black Marigolds" read by Doc at the second party, and on the "morning after." Doc, the focal/main character, recites the last stanza of the poem, wiping his eyes while the white rats run in their cages and "the rattlesnakes lay still and stared into space with their dusty frowning eyes." The only thing missing from the scene, the punchline as it were, is the actual last line of the poem: "The heavy knife. As to a gala day." Compare this to the lines in the introductory chapter of *Cannery Row* (regarding worms, the metaphor for the stories about to "crawl in"): "You must let them ooze and crawl of their own will onto a knife blade. . . ."

"Black Marigolds" was written by Kashmirian Bilhana in the 12th century, and is also known as "Chaurapanchasika" (the "Fifty Stanzas") and according to the introductory note by the editor of an anthology in which portions of E. Powys Mather's translation (the one used by Steinbeck)—including the crucial final stanza—appear:

> Tradition says—though without much historical war-
> rant—that the author of this poem loved a princess
> and, when their love was discovered, was condemned to
> death. Whereupon he wrote the fifty stanzas from
> which these are taken. The king was so impressed that
> he forgave the poet, and bestowed on him the hand of
> his daughter. (303)

So the poem's point of view asks the reader to be a condemned man, waiting for the sun to rise on the morning of his
execution. But the memory of his love makes the occasion
something of a party. *Cannery Row* invites the (male) reader to
adopt this stance, transposed from romance and pastoral to
irony, as a viable long-term relationship with the Other, both
World and Woman, using a tableau-device ending: the worms
of the opening pages have "become" the snakes staring out (as
Andy the boy had stared through the eyes of the Old Chinaman
in an early intercalary chapter) at the executioner's block.
Through Doc, we stand in the same relation to the Author as,
within the work, the cook stood to William the pimp as he held
the ice pick he was about to plunge into his chest.

St. John's Gospel begins "In the Beginning was the
Word." Any work in Western literature that deliberately includes biblical echoes (as *Cannery Row* does with its "Our Father
who art in Nature" and *Sea of Cortez* does with its Easter Sunday
allusion) and plays with the concept of "the Word" invites this
Gospel echo. But the concept of Beginning is a concept of Time
that raises the issue of causality. Fontenrose criticizes Stein-
beck/Ricketts for confusing levels of causality (Aristotle's) in *Sea
of Cortez*, an issue related to the perception of Time as one item
in a traditional Art-vs-Science debate. (See Meyerhoff for a conventional summary of the debate.) What that debate conventionally ignores, one of the points raised in the present paper,
is the fact that both approaches produce narratives, stories,
structures of words to explain "what-is." The Thing-becomes-a-
Word-and-back-to-Thing is only one cycle within wider and
deeper circles.

This struggle with the Other, on the level of human experience of the World, explains the manipulation of Time found
in *Cannery Row*. That manipulation occurs on several levels of
Authorial intervention—flash-backs and -forwards overtly sig-
nalled ("But back to that evening") and abrupt tense shifts (as
when the descriptions of Doc's lab, etc., are put in a kind of eter-

nal present tense). Such manipulation underlines the Author's role as *speaking* for the objects/characters of *his* story.

The "we" of *Sea of Cortez* seem intent on making some points about cultural diversity, and the stories about the Indians, their names or lack of names for things, their identification with Nature to the extent of thinking (in "our"'s view) "Of course I will rain," and, perhaps most importantly, the "timeless" quality of their existence, are all designed to argue for that diversity. But it is diversity seen from above, in traditional pastoral fashion, for "we" don't realize that the diversity is bracketed within the hegemony of the white western male narrator. Just as the narrative itself, while speaking of a "timeless" experience, is shaped to a very deadline-conscious beginning and end, and divided into chapters most of which are headed by the date on which that chapter's reported events occurred or commenced.

We are left with an unresolved contradiction: the World as thing, as other. The Other as object, the subject the Male Author, in control of the process of naming. Steinbeck claims to adopt, in *SC*, the "neutral-observer" stance of the scientist, without thinking through the results of a fact he acknowledges— that the observer controls/shapes/changes the thing named.

Levant argues that Steinbeck's career involves the struggle to effect a fusion of structure and materials, and that the end-result of his "what-is" stance toward Life is increasing disorder in his fictive world. The argument makes a good story, as are the stories in modern physics about entropy, counterposed to the information theory stories about information as a force opposed to disorder (a smuggling into science of the Romantic poets' notion of the importance of Art). In all these stories the silence of Death is the final disorder, and it is the logical (in a root-sense) end of Steinbeck's vision: that no matter how the sense of time is manipulated in *Cannery Row*, and how the Word/World division is played upon, the end is silence and "the heavy knife."

"Black Marigolds" is embedded in a tradition of poet-saved-by-his-poem. No such salvation is offered in *Cannery Row*. The Author asks at the start "how to set them down alive?" forgetting or ignoring that the specimens he calls on as metaphor are, in the process of being "saved," rendered quite dead. There is more irony than Ditsky seems to realize when he says:

For many of Steinbeck's novels, therefore, the ending
provides a last point of comparison with what "is"—a
sort of checking-in with the cosmic housemother. (62)

The Male Voice, in Steinbeck as elsewhere in the culture, creates
a world of silent objects. And the silence returns to claim its
own.

Works Cited

Alexander, Stanley. "*Cannery Row*: Steinbeck's Pastoral Poem." *Steinbeck: A Collection of Critical Essays*. Ed. Robert Murray Davis. Twentieth Century Views. Series Ed. Maynard Mack. Englewood Cliffs: Prentice-Hall. 1972. 135-48. Reprinted from *Western American Literature*, II (1968). 281-95.

Benton, Robert M. "The Ecological Nature of *Cannery Row*." *Steinbeck: The Man and His Work*. Ed. Richard Astro and Tetsumaro Hayashi. Corvallis: Oregon State University Press, 1971. 131-140.

Booth, Wayne C. *The Rhetoric of Fiction*. Chicago: University of Chicago Press, 1961.

Ditsky, John. "Music from a Dark Cave: Organic Form in Steinbeck's Fiction." *The Journal of Narrative Technique* 1.1 (1/71): 59-67.

Eagleton, Terry. *Literary Theory: An Introduction*. Minneapolis: University of Minnesota Press, 1983.

Fontenrose, Joseph. *John Steinbeck: An Introduction and Interpretation*. Gen. Ed. John Mahoney. American Authors and Critics Series. New York: Holt, Rinehart & Winston, 1963.

Frye, Northrop. *Anatomy of Criticism*. New York: Atheneum, 1969.

Kiernan, Thomas. *The Intricate Music: A Biography of John Steinbeck*. Boston and Toronto: Little, Brown & Co. 1979.

Levant, Howard. *The Novels of John Steinbeck: A Critical Study*. Columbia: University of Missouri Press, 1974.

Lisca, Peter. *The Wide World of John Steinbeck*. New York: Gordian Press, 1981.

Marks, Lester Jay. *Thematic Design in the Novels of John Steinbeck*. The Hague and Paris: Mouton, 1971.

Martin, Wallace. *Recent Theories of Narrative*. Ithaca: Cornell University Press, 1986.

Mathers, E. Powys (trans.). "Black Marigolds." *Poetry of the Orient: An Anthology of Classic Secular Poetry of the Major Eastern Nations*. Ed. Eunice Tietjens. New York and London: Alfred Knopf, 1928.

Meyerhoff, Hans. *Time in Literature*. Berkeley and Los Angeles: University of California Press, 1955.

Rimmon-Kenan, Shlomith. *Narrative Fiction: Contemporary Poetics*. General Ed. Terence Hawkes. New Accents. London and New York: Metheun, 1983.

Steinbeck, Elaine, and Robert Wallsten. *Steinbeck: A Life in Letters.* New York: Viking Press, 1975.

Steinbeck, John. *Of Mice and Men* and *Cannery Row.* New York: Penguin Books, 1987.

Steinbeck, John and Edward F. Ricketts. *Sea of Cortez: A Leisurely Journal of Travel and Research.* New York: Viking Press, 1941.

Timmerman, John H. *John Steinbeck's Fiction: The Aesthetics of the Road Taken.* Norman: University of Oklahoma Press, 1986.

Missing Women: The Inexplicable Disparity Between Women In Steinbeck's Life And Those In His Fiction

Mimi Reisel Gladstein

In 1974 Angela Patterson wrote a dissertation in which she evaluated the women of John Steinbeck's novels in light of humanistic psychology. Her purpose was to study Steinbeck's works to determine the way they reflected, not only the attitudes and opinions prevalent in the society of the times, but also Steinbeck's individual attitudes toward and opinions about women. She surveyed his works for self-actualized female characters, for women who were depicted as persons of worth in their own right. Finding few, she contented herself with the explanation that Steinbeck could not be held culpable for this deficiency as he was reflecting the society of his times, portraying the women of his world.

Patterson's rationalization is echoed by Steinbeck scholars as recently as the 1988 Winter/Spring *Steinbeck Quarterly*. Beth Everest and Judy Wedeles in "The Neglected Rib: Women in *East of Eden*" make a convincing argument for the centrality of the female characters in *East of Eden* though they excuse Steinbeck's restriction of women's activities by explaining that "Steinbeck was limited in the roles he *could* [emphasis mine] assign them" (23) because of "the historical realities of the times of both the writing and the setting" (23). A comfortable explanation, but not one that stands up to much scrutiny. The more we learn about the time of the writing of not only this, but most of Steinbeck's significant fiction, the less defensible this argument becomes. Therefore, it is disquieting that scholars writing in this generation should so readily echo discredited rationalizations of the past.

No, Steinbeck was not reflecting the society of his time, portraying the women of his world. No, Steinbeck was not restricted by "the historical realities of the times" in the "roles he could assign" women. Steinbeck's world was full of women who did not fit the *Godey Lady's Book's* prescription for proper feminine behavior, full of women who transcended traditional role restrictions. Indeed, the reality of his world included women professors, business representatives, strike organizers, labor sympathizers, writers, artists, and journalists. His formative days were filled with self-actualized, lively, and assertive women. Their numbers are many; their significance in his life is uncontrovertible. If one is to look to his life and times for an explanation for the dearth of women in his fiction, for a justification of the restricted roles he proscribed for the women who inhabit the pages of his major works, one will find that there is a great disparity between the women in Steinbeck's life and those in his fiction.

I will not rehearse here the full chorus of voices raised in question of Steinbeck's portrayal of women. A few examples will serve to illustrate the nature of the problem. Claude-Edmonde Magny was one of the first to note Steinbeck's exclusion of women from participation in the essential action of his plots. In a 1953 review of *East of Eden* Magny questioned the subordinate role of women in Steinbeck and his repeated focus on male couples. In her reading, the meaning of this was "expulsion of Woman from the true human community" (147). Shortly thereafter, Peter Lisca noted the close male relationships in eleven of Steinbeck's novels and the relegation of women to either home-making or whoredom (206). Robert Morsberger, noting a degree of misogyny in Steinbeck, traces the contradictions in Steinbeck's numerous portrayals of prostitutes. My own exploration of the problem in "From Ma Joad to Pilar: A Singular Scarcity" compares Steinbeck's deletion of the different kinds of women in his life from his fiction with Hemingway's singular focus on woman as sex object in his.

Perhaps one of the reasons Steinbeck's critics have so readily accepted the rationalization that Steinbeck was depicting his world, one which they assumed was strangely womanless, is explained by the dearth of biographical material on Steinbeck's life. Hemingway's life has been well-documented. Biographies abound. The man's life, his loves, his wives, are part of the public province. Not only have we learned of Hemingway's relations with women from his biographers, but we have primary sources. His sisters have written books; his wives have written books, and books have been written about them.[1] By contrast, Steinbeck's life has received little press. This was, during his lifetime, by his choice. He was not one who sought the limelight. There is but one comprehensive biography and a few minor ones. Steinbeck scholarship has, for the most part, remained focused on the work, although certain works have tended to lend themselves to biographical and historical treatments. As more is written, the details of Steinbeck's life will become more accessible. Still it seems important now, before the inaccurate image of the historical and personal realities of his life becomes too deeply imbedded in the general consciousness, to direct attention to the disparity between the woman-peopled world Steinbeck lived in and the masculine world he created in his fiction.

The families Steinbeck painted with words are predominantly male. A traditional patriarchal authority, such as is transferred from Cyrus Trask to Adam Trask or John Wayne to Joseph Wayne, is a staple ingredient of the novels. The fictional families are full of brothers, of boys relating to their male siblings, of boys relating to their strong and authoritarian fathers. From Joseph Wayne in *To A God Unknown* who is one of a family of brothers (Thomas, Burton, and Benjamin) to two generations of Trask brothers (Adam and Charles, then Aron and Caleb) in *East of Eden* the relationships of male siblings predominate in his fictional works. Yet John Steinbeck was an only son, born into a family of sisters, into a family dominated by its mother. If there are no brothers in the fictional family, then the male is an only child like Jody Tiflin, who marched alone at the head of his imaginary army. Six schoolmates, all boys, follow him home to admire his pony, Gabilan, feeling the inferiority of footmen to a horseman. The pony in young John Steinbeck's life was one he played with with his sister. They recreated Arthurian tales, with Mary playing the role of squire and the pony Jill standing in for a knight's gallant steed. In fiction not only is the sex of siblings and playmates changed, but even a female horse is transformed into a male. During their childhood and through their college years, Mary was an athletic and adventuresome companion for John. Benson describes their closeness as "more typical of identical twins than of brother and sister" (853). There is no analagous brother/sister relationship in any of Steinbeck's fiction. It is appealing to speculate that perhaps Steinbeck felt some guilt for excluding Mary from his many Arthurian-inspired fictions. But it was not until after he died that acknowledgment of her participation in that significant aspect of their childhood, the Arthurian playacting which so inflamed the young Steinbeck's imagination, was made public. That acknowledgment came in the dedication of his final work, *The Acts of King Arthur*, a work he never completed. In his dedication to Mary, he notes that "It happens sometimes in sadness and pity that those who faithfully serve are not always as faithfully recognized" (853). Thereupon he takes the opportunity to make amends and in the dedication he raises Mary to knighthood, dubbing her Syr Mayrie Stynebec of the Vayle Salynis. This failure to recognize woman's knighthood was a lifelong pattern.

In the Steinbeck family, both John and his sisters were expected to do well in school and go to college. The women in the fiction have few aspirations beyond marriage and children. Like John, Mary went to Stanford. Unlike John, she got her degree. Carlton Sheffield remembers her as a fun-loving companion in many adventures. She was often part of their high-jinks, drinking with them, shocking more sober citizens with their "indecent dancing" and playing around with firearms. Mary's conduct suggests anything but the stereotype of decorous and homebound passivity or bovine innocuousness that characterizes the traditional images of what passes for appropriate sisterly or daughterly behavior. Though their married lives took John and Mary into opposing political and social directions, up to and through their college years, Mary was John's boon companion and trusted confidante. Steinbeck's rare depiction of college-educated women is not a very favorable one. Mildred Pritchard of *The Wayward Bus* is portrayed as a foolish girl whose "liberal" learning does not teach her enough to know when she is being made fun of or used by a man such as Juan Chicoy.

In Steinbeck's fiction men are mostly mentored by or taught by men. In Steinbeck's life it was mostly female teachers who played important roles in the encouragement of his writing. And Steinbeck was not unaware of the significance of these mentors. As a young writer he expressed his admiration for Edith Mirrielees in a letter to Robert Cathcart. "Miss Mirrilees is very good for one. She does one thing for you. She makes you

get over what you want to say. Her only really vicious criticism
is directed toward turgidity and that is a good thing. I like Miss
Mirrielees as a person and admire her as a critic" (Benson 59).
Steinbeck was not the only student inspired by Mirrielees. She is
one of a handful of Stanford teaching legends, tiny but tough, af-
fectionately referred to in the *Stanford Observer* as Stanford's
"first 100-pound heavyweight." Generations of students were
given the advice to take everything that Edith Mirrielees taught.
Later in his life, reflecting on the importance of such instructors,
Steinbeck wrote in the *CTA Journal* of his good fortune in finding three inspiring teachers in his life. He mentions Edith Mirrielees, though not by name, and Ed Ricketts, but the heart of the
article is a rhapsody to Emma Hawkins, his high school science
and math teacher. She inflamed him with curiosity and encouraged him in his independence and uniqueness. He concludes, "I
suppose that to a large extent I am the unsigned manuscript of
that high school teacher." In Steinbeck's reflections, Hawkins
and Mirrielees rank with Ricketts as teachers of "deathless
power." In his fiction, only Ricketts makes an appearance.

Female teachers played key roles throughout his academic
career. In high school, before he entered Miss Hawkins' class,
his writing was encouraged by Miss Cupp, his freshman composition teacher. Though he may not have been an outstanding
student in other subjects, in her class his works were used as
models for the other students. She was there at a crucial time
when his desire to be a writer was in its nascent stage. Positive
reinforcement during the tender early years when the ego is
most vulnerable should not be undervalued. On his second go-
round at Stanford Steinbeck joined the English Club where he
came under the influence of Margery Bailey who is described by
students of the time as something of a fire-eater. She was a Yale
Ph. D., opinionated, fierce, strong-willed, and a forceful and in-
spirational teacher. She helped establish the Ashland Shakespeare Festival and was not only a full professor, but an actress of
some ability. The *Palo Alto Times* obituary describes her teaching as "a drama in itself." Steinbeck and Bailey were often at
odds, their relationship marked by battle and disagreement, but
he thought enough of her to write her on the occasion of her re-
tirement in 1956. It is not a perfunctory congratulatory note, but
a five-page handwritten letter. In it he recalls her "sharp rapier
thrusts" and "acid, wise funny work." He reminisces: "I can hear
your bawdy laughter."[2] Her like is nowhere in his fiction. There

are strong women there, but they are usually uneducated and theirs is a quiet strength. Given the general level of education of women in Steinbeck's works, a woman of professorial rank is hardly a possibility. Yet the percentage of female professors in the late twenties was 28% of all faculty, greater than in the early nineteen-eighties when the percentage was only 26.3. Moreover, this is not just a question of statistics; female professors were a significant part of Steinbeck's university education.

Steinbeck does sprinkle his literary landscape with a few female school teachers, but they are hardly exemplary. Miss Martin wants Tularecito whipped because she lacks understanding of his nature. Molly Morgan, who succeeds her, shows little more insight. She fires Tularecito's imagination to disastrous results. Unlike Steinbeck's real-life teachers who were strong-minded and resolute, Molly Morgan daydreams and cannot face the reality of her father's alcoholism. Her solution to her problem is to run away.

When Steinbeck left school and married, he chose a woman who was in every sense of the word a partner in his life. While they were engaged he described her as having a "sharp and penetrating" mind (Benson 155). And after they were married she made use of that mind as both editor and critic of his work. In the opinion of those who knew them, Carol Henning Steinbeck was a crucial element in her husband's success. In Richard Albee's opinion she was "as good a wife as a writer in those times could ever have wanted. She kept things going with so little money . . . she was a source of all sorts of imaginative flights of fancy . . . and a good critic. She kept them fed and clothed and never expected John to get out and work" (Albee interview, 1975).[3] According to Thom Steinbeck it was Carol who made his father. In his opinion, manuscripts would never have gotten to New York without her (Detro 3). Ed Ricketts Jr. recalls that his father thought of Carol as "the backbone of John's writing" (Detro 3). In what may be one of his few fictional depictions of a woman modeled somewhat on Carol, Steinbeck describes Elisa who is, as Carol was, "handsome," and "able." However, her abilities are circumscribed in traditional feminine arenas— she grows flowers. In "The Chrysanthemums" Elisa is a woman who longs to live an adventuresome life, but is told that it is no life for a lady. When Henry offers to take her to the fights, where boxers break each other's noses and blood runs down their chests, Elisa declines and settles for the symbolic blood of wine instead. Carol Steinbeck was hardly so squeamish. Given to some violence herself, she is said to have opened up John's jaw with a left hook in one of their more furious melees (Detro 12). Rather than escaping the confinement of the pot-like valley, Elisa is defeated—ending the story by "crying like an old woman." Carol was by all accounts undefeated—in Joseph Campbell's words "resilient—full of fun" quite at home in a man's world of boistrousness, bawdy, and drink. No such wives occur in the fiction. The wives in the fiction tend to be Puritanical and restrictive, inhibiting their husband's and their children's natural high spirits. They do not share in their husband's partying and drinking. When Juan Chicoy's wife Alice drinks, she is alone and Steinbeck depicts her as anything but fun. It is a venomous portrait.

In the years of his marriage to Carol, Steinbeck associated with many active and assertive women, women who provided him with materials for his writing—women whose work was not in traditional spheres. They are nowhere to be found in his fiction, even when that fiction grew out of activities in which they were crucially involved. During these years of growth and productivity, (it could easily be argued that the novels of the 30s were Steinbeck's finest works), Carol and John lived in and near Pacific Grove where they were associated with many bright and creative people. One of the main centers for gatherings, both intellectual and convivial, was Ed Ricketts' legendary "lab" on old Ocean View Avenue. Joseph Campbell, who lived in the area for a brief period, remembers the fun they had, even though everyone was broke. Everyone was generous with whatever they had (Campbell interview). Carol recalls evenings of sitting around in a circle on the floor, sharing a jug of wine (Brown interview). If newcomers wished to join the group, they were judged, not by their sex or social class, but by what was in their minds (Scardigli interview). Among the women who were part of what some Steinbeck scholars have referred to as "the inner circle" were Virginia Scardigli, Margery Lloyd, Toni Jackson, Jean Ariss and Dr. Elizabeth Ott. Scardigli, Jackson, and Lilith James, a later addition, were part of the group of gifted children studied for Dr. Lewis Terman's landmark work on the effects of exceptional IQ. Bruce Ariss was also one of the "termites." As individuals with this level of IQ make up but one half of one percent of the population, it is statistically extraordinary that four should have been part of the lab group and not unnoteworthy that three of those four were women.

The lab group were an exceptional lot by any standards, and the women more than held their own. Scardigli remembers that the women were every bit as active in the conversations as the men, and that when someone from the outside would come in and act as if his opinion carried more weight because he was a man, the women would, in her words, "pooh-pooh" him, finding his attitude ridiculous. The women in the group were not only talented, they were also well-educated. Virginia Scardigli had graduated from Berkeley with a degree in anthropology. Margery Lloyd's degree was from McGill. Lloyd later became the editor of the *Carmel Pine Cone*. Jean Ariss published two novels. Elizabeth Ott was a psychiatrist. Lilith James co-authored, among other things, *Bloomer Girl*.

While women may have been an important component in the real life at the lab, Steinbeck's nostalgic recreation of these times in *Cannery Row* and *Sweet Thursday* is hardly egalitarian. In both books he panders to time-worn sexist clichés. In *Cannery Row* the only recurring female characters are Dora Flood, the madam of the Bear Flag, and Mrs. Molloy, the impossible wife who wants curtains for the boiler which has no window. There is also the strangely poignant story of party-loving Mary Talbot, who tries to keep despondency away from her writer-husband and gives six birthday parties a year. She ends up with the most stereotyped of solutions to her problem—pregnancy. Though friends from the lab period insist that Mary Talbot is modeled after Tal Lovejoy, there are also similarities between the Talbots and the Steinbecks. Like Carol and John at the time, the Talbots are very poor. Like John, Tom Talbot is a brooding young writer. Like Carol, Mary is a woman of irrepressible gaiety, who loves parties. But unlike Carol who worked to support the family and then came home to type the manuscripts, Mary Talbot stays home giving tea parties for cats while Tom works.

Much is made, both in the fiction characterization of Ed Ricketts as the Doc of both *Cannery Row* and *Sweet Thursday* and in his earlier prototype as Doc Burton in *In Dubious Battle*, of his far-ranging intellect, his fascination with novel ideas and extravagant theories. As the narrator explains, "His mind had no horizon." In the fiction these ideas are shared with men. When philosophizing about the row, it is Richard Frost who listens to Doc's views. When, in *Sweet Thursday* Doc takes a female companion with him to hunt octopi, the nameless girl is portrayed as interested only in Doc's romantic attentions, not at all in zoology. She gets angry when Doc becomes passionate about his subject. The women who visit Doc at the lab are portrayed, more or less, as hot and cold running bedmates. When Henri the painter visits Doc with his ghost problem there is a nameless girl in his basement who easily transfers her sexual interest from Doc to Henri. Of the women portrayed, there is not even a hint of any intellect to go with the sexuality. The only women who come to the parties that are thrown for Doc are the "girls" and Dora from the Bear Flag.

In reality, the women who attended parties at the lab were passionately interested in ideas. More than one, when recalling the period, mentioned Ed Ricketts' wall diagram of historical and artistic cycles. Dr. Evelyn Ott, who had been a student of Jung, loaned the group *Modern Men in Search of a Soul*, from which John and Ed derived theories of writing based on Jung's theses about levels of consciousness (Ariss 54). Bruce Ariss describes Evelyn Ott and Ed Ricketts as the Yin and Yang of the lab group, the only two who had achieved the rarified third level of Jung's categories, the Conscious level (56). Ott and John and Ed often discussed Jung's theories and Ariss thinks these discussions had a profound influence on John. Ott was a strong advocate of Steinbeck even after others in the lab group thought he had gone high-hat with success.

Another of the more vocal contributors to conversations at the lab was Beth Ingels, Carol's business partner at one time. Ingels was a talented journalist with a lusty sense of humor. She had grown up in Corral de Tierra, a valley off the road between Salinas and Monterey, and often told stories to the group about her childhood and the people in the valley. Steinbeck used these stories as the basis for *Pastures of Heaven*. Some years later Beth Ingels published her own versions of these tales in the *Monterey Herald*. Ingels was not the only woman who fed Steinbeck story matter. Sue Gregory, a Spanish teacher at Monterey High, was the source for many of the stories that became the basis for *Tortilla Flat*. Interpretations vary about what Steinbeck got from whom in terms of material for this book, but as the dedication is to Susan Gregory, one can deduce that she was the main source. Gene Detro claims that Gregory handed over to Steinbeck transcriptions of the tales she had collected over the years about the Spanish-speaking inhabitants of certain areas in New Monterey, but that when it came to giving her credit it was Carol who insisted on the dedication. Margery Lloyd remembers Steinbeck's friendship with Harriet Gragg who lived in a big abode at the end of Alvarado Street. Gragg was known as the "patrona" to the Mexican people in the area and had many stories about their traditions and values. A remarkable woman, she resembled Steinbeck's mother, physically. To this day her daughter-in-law contributes to the well-being of the itinerent workers in the area, collecting clothes, food, and furniture for them.

Still another woman led Steinbeck to the sources for much of the material that went into *In Dubious Battle*. Sis Reamer took Steinbeck to meet Carol McKiddy who told him much about Pat Chambers, one of the more active strike leaders of the period. Steinbeck's initial interest was in writing a first-person diary-like narrative of a strike leader. Jackson J. Benson suggests that when Steinbeck switched from the diary-like narrative to the novel form, he used much that he had learned about Pat Chambers to model the character of Mac. Various writers have suggested that the character of Jim is more of a composite. Like Jim, Cicil McKiddy had served some time as an apprentice of Chambers. Jim Harkins, to whom Steinbeck read passages of the novel, also contributed to Jim's characterization. But the most obvious model for Jim was neither of these men. Working with Pat Chambers as one of the main organizers of the Cotton Strike was a twenty-one year old woman named Caroline Decker. Benson and Loftis are also of the opinion that Chambers and Decker are the primary models for Mac and Jim (219). McKiddy had worked as a typist and errand boy, distributing leaflets written by Decker, so perhaps he contributed to Steinbeck's knowledge about her work. In many ways the relationship between Chambers and Decker suggests the relationship between Mac and Jim. The difference in Chambers' and Decker's ages parallels the difference in Mac's and Jim's ages. Like Jim, Decker was the more intense of the two, willing to push the situation to its limits. Benson and Loftis characterize her as "impatient for action," "tough-minded and more militant than Chambers" (219). Whether speaking to strikers, confronting sheriffs, or trying to elicit support from a comfortable Carmel crowd, Decker was an eloquent and impressive speaker.

At the emergency camp at Corcoran which, like the campsite in the novel, was donated by a strike sympathizer, Caroline Decker, like Jim, began to take over more and more of the leadership of the strike. This was due in part to the fact that

Pat Chambers had been arrested. Decker who, at her tender age, had already had strike experience at Harlan County, was one of the chief professionals on the scene. Her youth and good looks contributed to the consternation of the local papers, who complained about sinister communist organizers who looked like the girl next door. Later Decker went to jail under the California criminal syndicalism law and Steinbeck knew about this, using the particulars of her jailing to defend himself against Eastern cocktail circuit communists who protested that his depiction of the strike leaders was unrealistic, that no strike leader would carry a list of sympathizers.

Decker worked in the field, as did other women. Reports of the period confirm that a considerable amount of the strike activity was carried out by women who acted as "guerilla pickets," often running into the fields to encourage pickers to strike (Benson and Loftis 214). In recent years, *The Steinbeck Festival* has heard from women such as Jesse de la Cruz and Lillian Dunne who endured the privations of the strikes of the 30s and later became labor organizers themselves. Besides the women who worked in the field, there were women prominent in supporting the strikers. When Decker desperately needed pipes and faucets for sanitary facilities at the camp, she turned to Ella Winter. Winter, who had paid for some much-needed gasoline, brought a wealthy friend who wrote a check for the pipe.

Ella Winter and Lincoln Steffen's home in Carmel was a gathering place for idealistic young leftists and communists. It was through Winter that Steinbeck met Anna Louise Strong, journalist, poet, and supporter of radical reform. Strong spent a day with Steinbeck after the publication of *The Grapes of Wrath*, sharing with him her concerns about the new underclass being created in America (Strong 186). Yet, in Steinbeck's strike books, the only female strike sympathizers are those seduced by Dick, the bedroom radical.

Now there is no requirement that a fiction writer be realistic, even in what appears by most standards to be a realistic work. Many critics have pointed out the license that Steinbeck took with the data he compiled about the various farm strikes. However, it does seem amazing that half the human race is so thoroughly obliterated from activities in which they were so significantly involved. The only significant female character in *In Dubious Battle* is a silly, bovine, baby-laden young woman with no understanding of the political situation. She is incapable of abstractions or ideals, her desires do not go beyond the physical—"I like to have a cow—I like to have butter an' cheese like you can make."

Just as Steinbeck removed women from the families and political situations he created, so there is no evidence in his novels of women functioning in the business world. And yet, throughout his career, he had close contact with able and competent business women whose expertise was crucial to his professional well-being. After a short period of time when Ted Miller unsuccessfully represented his work, in 1931 Steinbeck turned his unpublished manuscripts over to Mavis McIntosh of McIntosh and Otis. This partnership of women represented him for the rest of his life. Elizabeth Otis became much more than a literary agent. He trusted her implicitly and she was mentor, guide, friend, and confidante. He shared with her everything from complaints about the hysteria engendered by *The Grapes of Wrath* to confidences about the psychologist he was seeing in the 50s. His intimacy with Mavis McIntosh allowed him, a normally very private man, to communicate, during the difficult period of the breakup of his first marriage, "Guess I was pretty close to a complete crack up . . . I'm trying to pull myself together but pretty bruised as everyone is" (*SLL* 227-8). This he told her she could share with Otis or not, as she saw fit. About Annie Laurie Williams, who represented his plays at McIntosh and Otis, he wrote, "She is the most amazingly intuitive woman I have every met. She knows everything about everyone." He believed in her closed-mouth reliability. No bright, able and dependable business women inhabit his fictional world.

Steinbeck's life, from beginning to end, was filled with women. He married three times and had numerous affairs. Attended by women all his life, he was surrounded by them when he died. In the room with him were his wife Elaine and Nancy Kester, a doctor friend. A nurse was there also. Elizabeth Otis and Shirley Fisher were in the living room.

There is no requirement that a fiction writer be autobiographical—his fictional world need not replicate his personal world. Art is selective. Its focus is restricted. Still it seems oddly inexplicable that every time Steinbeck selected, he chose to leave women out of a landscape they so prominently inhabited. Steinbeck was not unaware of this problem area in his writing. He broached the subject in a letter to Katherine Beswick, another woman with whom he had an intimate and intellectual relationship. Having sent her his manuscript to edit, he asks that she "kick the lame sentences into shape" and for her to "brace up punctuation and spelling" (Ltr 2/27/28).[4] He tells her that he knows no one else on the earth that he would trust with his sentences. When he married Carol, she was accorded these privileges and more. The manuscript Beswick had was *Cup of Gold* and in his discussion of the female characters, Steinbeck claims that he has played it safe by not attempting to enter their minds.

In his letters to Beswick, Steinbeck makes some statements that are amazingly similar to those of feminist critics in our decade. His response to Beswick's suggestion that she support him so that he can be free to write is refused because he considers her work as important as his. This may have been simply a convenient way to reject her offer, but other statements in the letters are of a curiously feminist tone. He declares that women have been forced into patterns of conduct by men and that most male writers cannot portray them well. In his analysis of the depiction of women in literature, he explains that most literature is written by men who have given other men erroneous characterizations of women, using Cabell, Conrad, and Lawrence as examples of writers who knew little if anything about women. To avoid this pitfall in his own writing, he claims that in creating female characters he uses only the "outward manifestations of some I have known." His scarce use of female characters in his subsequent works might have resulted from his insecurity about his ability to understand a woman's motivations or viewpoint. The sources of Steinbeck's insecurity about women are not clear. Perhaps the very importance and power they had in his life is the reason he turned the tables so completely in his fiction, the one area in which he was in complete control.

Throughout his life Steinbeck expressed the belief that he had a negative effect on women. Before his first marriage he wrote Katherine Beswick that he wouldn't marry Carol because he "would not make her happy." In a letter to Bo Beskow he expressed the feeling that men and women "should never come together except in bed. There is the only place where their natural hatred of each other is not so apparent" (*SLL* 313). To Beskow he also confided that he was not good for wives, claiming that he liked women, it was only wives he had trouble with (*SLL* 322). Again to Beskow, "Two women were turned to hatred and pain by marriage with me" (*SLL* 343). Still this explanation is not totally satisfactory, for it does not explain his exclusion of educated and professional women even outwardly presented. Nor does it account for such deliberate omissions as the deletion of Carol from *The Log from the Sea of Cortez*.

There are admirable women in Steinbeck's works, but they do not represent the women in his life. Unlike the women in his life, the women in his novels are from the lower classes, uneducated and domestic. Their spheres of influence are the home and the brothel. Angela Patterson in her desire to exculpate Steinbeck offers the opinion that "it is very doubtful that Steinbeck set out deliberately to 'put women in their place.'" It is more likely that he found them there already and described what he saw" (184). Patterson's comment is instructive for its unintended irony. As has been clearly illustrated Steinbeck was not at all describing what he saw, the world he knew. As a careful and conscious artist he was in control of the worlds he created, worlds in which he very deliberately put women in the places and positions he wanted them to inhabit.

Notes

[1] Two Hemingway sisters wrote books: Marcelline Hemingway Sanford published *At the Hemingways* in 1962. Madelaine Hemingway Miller published her memory, *Ernie*, in 1985. Mary Welsh Hemingway, the last wife, published *How It Was* in 1976, while Alice Hunt Sokoloff published her biography of the first wife *Hadley* in 1973. Bernice Kert's *The Hemingway Women* covers all the women: mother, sisters, sweethearts, wives, and lovers.

[2] This letter from John Steinbeck to Margery Bailey dated February 29, 1956, is housed in special collections at the Stanford Library.

[3] All quotations that are not followed by a page reference come either from taped interviews stored at the John Steinbeck Library in Salinas or from telephone interviews with Virginia Scardigli on 2/3/89 and Margery Lloyd on 2/13/89.

[4] Steinbeck's letters to Katherine Beswick are housed in special collection at the Stanford University Library.

Works Cited

Ariss, Bruce. *Inside Cannery Row*. Lexikos, 1988.

Benson, Jackson J. *The Adventures of John Steinbeck, Writer*. New York: Viking Press, 1984.

— and Anne Loftis. "John Steinbeck and Farm Labor Unionization: The Background of *In Dubious Battle.*" *American Literature* 52 (May 1980): 194-223.

Detro, Gene. "Carol—The Woman Behind the Man." *The Sunday Peninsula Herald Weekend Magazine* 10 June 1984: 3-6.

___. "The Truth about Steinbeck (Carol & John)." *Creative States Quarterly* 2: 12-13, 16.

Everest, Beth, and Judy Wedeles. "The Neglected Rib: Women in *East of Eden.*" *Steinbeck Quarterly* 21.1-2 (Winter-Spring 1988): 13-23.

Gladstein, Mimi R. "From Lady Brett to Ma Joad: A Singular Scarcity." *John Steinbeck: From Salinas to the World*, ed. Shigeharu Yano et al. Tokyo: Gaku Shobo, 1986. 24-33.

Lisca, Peter. *The Wide World of John Steinbeck.* Brunswick, NJ: Rutgers University Press, 1958.

Magny, Claude-Edmonde. "Book Review of John Steinbeck's *East of Eden.*" Trans. Louise Varese. *Perspectives USA* 5 (Fall 1953): 146-49.

Morsberger, Robert E. "Steinbeck's Happy Hookers." *Steinbeck's Women: Essays in Criticism.* Ed. Tetsumaro Hayashi. Steinbeck Monograph Series, No. 9, 1979, 36-48.

Patterson, Angela. "The Women of John Steinbeck's Novels in the Light of Humanistic Psychology." Diss. United States International University, 1974.

Sheffield, Carlton A. *Steinbeck: The Good Companion.* Portola Valley, CA: American Lives Endowment.

Steinbeck, Elaine, and Robert Wallsten, eds. *Steinbeck: A Life in Letters.* New York: Viking Press, 1975.

Steinbeck, John. ". . . like captured fireflies." *CTA Journal* 51.8 (November 1955): 7.

Strong, Tracy B., and Helene Keyssar. *Right In Her Soul.* New York: Random House, 1983.

Fallen Adam: Another Look At
Steinbeck's "The Snake"

Michael J. Meyer

Although John Steinbeck's consistent use of Edenic imagery has been long acknowledged by critics, only a few have traced his equally persistent preoccupation with moral ambiguity, the distressing condition which occurred after man's fall to sin.

As a result of moral ambiguity, fallen individuals are no longer able to distinguish right from wrong. Rather these formerly polar absolutes have become blurred and indistinct. In a post-lapsarian world, in fact, good can beget evil and vice versa; and it was such a perception of duality which Steinbeck often unveiled in his stories about Eden.

However, since Steinbeck's work contains many levels of rich soil for the probing critic, too often his stress on man's moral condition was overlooked in an attempt to examine still other potential interpretations. This tendency was particularly true of Steinbeck's short story "The Snake" which appeared in the collection *The Long Valley*, published in 1938.

According to Steinbeck, "The Snake" was based on an actual experience of Ed Ricketts, Steinbeck's closest friend and well-known resident of Monterey peninsula. More significantly, in his description of the actual event in *The Log from the Sea of Cortez* (xxiii-xxiv), Steinbeck acknowledged that the meaning of the tale remained a mystery to him although he recognized its power and appeal.

Yet despite Steinbeck's unwillingness to categorize "The Snake" by assigning it a specific significance, critics were not so hesitant. Edmund Wilson commented that "This tendency on

Steinbeck's part to animalize humanity is evidently one of the causes of his relative unsuccess at creating individual humans" (Wilson 38, 41). Obviously, Wilson's concentration settled on the lady in black, whom he considered to be an inhuman freak.

Others noted deep psychological meanings and quoted Freud and Jung, but only Warren French came near the story's meaning when he stated that the central focus of the story was not so much the woman as "what she allows us to learn about another" (French 82). However, French's further comment that "The Snake" condemns "those who seek scientific knowledge of the world they live in" (French 82) only serves to divert attention from his important initial insight.

French's initial comment is on target. The mysterious woman does allow us insight into another. In fact, she helps us to understand the protagonist of the story. Like Jay Gatsby in Fitzgerald's *The Great Gatsby*, who helps the reader see the true personality of the narrator Nick Carraway, the character of the woman serves as a mirror to Dr. Charles Phillips, the scientific researcher who was patterned after Ricketts. In exposing the doctor to this strange encounter, Steinbeck seems to suggest what outward appearance would deny: that mankind is still drawn toward primitive "evil" and mystical explanations of the universe despite our intent to progress toward "good" and success through science.

Dr. Phillips is presented as an Adamic figure, who as the original first man, has control of all the animals in an ironically prison-like Eden. Even the rattlesnakes recognize Adam (Phillips) and draw in their tongues as if not threatened by his presence. Unlike his predecessor, this Adam is scientifically oriented and believes that he can discover answers to the meaning of life through experiments. In fact, in Phillips there is also an echo of such Hawthorne characters as Aylmer, Rappaccini and Dr. Heidegger who also tried to reattain perfection for mankind. For Phillips these scientific trials are the forbidden fruit. He denies long-buried emotions and feelings, and instead exalts knowledge. In fact, he has progressed from an Adam to a kind of God. His specimens can be tested, regulated and explained by using the scientific method, a method which requires Phillips to be uniformly unfeeling. All his actions are head-controlled, rather than heart-controlled, and he is able to rationalize his "evil" experiments as justified by the potential "good" which may be realized from them.

For example, his starfish experiment requires random destruction of the ova in various stages of development. This casual extermination is justified as necessary for science, and later in the story Phillips proceeds callously to gas a cat as yet another indicator of his ability to separate feelings and emotions from his work. In each case, Phillips continues his experiments with little recognition or perception that his actions intermingle good and evil. He maintains that the prerequisites of death and destruction are sometimes necessities for gaining knowledge or insight. Maybe he has continued the original fall by maintaining that knowledge is all-important.

As the tale begins, Phillips appears to be fascinated by the nature of his job and anxious to get started with his task. As the reader watches his movement in the lab, he quickly senses that the doctor's efficient manner illustrates the duality of his personality. For example, he seems to care for the cat, as initially he pets it and treats it kindly; however, the next moment he casually places it in a gas chamber. Similarly, after eating hurriedly, he proceeds to examine the starfish he has collected in true scientific curiosity; nonetheless, a few minutes later, he begins another sequence of death.

The appearance of the dark woman with black hair, black eyes and a dark suit begins a pattern of light and dark imagery which will later allow associations of the woman with both Eve/temptress and snake/devil. Such syncretic allegory allows Adam/Phillips to "see himself though darkly" in her later actions.

In the initial stage of the meeting, however, the Adamic figure is too busy elsewhere to notice the parallels. Ironically, he is stopped in the middle of his starfish experiment, which is totally dependent on an accurate time sequence. Although Phillips attempts to finish his work, he feels strange as the woman quietly and mysteriously watches him play God by artificially mixing the sperm and ova. Then just as quickly as he creates life, he prepares to destroy it by arresting the fertilization process in stages and by placing it on microscopic slides for biological study.

This exaltation of knowledge again downplays emotion, especially the dark emotion which the woman epitomizes. Thus Phillips is annoyed that when he scientifically explains the process, the woman is apparently uninterested in his terminology. Yet on another level, her strange manner is intriguing, and

Phillips soon finds himself as an observer rather than the one observed.

Subsequently the doctor is fascinated by the dark lady's appearance, which allows Steinbeck to repeat the light/dark imagery. The doctor notes the darkness of the woman's eyes with no color line between the iris and the pupil, and he speculates that these abnormalities indicate a sub-human character. Yet, perhaps Phillips is merely sublimating the recognition of his own dark traits and is unwilling to admit the woman's "evil" exists in a "normal" human being like himself. The woman's sexual appeal is also emphasized as Phillips comments on her sensuality and is drawn to her despite his denial of a physical attraction.

Since the so-called "good" starfish experiment draws no comment from the woman, Phillips is determined to gain her attention by displaying the dead cat. This ostentatious display reiterates Phillips' own preoccupation with death, but again he fails to see his "evil" and instead explains the embalming process and concentrates on the fact that the dead cat will be used to aid students in bloodstream dissection. Thus Steinbeck reintroduces the head/heart theme of Hawthorne and suggests that the search for knowledge at the expense of feeling is an all too frequent occurrence. Although at this point Phillips believes himself to be faultless in his work, the encounter will lead him to acknowledge his own dual nature. Here he must confess that neither extreme, pure intellect or primitive emotion, is a positive, and striving to attain either exclusively creates deformity rather than normality. "Normal" man will always be plagued by the struggle between his worldly and his heavenly nature. However, like Aylmer in "The Birthmark" and Dr. Heidegger in "Dr. Heidegger's Experiment," Phillips has attempted to usurp the powers of God and to assert his perfectibility. Sadly, like the aforementioned characters, he also is forced to observe man's limitations and depravity in the image of his double, the dark woman.

After another short moment of uneasiness, Phillips again becomes observer of the woman. He is nervous and upset by the inaction of her body and the haunting observance of her dark and dusky eyes. Perhaps for a second there is a brief recognition of her similarity to himself, but Phillips does not admit it.

When he finally finishes stage one of the starfish experiment, Phillips does begin a conversation with the woman. After reading Steinbeck's physical description of the woman and noting how often he associates her with reptilian qualities, the reader is not surprised that she is interested in a male rattlesnake. In fact, when Phillips identifies one, she noiselessly follows him to observe it. Her fascination with the snake is obvious, and almost immediately she offers to buy it. The Edenic symbols of Eve and Satan here are combined as the temptress, the dark lady, is portrayed as both animal and as sensuous human. Eventually a contest of wills begins between Phillips and the woman, and it is evident that the woman is interested in ownership rather than possession. Soon the eerie nature of her actions becomes even clearer. Again sexual images emphasize the lust and sensual concerns of the woman, who seems to derive some type of sexual climax or ecstasy from her dark observation of the snake. Yet despite her outward appearances and the vivid description of her obsessions, her actions are no worse than those of Phillips shown previously.

Meanwhile, Phillips' comments underscore the theme of moral ambiguity: "'Rattlesnakes are funny,' he said glibly. 'Nearly every generalization proves wrong. I don't like to say anything definite about rattlesnakes but yet, I can assure you, he's a male'" (*Valley* 79). Paraphrased to express the thematic emphasis the section might read, "Humans are unpredictable . . . You'd like to think you can categorize them like animals, but generalization often proves untenable, and ambiguity abounds." Thus Steinbeck implies that as a result of man's fallen condition, relative rather than definitive statements are best when analyzing human action.

Although the doctor still sees himself very positively, his duality is further exposed when the dark lady reveals her fascination with death. However, she does not cloud her interests by attaching positive motivation to her interest as Phillips does. The bad simply is attractive, and symbolically she wishes to feed a white rat to the dusky snake to indicate the power of darkness over light. Phillips' reaction is abhorrence since he has already informed the women the snake does not need to be fed. As a result, Phillips considers the action to be wanton sport, unwarranted and unjustified. Steinbeck writes, "He hated people who made sport of natural processes. He was not a sportsman but a biologist. He could kill a thousand animals for knowledge but not an insect for pleasure" (*Valley* 80). Ironically, Phillips himself is guilty of what he hates. He is, however, able to

rationalize and explain away his own fascination with death and
the life process as justified by his position. However, despite his
revulsion, the hypnotic eyes of the woman persuade Phillips to
let her have her wish. Adam, seduced by Eve, gives in to her
request. Immediately, like his original counterpart, Phillips'
eyes are opened and as a consequence, his attitude and perception of his own work begins to change.

> He felt that it was profoundly wrong to put a rat into
> the cage, deeply sinful; and he didn't know why. Often
> he had put rats in the cage when someone or other had
> wanted to see, but this desire tonight sickened him.
> (*Valley* 81)

After he has agreed to the feeding, Phillips vainly tries to
make good out of bad and to find excuses for his actions. Emotion and feelings have returned to his life and with them confusion. But his initial revulsion still persists, since he eventually
suggests that another victim be substituted. This suggestion implies a sympathy for the rats and is contradictory to his earlier
non-involvement in emotional matters. Here he states that he
would rather place a cat in the cage because at least it would have
an equal chance. At this point it seems that Steinbeck parallels
the 'felix culpa' of Milton's *Paradise Lost* by suggesting that good
(Phillips' self-recognition) will come of evil (his succumbing to
the temptation of the dark). In doing so, he is echoing and acknowledging with Milton the inseparability of good/evil in a
fallen world.

But despite Phillips' evident modification of his beliefs,
the woman/temptress prevails, and the innocent white rat is
dropped in the feeding cage to be devoured by the snake.
Phillips' sensitivity to its imminent death is again heightened.
It appears to him as if the woman's body crouches and stiffens as
she sighs. Again her animal lust is emphasized, and a sexual orgasm is implied. The rat, on the other hand, seems curiously
unaware of its fate. Ironically, it is similar to the starfish, the cat,
and Phillips himself.

The doctor, despite his momentary insight, remains
unwilling to interpret or see the woman's evil as his own;
denying his duality he proceeds to describe the attack in intellectual, rather than emotional terms. Yet inwardly and subconsciously, he recognizes the symbolic nature of this event. In
the snake's destruction of the white rat, Phillips has observed

how "evil" swallows up "good" and how the two are strangely
intermingled in man. Similarly, death is superimposed on life,
demanding its end. Phillips is fascinated by the inexplicable
duality of the event, stating: "it was the most terrible thing in the
world" (*Valley* 80).

As the snake approaches the rat, Phillips goes back to observing the woman. In his eyes it seems as though she is paralleling the actions of the snake, again combining the traits of Eve,
Lilith and Satan. She weaves slightly as the snake stalks its prey,
and Phillips is afraid to look at her as the snake unhinges its jaw
and swallows the rat. The intense identification of the woman
with the snake again has sexual overtones, and it is apparent
that Steinbeck views the primal sexual urges as one of the evidences of man's depravity. Yet the doctor's intrigue with evil
and death remains central to this scene from the story. Perhaps
he even averts his gaze because he senses his own tendency in
the woman. Although he tries to justify the rat's sacrifice by
asserting that its death was painless and quick, he cannot deny
his fascination with the woman and with the rat's death. This is
a part of his fallen nature—that he is at the same time entranced
and yet repelled by perversion. He somehow senses that despite
his protests to the contrary, the forces of science have been sub-
jugated to evil, and the first sin of the first garden has been reen-
acted in a modern garden/laboratory.

Phillips' vicarious experiment with the woman ultimately causes the starfish ova data to be inaccurately reported.
In disgust, Phillips destroys the contents of the petrie dishes and
pours them into the sink. He returns the starfish to the water
and stops the embalming process of the cat. It is as though his
whole world has been called into question by this single
happening. On the other hand, the woman, satisfied by the
event, leaves and promises to return, but not before she orders
Phillips not to take this snake's poison because "she wants him
to have it." This statement also implies moral ambiguity since
the extraction of evil/poison would be used to create a good
antidote or serum. Steinbeck asserts in these final sentences that
good and evil will always stay mysteriously intertwined, and
unknowingly perhaps this intertwining will work for man's
good. Not unlike Hawthorne's Young Goodman Brown,
Phillips is left stunned at the end of the story. He has seen the
two sides of man's character and subconsciously at least has
observed that his own positive nature has identified and

associated with a woman who is simultaneously his opposite yet also a part of him: innate evil stalking innate good.

As a result of the encounter, Phillips thinks of three potential acts: killing the snake, praying to and accepting a god, and refusing to see the woman ever again. Wisely, Steinbeck does not have him do any of these. The religious solution would of course be too pat and contrived, but it does serve to alert the reader to an underlying meaning of the story. The reader also recognizes that the other two options, while more simplistic, are really not solutions to Phillips' dilemma, and thus Phillips is left in indecision. The event is merely "something that happened" and the reader, like Phillips, is left free to interpret its significance and its meaning. The reader may choose to delve deep into its significance or to regard it as insignificant and inconsequential, no matter how puzzling it may seem.

Regardless of this decision, Steinbeck's Adam/Phillips has indeed been changed in some way. An awakening of great significance has occurred, an awakening that is in proportion to the original Adam's enlightenment after eating from the tree of knowledge of good and evil in the original Garden.

Although critics may be left puzzled by the story's true meaning and whether the emphasis is on Freudian sex or the animalistic traits of the dark lady, a reading which stresses Phillips' initiation into evil should not be overlooked. Even though he is an adult, he experiences a rite of passage in this story by which he redefines himself and recognizes that duality is the heritage of every fallen Adam, a duality which leads man to seek good, even though an underlying evil motive also accompanies his thoughts and actions.

As Richard Astro points out in his analysis of Steinbeck's relationship with Ricketts (the model for Phillips),

> a philosopher cannot hope to explain the many contradictions in the world unless he is inextricably involved in them. Rather his is a philosophy of understanding and acceptance in which he seeks to unify experience to relate the unrelatable so that even nonsense wears a crown of meaning. (Astro 28)

Motivated by his friendship with Ricketts, Steinbeck believed in "breaking through," in discovering that the whole is more than the sum of its parts, and in convincing his public that there is a "deep thing nameless, outside of time, near immortality" (Astro 37) which is communicated in fiction.

Through "The Snake" Steinbeck found a creative synthesis in words which presented the untainted thoughts and actions of his characters and thus led his readers to accept an inescapable truth of the human condition and the truth about themselves.

As Steinbeck so succinctly put it in the *The Log from the Sea of Cortez*, the truth is this: man's "strange duality . . . makes for an ethical paradox" (97). It is this paradox which provides "The Snake" with such power as a piece of short fiction and which enlightens Steinbeck's admirers regarding his moral purpose in writing.

Works Cited

Astro, Richard. *John Steinbeck and Edward F. Ricketts: The Shaping of a Novelist*. Minneapolis: University of Minnesota Press, 1973.

French, Warren. *John Steinbeck*. New York: Twayne Publishers, 1961. Also in second revised edition, 1975.

Garcia, Reloy. "Steinbeck's 'The Snake': An Explication in *A Study Guide to "The Long Valley."* Ed. Tetsumaro Hayashi. Ann Arbor: Pierian Press, 1976.

May, Charles. "Myth and Mystery in Steinbeck's 'The Snake'" *Criticism* 15 (Fall 1973): 332-35.

Steinbeck, John. *The Log from the Sea of Cortez*. New York: Viking Press, 1951. Penguin edition. New York: Penguin Books, 1976.

Steinbeck, John. *The Long Valley*. New York: P. F. Collier & Sons, 1938.

Wilson, Edmund. *The Boys in the Back Room*. San Francisco: Colt Press, 1941.

Degrees of Mediation and Their Political Value in Steinbeck's *Grapes of Wrath*

Michael G. Barry

The problem with analyzing Steinbeck's *The Grapes of Wrath* from a philosophic point of view is that two very basic premises contend throughout the novel. One is that humanity is valuable because it is like the animal world, and the other is that humanity is especially valuable because it is unlike the animal world. This split is manifested in several ways, such as the difficulty in the novel of reconciling an agrarian philosophy and a socialist philosophy, and Steinbeck's two conflicting views of human efforts to make progress—one view that says even endless change does not yield progress, and the other view that plans for a better world.

The insistence in *The Grapes of Wrath* on the close connection between humanity and nature is unmistakable. According to Muley Graves, the way to determine one's ownership of the land is whether or not one is born there. "Place where folks live is them folks," says Graves (71). Muley has recently been spending his time lying down on the ground on his old land, and placing his hand on the bloodstained ground where his father was gored by a bull, so he certainly feels the connection strongly. The connection posited by Graves' definition is particularly true of the older generation. Grampa Joad, for example, dies very shortly after he is yanked away from the land and put on the truck moving westward. This agrarian sensibility, so explicit in the first part of the novel, is corroborated by the settings of the novel, by the animal terms Steinbeck uses in describing the Okie farmers, and by the earthiness of the habits of these Okies.

Most of the compelling images in the book are dominated by either dust or mud. Animals hover at the edges of many of the Joads' stopping points. And for the people of the land, these animals' presence is a matter of course; they are usually oblivious to the animals' fates. Tom Joad crushes a grasshopper as he rides in the truck after he is released from McAlester. Cats eat the entrails of rabbits as Tom eats with Jim Casy and Muley. Dogs copulate in the path as Tom and Casy stroll to Uncle John's. Al tries to hit a cat with his truck. Ma kills a red ant. Winfield and Ruthie are repulsed by the freshly killed dog on the road as they come back with their reptile eggs.

Even more important than the presence of the animals in the vicinity of our protagonists are the terms in which people are described. Al is like a rooster in his promiscuous strut, Tom like a rabbit as he lives in his cave. The mayor of Hooverville is bull-simple. Ruthie and Winfield are like crabs, and the candy-hungry children who get a great price on the nickel candy dive into their car and burrow out of sight like chipmunks. The people in the burned-out camps are described as "just like gophers" (*Grapes* 494). The Okies in general travel across the country like ants.

The biological sensibility is strengthened by the earthiness of the Joads. Grampa Joad is always fumbling with the buttons of his pajamas, and when the Joads are staying at Uncle John's, Grampa sleeps in the barn. Steinbeck makes a point of telling us Tom's method for stopping the bleeding from a cut he incurs while working on the car—he urinates in the dirt and slaps a little newly made mud on his cut.

The politics of an intense connection between farmers and their land is usually backward-looking, if not feudal. Agrarianism supposes that money, specialized labor, cities, and the benefits of science are antagonistic to a more natural state of humanity. Furthermore, when nature's benificent influence gives way to society's corruption, greater possibilities for evil ensue. Such a philosophy holds an enormously strong attraction for Steinbeck.[1] But the attraction is not strong enough to keep him from undermining the agrarian message at some key points, even early in the novel, before Jim Casy's prison stay has enlightened him about the benefits of group action. For instance, Steinbeck makes clear that white men had not inhabited this hallowed Oklahoma ground for very long: "In Hooverville the men talking: Grampa took his lan' from the Injuns" (*Grapes* 323).[2] We get several looks at the Indians, among them the story told in the migrant camps by a recruit against Geronimo: a Messianic Indian silhouetted against the top of the hill like a cross falls at the hands of the armed white soldiers. Even the Mexican Cession, by which the U.S. seized California, is alluded to as one means by which land was obtained. Steinbeck thus casts doubt on the stasis of agrarianism before this dustbowl upheaval, for already these Americans have inherited complicity in the seizure of land from people who may have had special ties to it.

Other features of the story also remind us that life close to the land had its drawbacks, and was not a connection to be wished for: notably the ravages of nature, the poor land, which the Okies had a hand in ruining, and the attractiveness of plumbing.

The alternative to agrarianism, at least by the end of the Joads' summer-long odyssey, is socialism. Ma Joad suggests co-operation outside of family ties early on: "If we was all made the same way, Tommy—they wouldn't hunt nobody down" (*Grapes* 104). Jim Casy, of course, later makes the best pitch for revolt of the workers when he talks to Tom in the tent; he is leading the strike against the owners of the peach orchard. He knows that the Joads will have to give up something to get to their desired end, but he is willing to push them in that direction. The strange thing about Steinbeck's penchant for socialism in this novel is that his portraits of the endearingly selfish and stubborn, take-care-of-your-own Okies have been so compelling that we lack the faith in the typical Okie's ability to mind somebody else's business for long enough to help in the establishment of any co-operative movement.

The attitude of the Joads that has always enabled them to get through hard times is to put one foot in front of the other, to take things one day at a time. The Joads cling to this habit, and moreover, their family always comes first. Ma Joad deserves respect as the pillar of the family and the one who always stands up for its unity, for her insistence preserves what at the time is the Joads' only human connection. The Joads' ability to survive has been attributable to their narrowness of perception, and their concentration on the present. They are not socialist material. Furthermore, Jim Casy's statement of the inevitability of change, the holiness of whatever is, and the real lack of purposiveness in change are convincing arguments against his own strike rhetoric later on.

"I been walkin' aroun' in the country. Ever'body's
askin' that. What we comin' to? Seems to me we don't
never come to nothin'. Always on the way. Always
goin' and goin'. Why don't folks think about that?
They's movement now. People moving. We know why,
and we know how. Movin' 'cause they got to. That's
why folks always move. Movin' 'cause they want
somepin better'n what they got. An' that's the on'y
way they'll ever git it. It's bein' hurt that makes folks
mad to fightin.'" (Grapes 173)

Now, I have been presenting the forward-looking Socialism as a
theory irreconcilable with a lifestyle that emphasizes the present.
In fact, it is a difficult task to reconcile what critics have learned
to call "non-teleology" with a plan for the betterment of the
world.[3] Ma Joad just cannot put meals on the table every night if
her family is on strike.

A choice needs to be made, and so Steinbeck offers us socialism, the system in which the migrants will be required to sacrifice the unity of the family in order to attain or hope for some
greater unity which will topple the existing order; they are to
look ahead toward a better time when they have won their battle, rather than to look down at their feet, and perhaps plan dinner for the evening.

We can begin to bridge the gap between the two paths that
Steinbeck wishes to explore—dinner and social progress—by
carefully defining his notion of socialism. It does not always rely
on a vision of a perfect world. Steinbeck wants to make clear
that behind his socialist movement is not a grand philosophy of
Utopianism, but one of need, need to avoid inimical conditions.
The people will join communally when they are forced to. Radical change will be created from below, not called for from above.
At first, all social movements consist only of people who are laying their feet down all in the same direction:

"They's stuff goin' on and they's folks doing things.
Them people laying one foot in front of the other, like
you says, they ain't thinkin' where they're goin', like
you says—but they're all layin' 'em down in the same
direction, jus' the same. An' if ya listen, you'll hear a
movin', an' a sneakin', an' a rustlin', an'a res'lessness.
They's stuff goin' on that folks doin' it don't know
nothin' about—yet. They's gonna come somepin outa all
these folks goin' wes'—outa all their farms lef' lonely.
They's gonna come a thing that's gonna change the
whole country." (Grapes 237)

Without an overarching philosophy, Steinbeck's socialism is issue-oriented and ad hoc. Progress is toward a single goal. The "group," which Steinbeck sees as an organism, is never all of humankind (notwithstanding Casy's "Oversoul" rhetoric, which perhaps is more applicable to the natural world before this crisis). Much has been made of Steinbeck's belief that groups are different from their constituent parts. But a group only comes together to insure survival in a conflict of wills, and in one regard, groups and individuals are alike: they both respond to opponents, and the resulting clashes of will (or whatever the indomitable spirit is called) yield no long-term human progress toward a good, but rather an equilibrium.

A look outside of the novel can help clarify some of Steinbeck's priorities. In *In Dubious Battle*, Steinbeck's strike novel of three years earlier, Doc Burton is the part-time philosopher and full-time doctor and health inspector for the striking apple pickers. Burton's perspective on human activity is extraordinary in its aloofness. He does not believe in any philosophy in which the end justifies the means, because he has yet to see any difference between end and means (*Battle* 253). He does not always preach perfect morality—he doesn't condemn immoral means so much as he debunks illusions about the ends. He doesn't try to dissect an action and ferret out the bad, for then he would end up getting rid of the good also. "I don't want to put on the blinders of 'good' and 'bad' and limit my vision" (143). He helps the party agitators run the strike, but he does it in a fairly disinterested manner.

Burton does not encourage revolt from the capitalist fold, but he will not discourage it either, because he sees that it arises out of the state of things. "When group-man wants to move, he makes a standard . . . But the group doesn't care about [the standard of] the Holy Land, or Democracy, or Communism. Maybe the group simply wants to move, to fight, and uses these words simply to reassure the brains of individual men," says Burton (*Battle* 45). Like Steinbeck, he believes that any newly established idea will begin to change right away—"the same gradual flux will continue" (143). Change is a constant, as it is in *The Grapes of Wrath*. Socialism for Burton, like so many other things in Steinbeck's view of the world, *certainly* doesn't deserve blame, even if it doesn't deserve approbation either.

Steinbeck writes an exposé of the capitalist system in *In Dubious Battle*; the tragic death of the new strike leader, Jim

Nolan, betrays Steinbeck's allegiance to the strikers. But Steinbeck's greater allegiance is to Doc Burton, the student of "Group-
man" who tries not to limit his own vision. Steinbeck sponsors
Burton's philsophy in *In Dubious Battle*, and retains that philosophy, I think, in *The Grapes of Wrath*.[4] When Casy returns
from prison, he seems to believe in long-term human progress;
he has a hope for an improved humanity. But such beliefs are
just a standard thrown up in front of a mass movement, a philosophy that serves the brains of individual humans who participate in the movement.

I indicated earlier that a definition of Steinbeck's socialism
might bridge the gap between short-term desires and long-term
desires. Unfortunately, an ad hoc socialism as much as a
Utopian socialism is a movement where ends must justify the
means, and some of the same hopes must arise. There is still the
dinner question. But I wish to defer that for a moment, and discuss the origins of evil in Steinbeck's world.

Jim Casy, like Doc Burton, seems to evaluate humanity
from a distant perspective at the beginning of the novel; like
Burton, he is non-teleological. He turns to socialism while he is
in jail observing people. He changes from dwelling on the
premise that "All that lives is holy" to dwelling on those who
bust up the holiness. And he discovers that these latter are usually the ones in power. He has experienced a fall of sorts. With
industry and specialization and whatever else it is that separates
a farmer from his land come new prospects for evil in the world.
Now Casy studies the world from less distance, and he becomes
morally indignant. Casy has changed and grown, and we can be
sure that he has some of Steinbeck's sympathy; Steinbeck has
seen things from this close-up perspective too. Yet Steinbeck
may maintain the distant perspective toward the human struggle even as he narrows in on moral atrocities. He has two perspectives, somewhat related to his two styles of narration: one is
distant, deterministic, biological, and survival-oriented, and the
other is close-up and concerned with morality.

In the perspective that is closer, that sees in the advent of
industry something new, the farmers ask again and again where
evil is located. Before, it hardly existed. Life may not have been
paradise, but all that lived was holy and conflicts seemed to be
part of the plan. Now there is the new evil of institutions. An
individual's capacity for evil is limited. Feeding the family is
often the primary motive that Steinbeck ascribes to those who

take part in corruption. Seldom will he upbraid a strikebreaker, or one who does not think globally. In one of the interchapters of *Grapes of Wrath*, an Okie being victimized by a compatriot who is paid to drive a tractor over the newly repossessed land complains of the lack of a villain. He first suggests shooting the president of the bank, and is told that the president gets orders from the East. The conversation continues:

> "But where does it stop? Who can we shoot? I don't aim to starve to death before I kill a man that's starving me."
> "I don't know. Maybe there's nobody to shoot. Maybe the thing isn't men at all. Maybe like you said, the property's doing it. Anyway I told you my orders."
> "I got to figure," the tenant said. "We all got to figure. There's some way to stop this." (*Grapes* 40)

The above passage brings us from the unmediated struggle between men to the intrusion of the institution, of the system. The system always enables the people in power to have less of a human connection with the people whom they exploit—they are relatively unconnected geographically, for example. Steinbeck blames the buffer that the system provides for making a human less of a human in the first place, for land ownership makes a man *bigger* than he is when that ownership enables him to walk on the land and have a personal investment in it, but it makes him *smaller* when it is land that he does not see, when it is the title deed he owns instead of the dirt. In fact, it is institutions that are posed as the basis of evil in this novel, and in order to understand the resolution of Steinbeck's themes, we should investigate his feelings toward the mediation between the natural and the human; by mediation I mean simply the intrusion into human existence of that which is not strictly natural.

If *The Grapes of Wrath* places an especially high value on an agrarian, land-to-mouth existence, where human beings live perhaps in social situations, but as close to the land and their natural sources of subsistence as possible, then the book must manifest at best mixed feelings about the institutions that are far removed from living off the land. But there are degrees to which humanity's reality is mediated, and so Steinbeck's distrust varies in degrees. Indeed, it varies even as Steinbeck vacillates between a world-view that is sentimental and idealistic and one which must make the best of some systems that appear not to be leaving us.

The mixed feelings portrayed in *The Grapes of Wrath* for the economic systems of agrarianism on the one hand and socialism on the other are reflected by some quite self-conscious comments on various forms of mediation which distance civilization from the natural: money and language. Money is specifically suspect when banking is involved; language is suspect especially when written, or when it is not genuine, or when it involves the replacement of reality with a named abstraction, and therefore permits long-range planning.

We have seen the motives for exploitation of the Oklahoma farmer traced back to the profit system already, and indeed, it is the bank which is portrayed quite heavy-handedly as a monster in this drama (*Grapes* 45). The system—any mediated system of human government—causes evil. Money, of course, is part of the system. Money has no place in nature. Steinbeck attests to this belief when he follows the progress of a nickel in a diner jukebox: "The nickel, unlike most money, has actually done a job of work, has been physically responsible for a reaction" (214). Money, in a normal situation, only stands in for some agreed-upon understanding, and *does* nothing; it is therefore a mediator, and hence its identity as the root of all evil should not be surprising. In the system that the displaced farmer complains of, it is profit that calls the shots. The thing isn't men at all.

Nor are linguistic systems men, and written language is another major threat. Written language is distrusted because it is not close to the land. Tom, in a short but memorable explanation, tells Jim Casy why his father fears writing: "He don't even like word writin'. Kinda scares 'im I guess. Ever' time Pa seen writin', somebody took somepin away from 'im" (*Grapes* 74). Why should Old Tom Joad trust writing? Writing is a way of controlling a situation, and he was always on the controlled end rather than on the controlling end. Writing could never have put food on the table for him.

Steinbeck's unsteady hand in the organization of his novels may be a large unintended capitulation to the part of his psyche that distrusts written language. Steinbeck may write in one-syllable words, but a writer always wields control over his reader. As a novelist, he must manipulate reality, he must impose order on a world which he has created. In *The Grapes of Wrath*, Steinbeck uses language for a political purpose, and his role thus becomes even more ambiguous. If Steinbeck's material sometimes grows beyond his control, perhaps that reflects a hesitancy on Steinbeck's part to hold such power.

Spoken language, unfortunately, may have the same potential as written language. Language always takes reality and attempts to express it in some abstract, arbitrary way, and is therefore suspect. But Steinbeck realizes that language is also *constitutive* of reality, and is necessary for defining our humanity.[5] He would obviously be ambivalent toward such a tool. Language makes a being peculiarly human and yet sets it apart from the animal world, a world that seems valuable for its absence of premeditated evil and its long resistance to destruction. Steinbeck inserts a discussion of language's relationship to reality into several situations in the novel where language's role could easily be skipped. The awareness he exhibits at these junctures is worth studying.

Language conveys in varying measures in *The Grapes of Wrath*. Certainly fighting, eating, pissing, and making love are all more interpretable actions. Seeing is believing. Hearing may not be. When Tom comes home from McAlester prison, his mother, like doubting Thomas, must touch him, feel him. She continually looks for greater signs of reality, such as blood. She has to study him, "her eyes digging to know better." Steinbeck tells us "Her face looked for the answer that is always concealed in language" (*Grapes* 103). Above all, the novel's characters are leery of fancy language. Tom Joad's conversation with the truck driver indicates Steinbeck's grave misgivings about big words. Bureaucratic language, for instance, has a much greater distance from bare reality than does everyday talk.

The meaning of language in *The Grapes of Wrath* is commonly not really connected with the words themselves anyway, but rather with the spirit. "Okie means you're scum," a seasoned traveler tells Tom. "Don't mean nothing itself, it's the way they say it. But I can't tell you nothin'. You got to go there" (*Grapes* 280). What Okie means is in the manner in which it is leveled at you, not in the word. Sarah Wison recognizes the formative power of intent just as the man going East who defined "Okie" recognized it, and she recognizes in like fashion the relative powerlessness of words, this time in prayer: "Then say one to yourself. Don't use no words to it. That'd be awright" (298). Jim Casy has been muttering prayers ever since he joined up with the Joads, but not everybody listens. Like these other examples, words carried no content in the instance of Casy's first breakfast prayer either, but it was hardly intent that mattered here, so much as form. For Granma times the pauses, and says "Amen" when they come around, while the rest are "trained like dogs" to raise their heads at the "Amen" signal (110). Nobody really listens to the words. But whether spirit or form, in either case, it is not the relationship between the word and object that counts. Steinbeck seems to be investigating this relationship. He is tentative as he works with the process of language, seeing if it has any inherent qualities.

One of the key features of human language is its ability to displace—that is, to talk about what is not present to the senses. This ability is intimately tied up with a human's ability to imagine and to conceptualize. Steinbeck at first casts doubt on that ability. The man at Needles who is coming back East from California can't succeed in informing Tom. Tom has to go to California to find out what he needs to know. Language fails in this instance, and so history will not work, and the displacement that separates a person from any given situation can never be bridged. Uncle John voices this opinion later on, as the Joads bathe in the water at Needles: "We're a-going there, ain't we? None of this here talk gonna keep us from goin' there. When we get there, we'll get there" (*Grapes* 283). And Tom agrees with him. Steinbeck must disagree; otherwise he would not have written the book. But he views the situation with sympathy, and he understands that people are hesitant to admit what they have not experienced. Learning is difficult, and we do not want to do it. But it is not impossible. Tom's and Uncle John's reactions are still not conditioned by the demonstrated failure of their old way of life, and soon, Tom at least will believe in concepts that he has not seen. This is the movement of the novel: not only from family to larger social group, a movement which is made explicit, but from stubborn unmediated agrarianism to the acknowledgement of the mediations of communities and systems.

By the end of the novel, Tom has seen what we have seen: that language has a more affirmative side also. He attempts to follow the teachings of Jim Casy, who is, as Tom tells us time and time again, a great talker. Casy is also an advocate of the talking cure. When Muley Graves is confessing to crazy thoughts, Jim tells him "you should talk . . . Sometimes a sad

man can talk the sadness right out through his mouth. Sometimes a killin' man can talk the murder right out of his mouth
an' not do murder" (*Grapes* 72).   Casy believes that his own
newfound ability to cuss, now that he's no longer a preacher,
does him good too (94).   Language even serves as a way of
making something real, something that wasn't real until it was
articulated: Ma tells the store man at Hooper Ranches: "Tom, he
wanted sugar in his coffee. Spoke about it" (513). The Joads are
forced to articulate their reasons for acting at their little family
meetings.   Maybe this is to give us as readers a look at the small
decisions that have to make up their life; it seems equally valid,
however, to see these discourses as a way of airing out their tired
thoughts.   Here are some of the machinations of the family's
business before they leave Uncle John's:

> Noah asked, "Gonna take the water down there or
> bring the pigs up here?"
>   "Pigs up here," said Pa. "You can't spill a pig and
> scald yourself like you can hot water. " (142)

Ma contributes her wisdom similarly:

> "Don't do no good to take little stuff. You can cook lit-
> tle stuff in a big kettle, but you can't cook big stuff in a
> little pot. Take the bread pans, all of 'em. They fit
> down inside each other." (147)

And of course there is Al's good sense about the car, now that he
is settling down and offering his help:

> "She'll ride like a bull calf, but she ain't shootin' no
> oil. Reason I says buy her is she was a pop'lar car.
> Wreckin' yards is full a Hudson Super-Sixes, an' you
> can buy parts cheap. Could a got a bigger, fancier car
> for the same money, but parts too hard to get, an' too
> dear. That's how I figgered her anyways." (137)

Steinbeck is relenting on the issue of mediation. He is not
so naive as to pretend that the answer is to return to cave
dwellings. The tenant has now got to figure. If he never had to
figure before, because his life moved along according to the dictates of the seasons, now he has got to figure. These farmers
make plans; they place mediating space between present and future. "Figuring" substitutes abstractions for things felt, whether

by drawing symbols in the dust, or by some other means. Steinbeck bows to the pressure and admits that to fight mediation, one needs mediation. He doesn't trust institutions, and even organizations such as unions deserve that title, but they are all he's got, and an extension of the philosophy he presents in *The Grapes of Wrath* leads us to depend on institutions, for however flawed they are, they now seem to be the only hope.

The acknowledgement of the farmers' need for buying into the system that has victimized them comes slowly. The Joads begin to work with the car, for example, and understand it. Mechanization has ruined them, but the Hudson serves them well (readers certainly remember it fondly).[6] When Grampa dies, the Joads have to bury him by the side of the road, and they have to accept some of the changes that the tractors have wrought. One of these changes is to trust writing for helping them to survive. Tom leaves a note in a bottle to be buried with Grampa, that says he wasn't killed, but died of a stroke.

The Joads go into the struggling world of the migrant camps, and they continue to "figger" in order to survive. Floyd Knowles will be glad to sign some document that tells him how much he will be paid for picking fruit; in fact, he demands it. Meanwhile, the "figgerin'" that was necessary before the Joads left becomes the terrible burden for Tom and for us of whether abstractions and future benefits of a strike can have any weight next to having meat that night.

If Steinbeck's socialistic purpose seems to be brought out by an analysis of his attitudes toward mediation, then we are thrown back into indecision when we arrive at the brilliant ending of *The Grapes of Wrath*, in which Rosasharn breast-feeds the old man. It is true, as many critics have pointed out, that her agreement to save someone outside of the family demonstrates a growing of sensibility. But the car is gone, and the family has come to a barn. The strike appears to have been futile. And the last action could not be more direct and natural. It is pure and unmediated—earthy.[7]

At the end of the novel, rather than tempering the agrarianism with hints of socialism, Steinbeck tempers his socialist message with a glorification of the unmediated.

The process of reading this novel, especially reading it a second time, furnishes further evidence for a non-teleological message. Each action of this picaresque is hardly tainted by our knowledge of the end. The reader's progress is analogous to the prisoner's one-day-at-a-time attitude, the attitude that Tom prescribes for his family. We frequently read the book by appreciating one story at a time, not looking ahead too much.

Because the non-teleological interpretation is most attractive, and because even a successful strike may not significantly decrease the amount of evil in the world, ends and means being so often the same, Steinbeck's ideas can seem deeply conservative. This conservatism, which affirms the place of evil in the world, emerges in one of the more chilling passages in *The Grapes of Wrath*, when Steinbeck talks about evidence of man's spirit.

> Fear the time when the bombs stop falling while the bombers live—for every bomb is proof that the spirit has not died. And fear the time when the strikes stop while the great owners live. . . And this you can know— fear the time when Manself will not suffer and die for a concept, for this one quality is the foundation of Manself, and this one quality is man, distinctive in the universe. (*Grapes* 205)

It seems that one person's spirit is another person's evil, and the desired state of things is a conflict of spirits, an equilibrium of human nature. We have here shed the blinders of good and evil. The very beginnings of the migrants' plight are attributable to spirited human beings who believed in a concept—their freedom to achieve it brought about the enslavement of others. The same freedom that the oppressed people strive for, apparently, is the freedom that permitted the failure that "hangs over the state like a great sorrow." The spirit that we need so much if we are to extricate ourselves from a mess is the same as the spirit which brought it,[8] just as institutions might be the answer to the woes of other institutions.

Man's distinction in the universe is an interesting point of departure in trying to correlate all of the themes in this epic novel, for within the distant perspective that Steinbeck adopts, with its non-teleological component, humanity is animalistic; whatever is peculiarly human is de-emphasized. Many human actions would be best if governed by the dictum that "A man's gotta do what he's gotta do." This reduction of human behavior removes the basis for morality. If all behavior is "got to's," then responsibility for that behavior goes by the way, and we have no judgment of what is evil (and not so incidentally, also none of what is good). "A man's gotta do what a man's gotta do" is also a deterministic philosophy, one that implies that a man's hand is always forced by circumstance. Because each human acts the same as the next, individuality is de-emphasized, and humans are valuable mostly as they make up the collective. Here there is a total annihilation of a good/bad spectrum, of any axiological system. The same is true of the philosophy that "All that lives is holy." The universe has much less meaning. But eradication of meaning in this case is in turn a meaning, since the only meaning we had before was a pessimistic one. Rather than disillusionment, lack of meaning is a victory.[9] Now nobody has a malevolent will either, and the battle is only one of survival. Consider Doc's speech in *In Dubious Battle* (143). Is there really an eradication of meaning? Or is his keen interest in process in turn a meaning?

Humans are like animals, and yet in the face of Casy's determinism, Steinbeck has averred that only humans can suffer and die for a concept, and that "in the whole universe only man can change" (*Grapes* 267). Casy has said that they change when they have to. But can not animals also do that? The key is that animals cannot plan, they cannot "figger," they may communicate, but they cannot talk about what is not in the room. For that, they need to conceptualize, to have words for that which is displaced.

I return now, with some trepidation, to Casy's belief in the peach pickers' strike, and what I feel is his concurrent belief that one climbs fences when he's got to, and it's the best way. Does one work as a scab to have dinner?

Part of the way out of the problem is to say that the deprivation of the planning stage is sometimes not so distinguishable from the luxury of an immediate reward because so often there is no reward. But there is another possibility, and that is that the hope of future rewards *becomes* the immediate reward. Man is unique in his ability to change not because he is free and independent of his "got to's." His "got to's" can be incorporated into conceptual choices, because humanity can actually feed itself on abstractions and hope. Jim Nolan knew what he was about when he told the migrant apple pickers of *In Dubious Battle* that not striking would mean the wage for the cotton would go down next. He was changing the perception of what the workers "got to" do, by changing their hopes for the future. Tom Joad's father may want to have meat tonight and mind his own business, but as a human being, he can look into the future, and gauge whether or not some day he is going to say "Tonight, I got to go without."

The Grapes of Wrath has been considered a problematic book by many because the colloquial philosophy of its farmers seems to be merely a translation of some of Steinbeck's thoughts, because its symbolism is overdone, and because the mass of mythic images employed in it are confusing more than enlightening. But it has a project much larger than merely the sociological exposé of the migrants in California. It obviously wants to encapsulate some large theory of humanity. It is not a religious book. Its use of the religious framework is a way of showing the way that socialism can be posed as an alternative to religion, and serve some of humankind's basic needs for hope. Religion also has a touchy flirtation with affirmation of the evil in the world that is akin to Steinbeck's philosophy. It seems that we should be trying to solve the world's problems, and yet we know that there is something infinitely precious about the conflicts of the world as it is. The attitudes toward language, and even language's clumsy self-consciousness, are part of a larger project, an admirable project, and one that rewards careful reading.

Notes

[1] In "The Ambivalent Endings of *The Grapes of Wrath*," a thoughtful and comprehensive essay on the political stances of the novel, Jules Chametzsky maintains that an agrarian society with an "almost pastorally simple relation of man to the soil" is something that Steinbeck was committed to, that "such a vision and commitment go[es] deeper in Steinbeck—is certainly more emotionally charged. . . than any commitment to reform based on a planned economy" (39).

[2] Leslie Fiedler once commented that the novel is narrow in scope considering its epic pretensions, for it leaves out the racism of the peasant and the truck driver, does not mention that the owning class has also encountered hard times, and avoids the subject of black, Mexican, and Asian competition among workers (lecture at SUNY Buffalo, October 1988). It is thus the more remarkable that Indians are mentioned at all.

[3] In *Twentieth Century American Literary Naturalism: An Interpretation*, Donald Pizer mentions the oft-perceived incompatibility of the ideas of non-teleology and of the phalanx, or the group. "An 'is' thinking in particular seems to be foreign to the moral indignation present in much of Steinbeck's fiction of the decade." But Pizer goes on to cite Richard Astro's *John Steinbeck and Edward F. Ricketts: The Shaping of a Novelist* and Elaine Steinbeck and

Robert Wallsten's *Steinbeck: A Life in Letters,* asserting that non-teleology has been discovered to be mostly Ricketts' idea—that Steinbeck was interested in the phalanx idea during the thirties, as his letters reveal. Pizer believes after reading these books that "the problem in fact does not exist" (67).

[4] Both Howard Levant (in *The Novels of John Steinbeck*) and Sylvia Jenkins Cook (in "Steinbeck, the People, and the Party") point out a shift in Steinbeck's attitudes toward groups in the years between *In Dubious Battle* and *The Grapes of Wrath*. They are no doubt correct, especially when we consider the flawless administration of the government camp where the Joads stay, an administration that should be tainted by some of Steinbeck's insights into institutional action. Still, the difference between the two novels, to me, seems to be largely a difference in emphasis. If Steinbeck maintains an objective perspective and a moral perspective in both novels, he perhaps moralizes more in the later one.

[5] In his biography of Steinbeck, Jackson J. Benson points out the role of language that Steinbeck must have had to consider: "Language. . . starts by purporting to describe reality and ends up becoming reality" (65).

[6] I agree heartily with Benson's comment that Steinbeck's knowledge of and experience with such things as carburetors "has been part of the conduit of sympathy that Steinbeck has established with his readers. He gives a great deal of attention to small things which have meaning for ordinary people . . . " (166).

[7] Chametzsky believes that the ending of the novel may provide us with an insight into Steinbeck's politics; the book could have ended in the government camp, affirming the New Deal, or could have ended with Old Tom Joad's building the dike, affirming a proletarian theme. Instead it ends in the barn. Steinbeck's ending is an "evasion" of a stance, but an honest evasion, says Chametzsky.

[8] Although some readers, such as Agnes Donohue, have seen Original Sin played out in *The Grapes of Wrath,* R. W. B. Lewis, in "John Steinbeck: The Fitful Daemon," complains that Steinbeck demonstrates "an inability to confront tragic truth" and that "Death is always the end of experience in Steinbeck, never the beginning" (134-135). In other words, there is no vice in most of Steinbeck's characters. He aptly points out that *The Moon Is Down* is "woefully limited by the absence of anything but the slightest hint that the fault, the guilt, the very Fascism, is a manifestation of the human heart, and so detectable on all sides on the conflict" (136). Although these criticisms of Steinbeck are insightful, they do not account for hints in Steinbeck's work that evil is on all sides (*The Moon Is Down* may be exceptional), that human spirit is often responsible for a banal kind of evil. Lewis also believes that we must wait for *East of Eden* to find an instance in Steinbeck of the upholding of individual glory at the expense of group movement.

[9] Benson believes that Steinbeck had an "affection for the alternative to the anthropocentric view of life" that was unique among American Naturalists (244).

Works Cited

Benson, Jackson J. *The True Adventures of John Steinbeck, Writer.* New York: Viking Press, 1984.

Bloom, Harold, ed. *John Steinbeck's* The Grapes of Wrath: *Modern Critical Interpretations.* New York: Chelsea House, 1988.

Chametzsky, Jules. "The Ambivalent Ending of *The Grapes of Wrath.*" *Modern Fiction Studies* 11.1 (Spring 1965): 34-44. Reprinted in Donohue, *Casebook,* 232-244.

Cook, Sylvia Jenkins. "Steinbeck, the People, and the Party." *Literature at the Barricades: The American Writer of the 1930s.* Ed. Ralph Bogardus and Fred Hobson. Tuscaloosa: University of Alabama Press, 1982. Reprinted in Bloom, 67-81.

Donohue, Agnes McNeill, ed. *A Casebook on* The Grapes of Wrath. New York: T. Y. Crowell, 1968.

—. "'The Endless Journey to No End': Journey and Eden Symbolism in Hawthorne and Steinbeck." *Casebook,* 257-266.

Levant, Howard. *The Novels of John Steinbeck: A Critical Study.* Columbia, MO: University of Missouri Press, 1974.

Lewis, R. W. B. "John Steinbeck: The Fitful Daemon." *The Young Rebel in American Literature.* Edited by Carl Bode. London: Heinemann, 1959. 121-141.

Pizer, Donald. "John Steinbeck: *The Grapes of Wrath.*" *Twentieth Century American Literary Naturalism: An Interpretation.* Carbondale, IL: Southern Illinois Press, 1982. Reprinted in Bloom as "The Enduring Power of the Joads," 83-98.

Steinbeck, John. *The Grapes of Wrath.* New York: Viking Press, 1939.

—. *In Dubious Battle.* New York: Random House; Modern Library, 1936.

Steinbeck's Poor in Prosperity and Adversity

Sylvia J. Cook

> Most men, even in this comparatively free coun-
> try . . . are so occupied with the factitious cares
> and superfluously coarse labors of life that its
> finer fruits cannot be plucked by them . . .
> Actually, the laboring man has not leisure for a
> true integrity . . . We should feed and clothe
> him gratuitously sometimes, and recruit him
> with our cordials, before we judge of him.
> Thoreau, *Walden*

In 1939, according to Jackson J. Benson's biography, Steinbeck prepared a script for a radio interview in which he wrote:
"Boileau said that kings, gods and heroes only were fit subjects
for literature. The writer can only write about what he admires.
Present day kings aren't very inspiring, the gods are on a vaca-
tion, and about the only heroes left are the scientists and the
poor" (401-402). At the time of this remark, Steinbeck had already written three novels dealing specifically with poor people,
Tortilla Flat (1935), *In Dubious Battle* (1936), and *The Grapes of
Wrath* (1939), and he would publish a fourth, *Cannery Row*, in
1945. Two of these four novels, *Tortilla Flat* and *Cannery Row*,
examine the lives of poor people largely outside the contemporary economic impact of the Great Depression while the other
two make that historical situation central to their concerns. Together the four novels display a wide range of literary types and
forms, from the mock-heroic paisanos of *Tortilla Flat* to the
tragic Joads of *The Grapes of Wrath*; from the grim naturalism of
In Dubious Battle to the comic playfulness of *Cannery Row*.
They are unarguably all books *about* poor people, but if any more

precise definition of the common condition of these poor were to be sought, it might be tempting to say of them as Richard Frost does in *Cannery Row*, "'I think they're just like anyone else. They just haven't any money'" (129). We sense that Frost is wrong in Steinbeck's eyes, just as we know Hemingway was wrong in Fitzgerald's for his parallel comment about the rich— having or not having money *does* make a difference. Indeed Steinbeck's poor may generally be separated from his middle and upper classes by their vitality, vulgarity, and resistance to pru- dence and conformity, for such qualities do not co-exist in his world with the possession of money and property. However, Steinbeck's poor, beyond these distinctions from his rich, also exhibit an almost bewildering range of differences both among these four novels and within the individual books as well. This variety suggests either a series of changes and fluctuations in Steinbeck's conception of subject and form, in the context of the decade between 1935 and 1945, or a more complicated vision of human nature than he has usually been credited with. Since these different versions of the poor *among* the novels have been greatly emphasized, while the tensions and oppositions *within* the novels have received less attention, the main victim of this process has been Steinbeck's reputation as a thinker with a seri- ous vision of the meaning of poverty in America.

Alfred Kazin felt, for example, that Steinbeck's mind moved "happily in realms where he [did] not have to work in very complex types" (398); Robert Murray Davis argued that he "embraced one simplicity, whether an idea or character, at a time," that he lacked a tough mind, and that he never really "knew what thinking meant" (6-7, 6). Howard Levant found in Steinbeck's opposed views of the poor evidence that he was "not interested in rendering the materials in any great depth" (118), and Joseph Fontenrose concluded from his "fitful" vision of the migrants that he had "an inadequate philosophy for a novelist" (133). Steinbeck himself undoubtedly helped contribute to this sense that he was manipulating simple types for extreme effects by his introduction to *Cannery Row*: "Its inhabitants," he wrote, "are, as the man once said, 'whores, pimps, gamblers, and sons of bitches,' by which he meant Everybody. Had the man looked through another peephole he might have said, 'Saints and an- gels and martyrs and holy men,' and he would have meant the same thing" (1). Steinbeck's implication here is that a different "peephole" or a new perspective would completely change the judgments on his characters. However, not only did he change "peepholes" among his four novels of poor people, he also changed literary form, setting and circumstances and thus appeared to be offering four quite distinct versions of the experience of poverty.

The earliest of these versions, *Tortilla Flat*, offers a comic and mock-heroic account, in formal language, of the lives of a group of men of mixed Spanish, Indian, Mexican and Caucasian blood, Catholic religion, and common history and culture. They abhor equally work and hygiene, obtain the necessary food and alcohol for their daily sustenance by theft, providence and conniving, and display variously loyalty, generosity, shrewdness and wildness. Outside this central male group in the novel is a larger and not antagonistic community of almost equally poor people. These include Teresina Cortez, whose eight children subsist on a diet of beans which their grandmother dips from a kettle and scatters on the floor for them. Not only has the school doctor "'never seen healthier children in [his] life'" (227), but the children rapidly begin to sicken when given a richer diet of fish, fruit, vegetables and milk. There is also Sweets Ramirez who delights in a motorless vacuum cleaner, and Cornelia Ruiz who is "nice" (243) to men who bring her gifts, but just as willing to "comfort" (192) those who come empty-handed. In this whole community, wealth and material possessions prove merely burdensome and exhausting for their owners: Danny feels only relief when his second house is burned, and the Pirate's great joy comes in giving away a thousand dollars for a gold candlestick for a saint. Torrelli, the single acquisitive businessman in the community, is constantly bested in his dealing with the paisanos and pays dearly for his few successes in frustration and suspicion. Insofar as poverty is a pervasive presence in the world of *Tortilla Flat*, it appears not merely endurable but even attractive and healthy for both body and soul.

In 1936, only one year later, Steinbeck presented, by contrast, in *In Dubious Battle*, a cold detached enquiry into poverty in the lives of a very different group of poor people in a dramatically changed context. These poor consist of migrant fruit-pickers, not men alone, but with wives and children whose only common bond lies in a strike which brings them physically and purposefully into a brief communion. They live in organized proximity, work grimly, eat greedily, and fight viciously together as a group, but share neither culture nor traditions. They are

greedy, selfish, filthy, cowardly, bloodthirsty, brutal and gullible.
They speak a coarse, vulgar and limited language which can
readily descend to growls and snorts in concert with their bestial
behavior. When Danny and his friends in *Tortilla Flat* refrain
from cleaning their house, the result, Steinbeck says, is a pleasant curtain of dust and cobwebs on the windows which makes it
"possible to sleep in a dusky light even at noonday" (239), but
when the "bums" of *In Dubious Battle* go without washing, they
smell bad, their untended camp looks bedraggled and littered,
their latrines become unsanitary, and no advantages whatsoever
attend their laxness. The women in *In Dubious Battle*, unlike
Cornelia, Sweets, and Teresina, find providence to be an ungen-
erous supplier, and are discontented and divisive among the
men. There are none of Steinbeck's "happy hookers" (Morsberger) among the women of this novel, and indeed there is
even a suggestion that Jim's 14-year old sister, Mary, has run
away to become a prostitute, and has thus been "'ruined by the
system'" (13). Unlike the paisanos, the fruitpickers are surrounded by a hostile community of prosperous people whose
emissaries and newspapers try to control them and whose armed
forces threaten to destroy them. They are unlikely to appreciate
the glories of the veteran's funeral that is given to Danny in *Tortilla Flat* for they live in a society that has burned veterans out of
their tent colony in Washington (255). They quarrel over the
minuscule items of property they own, whether a cushion of
newspapers or a can of peaches. Even the weather appears ugly
in *In Dubious Battle*, where a steady rain dampens both the spirits and the meager shelters of the strikers. Poverty in this novel
goes hand in hand with neither raffishness nor nonchalance but
reveals instead the sullen indignities and degradations of its
sufferers.

However, three years later, in *The Grapes of Wrath*,
Steinbeck wrote another novel of the migrant workers in California that provided them with their own version of the history
and culture of the paisanos of *Tortilla Flat*. Though, as in *In Dubious Battle*, they are once again uprooted families in an alien
land, they are no longer so utterly detached from the conventions and customs of a more traditional rural life. The Joads
bring skills, superstitions, standards of conduct, memories and
personal eccentricities along with them and their behavior encompasses a broader spectrum than the debased strikers, from
violence and vulgarity to hard work and decency. Though cre-

ated later, the Joads appear to come from an earlier stage of the transition into rootlessness than the strikers of *In Dubious Battle*, even though they reach a far lower point of destitution in the end. Like the paisanos, the Joads can be generous, comical, shrewd and wise; like the strikers they can be exploited, ostracized and demeaned. Unlike the paisanos, however, there are no miracles of sturdy good health among children on poor diets, no windfalls of money, no Torrellis on whom to practice tricky dealings for food and drink. Unlike the complaining women who threaten the solidarity of the strikers, the Joads now have a woman as the focal point of both their unity and endurance, and a tragic dignity even in the depths of their misery, derived largely from her presence.

Steinbeck's fourth novel about poor people, *Cannery Row*, returned again to a comic mode though not to the allegorical form of *Tortilla Flat*. It is once again about a group of men who have in common "no families, no money and no ambitions beyond food, drink, and contentment" (7), but now paralleled by a somewhat comparable group of women, the prostitutes in Dora's brothel. These two groups, in the Palace Flophouse and Grill and in the Bear Flag Restaurant, lead "decent" and "virtuous" lives (13) at the boundaries of civilization (10), borrowing some of its niceties but avoiding its traps and burdens. Although Mack and the boys do not embrace the predominant values of their environment, they are not opposed vigorously either: Steinbeck says of them, "In the world ruled by tigers with ulcers, rutted by strictured bulls, scavenged by blind jackals, Mack and the boys dine delicately with the tigers, fondle the frantic heifers, and wrap up the crumbs to feed the seagulls of Cannery Row" (12). Such a peaceable co-existence is simply not feasible in the worlds of *In Dubious Battle* or *The Grapes of Wrath* where there are no crumbs left to feed the poor, much less the seagulls. Like the paisanos, Mack and the boys can sustain themselves on the gleanings of a bountiful nature and the detritus of a comfortable society; unlike them they are able and even willing to work when necessary to supplement their wants.

If one considers the variations in circumstance, behavior, perspective and literary form in these works, it is tempting to recall Edmund Wilson's comment on Steinbeck, "when his curtain goes up, he always puts on a different kind of show" (36). However, so different did these kinds of shows appear to some of Steinbeck's other critics that he appeared to them to be engaged in an indefinite empirical observation of the poor that was producing not only contradictory literary consequences but also conflicting ethical and ideological judgments about their situation. One of the first critics to comment on this "discrepancy" was Edwin Berry Burgum who found in Steinbeck's work "an oscillation between the decadence represented by an amused tolerance for ignorance, poverty and depravity and a recovery from decadence in the social novels" (105). Frederick Carpenter labelled *Tortilla Flat* and *In Dubious Battle* "fundamentally opposite" novels (75), and F. O. Matthiessen found himself puzzled as to why Steinbeck should have written such a book as *Cannery Row* after the social and political engagement of *The Grapes of Wrath* (Lisca 197-98). Critics noted and pondered Steinbeck's ability to be by turns frivolous and somber about misery and degradation and to see poor people alternately as more purely human than other social groups or as inhumanly degraded by their deprived circumstances and hence in need of radical change.

In seeking to account for such variations, these critics proposed theories both nonliterary and literary, historical and formal about Steinbeck's changes in this decade. The most obvious historical theories suggest that some time between the writing of *Tortilla Flat* and *In Dubious Battle,* that is, in 1934, Steinbeck rather suddenly became conscious of the larger economic crisis of the nation and particularly of the plight of migrant workers in California. Thence he abandoned his endorsement of amoral poverty for the social commitment to eradicate hunger and want that underlies *In Dubious Battle* and *The Grapes of Wrath.* Blake Nevius found both of these novels to have been "generated by the impulse for social change" from which Steinbeck afterwards returned to an earlier and a "more characteristic point of view" (203), and Woodburn Ross similarly considered these two novels "products of the great depression" and noted that "Steinbeck shows a distinct tendency to shift his apparent interests with the times" (207). However, while it is true that Steinbeck became very closely involved with the migrant poor in California during the middle years of the Depression, Benson's biography suggests that, virtually from his childhood, he had observed and reacted to the lives of the poor, "had broken out of the mold of middle-class sensibility, had lived among those who actually did lack food and the means to obtain it, and

had developed a strong sense of social justice, giving vent to the
same indignation he was to express so forcefully in *The Grapes
of Wrath* nearly two decades later" (44). As a young man, Steinbeck had also become acquainted with bindlestiffs and casual la-
borers, and had collected anecdotes from Mexicans that he would
use many years later in *Tortilla Flat* (Benson 41). Thus the seemingly apolitical poverty of the paisanos and the highly political
poverty of the migrants were not separate historical discoveries
of the 1930s for Steinbeck but part of a longstanding interest in
the value and quality of the lives of the poor.

The more literary and formal theories about the differences in Steinbeck's depiction of these lives came from critics
who noted disparities between the two social novels themselves,
and who did not find *Cannery Row* to be simply a repetition of,
or return to, *Tortilla Flat*. Warren French saw Steinbeck writing
in a naturalistic mode in *Tortilla Flat* and *In Dubious Battle*, and
changing in *The Grapes of Wrath* to an anti-naturalist "drama of
consciousness" which he then continued in *Cannery Row* (43-
44). Howard Levant looked even more closely at the formal
structures of Steinbeck's novels and found the opposed and
varying attitudes in his work to be a consequence of his failure to
find forms appropriate to his ideas, and of his tendency to adopt
such rigid schematic devices as allegory and myth which inhib-
ited rather than enhanced complications of thought (128-29).
Even Edmund Wilson, who *applauded* Steinbeck's formal dex-
terity, acknowledged that "his virtuosity in a purely technical
way" had "tended to obscure his themes"; but Wilson was, nevertheless, one of the first of Steinbeck's critics to insist that there
were consistent themes underlying the surface variety and that
these were biological in nature (35, 36).

Critics who followed Wilson in exploring this biological
naturalism tended, like him, to see Steinbeck creating rudimentary and primitive human types so close to animals in their nature that they relieved Steinbeck of the need to explore their
more human qualities. By these biological criteria, the resilience
of Steinbeck's poor could be seen to derive from their capacity to
endure as a group, to reproduce and to adapt to changing envi-
ronments. However, even allowing for Steinbeck's tender and
approving vision of these natural processes, such features of the
poor hardly seem to merit his own label of "heroes." His fiction
is undeniably naturalistic, but like most literary naturalism, despite the myriad analogies between people and animals, its main

interest derives as much from exploring the behavior and attitudes that distinguish the two groups as from those that are mutual. Frederick Bracher notes in *Cannery Row* Doc's tip of his
hat to a dog as a sign of Steinbeck's "respectful tenderness toward
living things" (185) yet Doc, himself a biologist, makes clear dis-
criminations among those living things. He makes his living
collecting and selling marine biological specimens but when, on
one of his expeditions, he finds a woman's body in the ocean, he
is appalled by the idea of claiming the bounty that is paid for
such finds. Bracher himself reveals how easily an emphasis on
Steinbeck's biological vision may disguise a more typical interest
in character—he signals out Ma Joad as a prime biological spec-
imen of survival and then notes that the elements of her superiority are "humor, generosity, and tolerance" (193), not especially rudimentary or animal characteristics at all. In his four
novels about poor people, Steinbeck distinguishes similar qualities in them that are quite separate from mere animal spirited-
ness or endurance and reveals how those qualities, enhanced in
some circumstances, distorted in others, are vital to the heroic
possibilities of human nature.

   Prime among these qualities is, not surprisingly, a rather
cerebral one—a certain kind of cunning and scheming ingenuity
that permits Steinbeck's poor to survive by their wits in an environment where they have no material authority. Though there
are some simple people and some genuine simpletons in his
novels, these are more than balanced among the poor by the
endlessly resourceful connivers and manipulators who, like
Huck Finn in his "borrowings," can usually find soft words for
their questionable actions and cover their true motives with the
guise of benevolence. Even the paisanos who appear to live by
providence and concern for each other's welfare are clearly as
clever and deceptive as is necessary to provide for themselves
and give providence a helping hand. Their philanthropy flour-
ishes largely because they are all such willing objects of it: "Let
Pilon come by a jug of wine or a piece of meat and Danny was
sure to drop in to visit. And, if Danny were lucky or astute in
the same way, Pilon spent a riotous night with him" (35-36).
Though Steinbeck declares the paisanos "Clean of commercialism" (11), they are nevertheless first-class cozeners who operate
"with conscious knowledge of their art" (68). They victimize
and exploit one another with style and, like the best con-men,
acknowledge this style when they see it in others. When Pablo

and Pilon pretend a false concern for the welfare of Jesus Maria, Steinbeck says, "There was not the slightest tone of satire" in their voices, "but Jesus Maria knew it for the most deadly kind of satire" (72). Far from being primitives, the members of Danny's household are, in Peter Lisca's words, "extremely civilized" (88) in that they have developed "an intricate pattern for satisfying [their] wants" (88) that converts essentially anti-social behavior into altruism, or at least the appearance of it.

This capacity to dissimulate, scheme, extort and exploit reappears at full strength in the character of Mac, the Communist strike leader in *In Dubious Battle*, who proves endlessly inventive with the most meager resources. Mac, like the paisanos, can turn any person or situation to his advantage, can contrive and conceal and perform, work a crowd, imitate any form of speech, and conjure food and shelter for hundreds of people out of a much less sympathetic environment than that in *Tortilla Flat*. Mac is even able to vindicate his expedient behavior by claiming a higher purpose than the paisanos—it is to help others—yet his actions bring none of the pleasure of those of the members of Danny's household. His use of his old friend Joy's murdered body to provoke the strikers to violent action is strategic, justifiable and, certainly, morally superior to Pilon's plans to exploit the gentle Pirate for his hard-earned money. However, it is the very necessity of Mac's expediency that makes it so ominous, even to one of the strikers for whom he acts: "'Pal of yours,'" the striker says, "'and you won't let him rest now. You want to use him . . . You're a cold-blooded bastard'" (170). Mac is, in fact, far from being cold-blooded—after he has viciously beaten up a boy and commented, "'he's not a kid, he's an example'" (278), his muscles begin to shudder and he turns pale and grey. When he finally uses his friend and pupil Jim's dead body as a goad to the strikers, it is only by an enormous act of will that he can overcome his revulsion from the task and "break his frozen jaws loose" (349) to address the crowd. Mac takes no delight in his own skillful machinations for, unlike the paisanos, he has not chosen this mode of poverty for his life but had it arbitrarily enforced upon him. Such involuntary poverty, rather than enhancing the natural qualities of the poor, serves to distort them, as in Mac's case, into a grimly determined mold, or, as in the case of the strikers, to repress them so that they have lost all their initiative. When Pilon, in *Tortilla Flat*, discovers that The Pirate's treasure trove is intended for a candlestick for St.

Francis, he and the others freely relinquish any claim on it, but such an act of personal honor is not possible for Mac who has been robbed of such choices by the poverty that has freed the paisanos. Mac still has the calculating moral acuity that appears to have shrunk in the strikers from despair and disuse, and he willingly dedicates it to the Communist cause, but only in order that his world may someday provide a more acceptable range of alternatives than it presently does.

In *The Grapes of Wrath* the Joad family moves from what might be called voluntary poverty on their farm to involuntary poverty as migrants and in doing so they demonstrate how poverty may change from a combative mutual game where people use their wits to extort what they can from each other, and share when they please, to a desperate dilemma that excludes any playful reversals of moral direction. At the beginning of the novel, Tom Joad manipulates a truck driver into giving him a ride in violation of his "No Riders" sign by saying, "'sometimes a guy'll be a good guy even if some rich bastard makes him carry a sticker'" (11). The driver knows he is being trapped by this and responds with his own kind of blackmail by boasting to Tom of his ability never to forget a face, especially of someone who seems suspicious. A little later, when Tom reminisces with Casy about the ways of the Joad family before they were tractored or dusted off their land, he describes a life of scrounging, conning and trading that is not so far from that of the paisanos. Pa had provided his family with their home by stealing it readymade, although he had only managed to cart off one half of the house before the rest of it was appropriated by a neighbor. However, while these sharp practices of the Joads are presented as essentially victimless, or at least equal in loss and gain, when Steinbeck shifts immediately to the business of the used car dealers, there is no play in their exploitations of these same poor people who must now, by the exigency of their situation, capitulate to them. Even among the Joads themselves, the deception and victimizing turn deadly serious when they are no longer a matter of choice—Granpa Joad's death seems a direct consequence of the way he has been doped and smuggled from his home and Granma's death is explicitly a sacrifice by Ma of the sick old woman for the larger good of the family. Although Casy directs the reader's reaction by saying, "'there's a woman so great with love—she scares me'" (313), Ma's act is a grimmer version of Mac's use of Jim's body in *In Dubious Battle*, an ugly last resort with none of the thrill that comes with the lying and cheating of *Tortilla Flat* and *Cannery Row*. Steinbeck rarely shows poor people whose poverty has caused the kind of extreme mental and moral degeneracy of, for example, Erskine Caldwell's characters in his novels of the same period. At their lowest point, the Joads still prove pragmatic and thoughtful, but Ma's comment at the end, "'They was on'y one thing to do—ever—an' we done it'" (604), suggests that they have indeed been diminished into mere reactors to their environment. Though they cling to the notion that they are making choices, right up to Rose of Sharon's final one to feed the starving man in the barn, even this is clearly an act of necessity—the exchange of milk for a blanket, a moment of desperately needed relief for both participants. Ma kisses her daughter approvingly before the act, and the young woman smiles, but its virtue stems not from any deliberate altruism but from a certain nobility in accepting this gro-tesque fate.

In turning in 1945 to the much less stringent conditions of life on *Cannery Row*, Steinbeck did not wholly abandon the exigencies of the Joads' world for the irresponsible freedom of another group of single men. The tale of Joey's father, who killed himself with rat poison because he failed for a year to find a job, is in striking contrast to the lives of Mack and the boys who boast of their ability to get a job when they need one because they have the reputation of sticking to it for at least a month. The first of several suicides in the novel is also that of a husband and father, Horace Abbeville, who has two wives, six children and an intolerable grocery debt. Neither Joey's father nor Horace can avoid the tigers and jackals that beset the Joads, even in the different economic context of Cannery Row, for their families and dependents exacerbate every degree of deprivation that is not of their own accord. By contrast to the determinism of these two men, Doc affirms that Mack and the boys in *Cannery Row* have so arranged their lives that they "'can do what they want'" (129), and his admiration of them stems from their refusal to "'fight to secure certain food'" (11-12)—a fight that the Joads could not opt out of. Mack, who has "'qualities of genius,'" and the rest who are "'all very clever if they want something'" (130), do not allow themselves to be trapped in this worldly kind of wanting. They use their cleverness in chicanery and extortion and sometimes even in working to accommodate their most basic physical needs, but since these are relatively easily obtained in *Cannery*

Row, both their self-serving and their subsequent expansiveness and generosity appear as the products of wisdom and a highly sophisticated sense of priorities rather than as an acquiescence to brute necessity.

Besides this cunning and cleverness that separates Steinbeck's poor from their bourgeois fellows, they also share a pervasive humorous sensibility that is linked partly to a self-consciousness about their own conniving and partly to a disrespect for the pieties of others that enables them to parody and satirize them. The paisanos of *Tortilla Flat* direct a broad double irony towards themselves and their world, covering their thefts with tongue-in-cheek benevolence and the behavior of others with an extravagant cynicism. Even in the gloomier atmosphere of *In Dubious Battle*, Albert Johnson, a loyal striker, and Mac, the Communist leader, can banter about their cause and deflate its pretentious language, mocking the notion of the nobility of labor and claiming they have nothing to lose but their hair (243). In a reverse situation where Mac has solemnly lectured a bum riding a freight train on the virtues of sharing, the man makes a gracious formal apology before he swings out of the train. Then, as he hits the ground, he yells back to Mac, "'You dirty son-of-a-bitch'" (44). Tom Joad notes the same rude impulse in the behavior of children who throw stones at windows, in a metaphor reminiscent of Mark Twain, who also approved the disposition to sass and "heave clods" at symbols of power and pretension. Steinbeck's poor seem defiantly alert to all signs of sermonizing and humbug in themselves and in their world. Ma Joad quickly deflates Pa's rhapsodies on the superior plumbing at Weedpatch camp by reminding him, "'we can't eat no toilets'" (479), and Granma, for all her lip-service to preachers, punctuates Casy's ponderous transcendental graces with premature "amens" so she can get to her food (110). The final extension of this irreverent ridicule of false deference comes in *Cannery Row* in Monterey's efforts to rescue the intestines of its now deceased leading literary man from being made into bait to catch mackerel. The essentially subversive nature of this humor evokes Emerson's comment on the value of the pit in the playhouse—it is "independent, irresponsible . . . interesting, silly, eloquent [and] troublesome" (48-49)—but, it must be added, progressively less so in those novels of Steinbeck's where the poor find their anarchic energy drained or absorbed in the struggle merely to preserve their physical existence.

Even such an apparently inexhaustible quality as idle curiosity, which typifies all of Steinbeck's poor, requires the leisure from getting and doing that is lacking in his middle class but also in the migrant poor in their direst straits. The problems of obtaining shelter and food preoccupy them largely to the exclusion of the kind of luxury the paisanos have to live outside of time in passive contemplation of the world. After listening to a long story in *Tortilla Flat*, Pablo declares that he likes it "'because it hasn't any meaning you can see, and still it does seem to mean something, I can't tell what'" (257). By contrast, Mac in *In Dubious Battle* responds to Doc's philosophical speculations by insisting, "'We've got a job to do. We've got no time to mess around with high-falutin ideas'" (153), despite the fact that Mac clearly does find ideas engaging. In *The Grapes of Wrath* the only respite for Tom Joad from the burden of his daily search for food and shelter comes as the enforced consequence of his murder of Casy's killer. When he has to take refuge in a cave in absolute solitude, with no peaches to pick, no truck to fix, no family to care for, he is able for the first time to meditate on the meaning of everything he has witnessed, though Tom, unlike Pablo, is forced to resolve ambivalence and, like Mac, translate his new ideas into action. For the other Joads, the journey to California is accompanied at first by the great stimulus to curiosity of meeting new people and discovering their customs, history and even modes of speech. However, as they move inexorably towards absolute hunger and homelessness, their curiosity is ultimately replaced by a grim indifference to everything that is not pertinent to their material survival. In the final scene between Rose of Sharon and the starving man, not even names are exchanged, nothing but the blunt requirements of their physical necessities. Earlier, when Ma had pierced Rose of Sharon's ears, she had asked wonderingly, "'Does it mean somepin?'" and Ma had assured her, "'Why 'course it does'" (484), but the young woman's interest in symbolism, like her petulance, vanity, timidity and modesty, are all in the end displaced by the immediacy and acuteness of her plight. Not all of the curiosity of Steinbeck's poor is of a grandly philosophical nature—in *Cannery Row* Doc is obsessed by what a beer milkshake would taste like and the entire population of the town displays a prurient and trivial fascination with the toilet habits of the flagpole skater outside Holman's Department

Store. However, these concerns, though whimsical and comic, are still at the core of that enquiry and speculation in which people are most themselves and without which they are in danger of becoming merely biological exemplars.

Although many of the qualities which Steinbeck emphasizes in his poor people are distinctly mental ones, what has been more often noted in them is a dionysiac element in their behavior that encompasses ready violence, drunkenness and sensuality, and thus might seem to vindicate the common sense of them as primitives. However, their violence is almost invariably linked to a sense of justice that is either highly personal or in direct opposition to the injustice they see practiced in society. The paisanos' methodical beating up of Big Joe, Tom Joad's two murders, and Doc's vicious punch in Mack's face are all performed in anger spurred by motives of honor and equity. As the title of *The Grapes of Wrath* suggests, Steinbeck sees such righteous fury as a vital element in the survival of poor people, but in the worlds of *In Dubious Battle* and *The Grapes of Wrath* the enemies of the poor prove very difficult to identify and thus anger is frequently diffused and misdirected. In *In Dubious Battle* the strikers require constant goading by their leaders since they have almost no direct contact with their real antagonists. They are quick to quarrel with one another rather than vent their hostility on the true agents of their suffering. In *The Grapes of Wrath* the Okies wonder in bewilderment, "'Who can we shoot?'" and though one of them swears, "'I don't aim to starve to death before I kill the man that's starving me,'" (52) they rarely find occasions for this kind of impulse to bear fruit, as it does in the anger of the paisanos. The wild release of drunkenness is shared by all of Steinbeck's poor, usually as a communal ritual, but even that loses its joy when it is forced by circumstances to be solitary or to become the source of guilt and misery. In *In Dubious Battle* Dakin's whiskey bottle is carefully corked and put back in the cupboard after it has gone one round, and later, when it is offered again, all his visitors politely refuse, in grudging respect of his private property. In *The Grapes of Wrath* Uncle John's notorious drunken benders are the subject of Tom's early comic anecdotes, but when the Joads are down to their last few dollars, Uncle John must humiliatingly seek everyone's permission before he walks forlornly off on his solitary binge. Sexual instincts must be repressed by Mac, the Communist leader, and by Tom Joad lest they distract them from their purposes, and indeed all pleasures of the senses tend to degenerate to grim opiates in proportion to combatting the stresses of hunger and destitution.

In the first chapter of *Walden*, entitled "Economy," Thoreau proposes that "None can be an impartial or wise observer of human life but from the vantage ground of what we should call voluntary poverty" (13). Thoreau concedes however that this condition presupposes a person's capacity to fulfill certain basic necessities of physical survival—Food, Shelter, Clothing and Fuel—arguing that "not till we have secured these are we prepared to entertain the true problems of life with freedom and a prospect of success" (11). Thoreau suggests, only a trifle facetiously, that one might find perfectly good shelter in a six foot railroad packing case; in *Cannery Row* Mack and the boys find it in a fish meal warehouse and Mr. and Mrs. Sam Molloy in a disused cannery boiler. Thoreau suggests one might live on beans and unleavened bread; in *Tortilla Flat* little Alfredo Ruiz dines happily at every meal on beans and tortillas. Thoreau throws three limestone ornaments out of his window in disgust to free himself from the chores of dusting them while his mind is undusted; the paisanos set fire to Danny's house and his one true feeling is "relief that at least one of his burdens was removed" (82). Steinbeck repeatedly suggests in these novels that the possession of property and the getting of money for any purpose beyond the most minimal physical necessities of life are both corrupting and restricting forces. Dakin, the proprietor of the whiskey bottle in *In Dubious Battle* is also the owner of a truck, a tent and a family which are his first priorities before the course of the strike, of which he is the ostensible leader. In *Cannery Row* the Molloys are happy living in their boiler until Mr. Molloy decides to rent out the abandoned pipes that lie around them. As soon as he becomes a landlord, his wife becomes discontented and gets the fever of acquisition and respectability, even procuring lace curtains for their non-existent windows. Steinbeck demonstrates everywhere that the freedom of indigence requires the maintenance of a fine balance between material sufficiency and ominous surfeit, a balance easily disrupted even among Mack and the boys on Cannery Row, as John Timmerman has shown, by the intrusion of a commercial civilization into the midst of their casual and communal practices (159-60). The making with chalk of simulated beds, giving each man "property rights inviolable in his space" (33), and the pride of the

boys in the "formal" and "cluttered" entrance to their home (35),
denote the pervasive tendency to own and to improve, even in
those who have supposedly avoided the trap, stepped over the
noose, and walked around the poison (12). "Voluntary poverty"
requires a certain diligence in its preservation from complacency
and ambition, from which not even the paisanos are wholly
immune, but Steinbeck clearly sees it, as Thoreau does, as the
prelude to the seeking of wisdom.

However, just as much as voluntary poverty is a condition to be desired, most of its advantages wither when people are
robbed, by forces beyond themselves, of any choice in their way
of life. Although Thoreau argues that anyone may live as well
as he does at Walden, Steinbeck, in the 1930s, is no longer willing to make that universal claim about the promise of American
life. By focusing, in *In Dubious Battle* and *The Grapes of Wrath*,
on wholly arbitrary and enforced poverty, from which there is
no simple escape for the self-reliant individual, he insists that
certain social and political goals must be accomplished to ensure
not the eradication of poverty and economic inequity but their
free election by those who do not want to pursue the ways of the
world. Richard Frost, once again, in *Cannery Row*, focuses
pertinently on the issue by asking Doc at one point, "'Who
wants to be good if he has to be hungry too?'" Doc corrects him
by saying, "'Oh, it isn't a matter of hunger. It's something quite
different'" (131), by which Doc explains that he means the refusal
to sell one's soul to gain the whole world. However, outside the
available abundance of Cannery Row, Steinbeck acknowledges
that it may indeed often be a matter of real hunger, rather than
worldliness, that stands in opposition to what Frost calls
"goodness."

Doc does not quarrel with the term "good" in Frost's question, but it is perhaps an even more misleading one, for
although Doc clearly endorses the moral superiority of those
who choose to be poor, Steinbeck appears to qualify Doc's view
on this as on so many other issues. The appeal of the willfully
poor for Steinbeck is not, largely, in the virtues Doc lists for
them—"'kindness and generosity, openness, honesty, understanding and feeling'" (131)—but much more in their disrespect,
contrivance, wit and ease. Steinbeck depicts the poor less as the
fully realized humans Doc admires than as people who are free
to loaf, scrutinize and enquire into life. The poor are Steinbeck's
heroes not because they have arrived at any superior moral

knowledge or conduct but because they are open, irreverently, to the possibility that there is no moral knowledge at all. They are engaged in, but have not finally resolved, the enduring conflicts between the virtues of society and those of solitude, between an active and a contemplative life, between the lure of the flesh and of the spirit, between responsibility and freedom. They are involved in those struggles within themselves whose conduct, according to Yeats, is the subject of poetry, but in order to be able to participate in this struggle within, the external, or rhetorical struggle with others must sometimes be encountered first. In taking up that external struggle in *In Dubious Battle* and *The Grapes of Wrath*, Steinbeck was not turning from decadence to wholesomeness nor from art to propaganda, but rather exploring those forces, generally absent in Thoreau, that keep the poor from being their cranky and extravagant selves. When the poor in Steinbeck's fiction are deprived of the freedom to choose, poverty becomes for them as destructive of human possibilities as property. With that freedom (and of course with many comic qualifications), poverty becomes, as in Thoreau, the first step towards an authentic and worthy life.

Works Cited

Benson, Jackson J. *The True Adventures of John Steinbeck, Writer.* New York: Viking Press, 1984.

Bracher, Frederick. "Steinbeck and the Biological View of Man." *Steinbeck and His Critics: A Record of Twenty-Five Years.* Ed. E. W. Tedlock, Jr. and C. V. Wicker. Albuquerque: University of New Mexico Press, 1957.

Burgum, Edwin Berry. "The Sensibility of John Steinbeck." *Steinbeck and His Critics: A Record of Twenty-Five Years.* Ed. E. W. Tedlock, Jr. and C. V. Wicker. Albuquerque: University of New Mexico Press, 1957.

Carpenter, Frederic I. "John Steinbeck: American Dreamer." *Steinbeck and His Critics: A Record of Twenty-Five Years.* Ed. E. W. Tedlock, Jr. and C. V. Wicker. Albuquerque: University of New Mexico Press, 1957.

Davis, Robert Murray. Introduction. *Steinbeck: A Collection of Critical Essays.* Ed. Robert Murray Davis. Engelwood Cliffs, NJ: Prentice-Hall, 1972.

Emerson, Ralph Waldo. *Essays: First Series.* Boston: Houghton Mifflin, 1968.

Fontenrose, Joseph. "Sea of Cortez." *Steinbeck and His Critics: A Record of Twenty-Five Years.* Ed. E. W. Tedlock, Jr. and C. V. Wicker. Albuquerque: University of New Mexico Press, 1957.

French, Warren. *John Steinbeck.* Boston: Twayne Publishers, 1975.

Kazin, Alfred. *On Native Grounds: An Interpretation of Modern American Prose Literature.* New York: Reynal, 1942.

Levant, Howard. *The Novels of John Steinbeck: A Critical Study*. Columbia: University of Missouri Press, 1974.

Lisca, Peter. *The Wide World of John Steinbeck*. New Brunswick, NJ: Rutgers University Press, 1974.

Morsberger, Robert E. "Steinbeck's Happy Hookers." *Steinbeck Quarterly* 15 (Summer-Fall 1976): 101-15.

Nevius, Blake. "Steinbeck: One Aspect." *Steinbeck and His Critics: A Record of Twenty-Five Years*. Ed. E. W. Tedlock, Jr. and C. V. Wicker. Albuquerque: University of New Mexico Press, 1957.

Ross, Woodburn O. "John Steinbeck: Naturalism's Priest." *Steinbeck and His Critics: A Record of Twenty-Five Years*. Ed. E. W. Tedlock, Jr. and C. V. Wicker. Albuquerque: University of New Mexico Press, 1957.

Steinbeck, John. *Cannery Row*. New York: Viking Press, 1945.

—. *The Grapes of Wrath*. New York: Viking Press, 1939.

—. *In Dubious Battle*. New York: Covici, 1936.

—. *Tortilla Flat*. New York: Covici, 1935.

Thoreau, Henry David. *Walden and Other Writings*. Ed. Brooks Atkinson. New York: Modern Library, 1965.

Timmerman, John H. *John Steinbeck's Fiction*. Norman: University of Oklahoma Press, 1986.

Wilson, Edmund. *Classics and Commercials: A Literary Chronicle of the Forties*. New York: Farrar, Straus & Giroux, 1950.

Rough People . . . Are the Best Singers:
Woody Guthrie, John Steinbeck, and Folksong

H. R. Stoneback

It would be difficult to say whether Woody Guthrie or John Steinbeck played the greater role in shaping the mythopoeic sense of the Okie experience, that mythic Dustbowl and the westering migration of the 1930s which occupies such a central place in the American imagination. Much has been said about both Guthrie and Steinbeck along these lines, yet the lines of discourse rarely intersect, for Steinbeck tends to be discussed by literary scholars who ignore Guthrie, as Guthrie is discussed by folklorists and students of popular culture or radical politics who pay little or no attention to Steinbeck. My primary concern here is to bring Guthrie and Steinbeck together, to study similarities, shared touchstones in their work, to examine possible influences and creative interaction, to clarify the record of their acquaintanceship, and to consider their relationship to the folk imagination, primarily through attention to folksong. In the remarks that follow I will steer a perilous course between literary criticism and folkloric observation together with some personal reminiscence based on extensive experience as a "folksinger" who followed some of the same roads travelled by Guthrie. But first it is necessary to assay Steinbeck's knowledge of folksong and to evaluate his uses of folksong in his writing.

II

In the evening a strange thing happened: the twenty families became one family, the children were the children of all. The loss of home became one loss, and the golden time in

> the West was one dream . . . A guitar un-
> wrapped from a blanket and tuned—and the
> songs, which were all of the people, were sung
> in the nights.
> *The Grapes of Wrath* (Chapter Seventeen)

From his earliest work Steinbeck employed allusions to
and descriptions of folksong, together with song-titles and fragments woven into the folkloric texture of his fiction. In *Cup of
Gold*, for example, Merlin is imaged as a man who once "made
songs—good, sweet songs." When Merlin is asked "Why are
you making no more songs?" he replies:

> I have grown to be a man . . . and there be no songs in a
> man. Only children make songs—children and idiots.
> Pest on him! It's an idiot himself, is the thought is on
> me. (32)

While Merlin may once have made and sung something like
"folksongs," he is now embittered and regards such activity as fit
for "children and idiots," which sets him apart from the narrator
here and separates him from the common humanity which
Steinbeck's work so often celebrates. Elsewhere in *Cup of Gold*
there are brief and specific but rather hackneyed descriptions of
folksinging, as in the passage which describes the "army of flat-
boats" on the River Chagres:

> The boats, in a long line, edged up the stream. The
> English shouted tuneless chanteys, swaying their bod-
> ies to preserve the rhythm; the French sang softly of
> the little loves they might have had; and the Ci-
> marones and blacks chattered their endless monologues
> directed at no one in particular. (169)

Such blurred folksong clichés, vague, non-explicit, and wielded
in a somewhat heavy-handed fashion typical of certain local-
color writers, are avoided by Steinbeck in his post-apprenticeship
fiction.

A few years later, Steinbeck brings to *In Dubious Battle* a
more specific knowledge and focused use of folksong. For example, in a passage which demonstrates the usefulness of folksong for organizing a group, the men march on the picket line
and "sing tunelessly": "It was Christmas on the Island, /All the
convicts they were there—" (160). In another scene, after Albert

and Mac preside over the slaughter of some cows, the men ride in the back of a truck, singing, appropriately

> Soup, soup, give us some soup—
> We don't want nothing but just some soup. (215)

Thus, in a context involving feeding the workers, Steinbeck aptly introduces one of the most popular left-labor songs of the 1930s. The "Soup Song" was frequently published in "Peoples" and "Workers" songbooks. In one such collection, *Songs of the People* (an official Communist Party publication), it appears with "The Internationale," and, interestingly enough for possible implications concerning *The Grapes of Wrath*, in sequence with "Solidarity Forever" (i. e., the Left/Party version of "The Battle Hymn of the Republic"—evoking the "final victory for One Big Solid Union," etc.), and "Song of Wrath," an insistent chant and harangue against the "fascist dogs" which urges the "workers in masses" to "boldly rebel." Steinbeck may well have gleaned some of his "folksong" knowledge from such a volume. The words to the "Soup Song" were written in 1931 by Maurice Sugar and it is sung to the tune of "My Bonnie Lies Over the Ocean." It passed quickly into leftist oral tradition as the Depression deepened and, as is suggested by the variant words printed by Steinbeck above, it was modified, as folksongs always are, by oral tradition. The chorus, as published, is

> Soup, Soup, They give me a bowl of soup
> Soup, Soup, They give me a bowl of soup.

The variant sung by the men in the truck may be a version that Steinbeck had heard sung by labor organizers and workers, or it may represent a faulty memory or a bad musical ear on Steinbeck's part, since the words as he presents them are hardly singable to the proper tune.

Nevertheless, this truck-ride passage is skillfully organized around the singing of the men, and fragments of two other songs suitable to the dramatic context are introduced. When a cop grins at the men in the truck one of them chants: "Whoops my dear, whoops my dear, /Even the chief of police is queer" (215); then, on down the road, all of the men sing "in chorus":

> Oh, we sing, we sing, we sing
> Of Lydia Pinkham
> And her gift to the human race—

This well-known satirical song exists in many versions and had been around for some time before the 1930s. One version appeared in Carl Sandburg's *The American Songbag* in 1927. Again, Steinbeck presents a variant chorus from the standard version as printed in the widely distributed Sandburg book, thus confirming the suggestion that he was *listening* to songs which were alive and well in oral tradition. Not a Thirties song, not a Left/Labor song, "Lydia Pinkham" is a general satirical blast against commercialism, false "love" and phoney "gifts" to the human race. The song-selection in the entire scene demonstrates Steinbeck's growing knowledge of folksong and his increasing skill in deploying that knowledge in his fiction.

In certain works, in spite of their rather deliberate folkloric quality, Steinbeck makes little or no use of folksong. In *Tortilla Flat*, for example, which earned him the reputation of "folk-humorist," the opportunity to employ folksong is passed up. In *The Pearl*, a quite deliberate "folktale," which, as Steinbeck noted in a perceptive commentary on folktale, he "tried to write as folklore, to give it that set-aside, raised up" quality of folktales, there is no use of folksong. This was probably a wise choice, for while folksong may have, above all other forms of folklore, that "set-aside, raised up" quality, it is most difficult to bring this across in prose, since it is the *music* that does the setting aside, the raising up. In another medium, however, folksong works naturally and well, as in Steinbeck's story and script for *The Forgotten Village*, where he effectively worked folksong into the film (e. g., "El Frutero del Sur" and "Save us, Santiago"). But the work in which Steinbeck makes his most effective use of folksong (and popular song) allusions is *The Grapes of Wrath*.

The first words we hear from Jim Casy are in song—an apt, memorable, and highly charged introduction to his character—as he sings "in an easy thin tenor" what might be called his "folksong" or "gospel" parody of the popular hit song:

> Yes, sir, that's my Saviour,
> Je—sus is my Saviour,
> Je—sus is my Saviour now. (25)

Throughout the novel, there are references to music—e. g., the

"glory-shoutin'" and gospel music of meetings, Tom Joad's playing in a "strang band" in prison, the woman in the camp whose
soft voice soothes the child to sleep singing "Jesus loves you in
the night," etc. But the two most important, complex, and sustained treatments of song occur in Chapters Fifteen and Seventeen.

Chapter Fifteen begins with an evocation of a typical truck
stop, a hamburger stand on Route 66, where the salient point of
definition is the jukebox, "the nickel phonograph with records
piled up like pies, ready to swing out to the turntable and play
dance music, 'Ti-pi-ti-pi-tin,' 'Thanks for the Memory,' Bing
Crosby, Benny Goodman" (208). Steinbeck images a world of
machines in a ruined "garden" through which people flee in
cars that whiz "viciously" by on Route 66; he catalogues the machines, the cars and trucks on the road, and inside "this dump,"
inside Al's place, is another world of machines: slot machines,
steaming coffee urns, chugging ice machines, humming electric
fans, griddles hissing with hamburgers, and—the most significant "machine in the garden"—the jukebox. Two truck-drivers
come in; one plays the slot machine, the other plays the jukebox
and

> watches the disk slip free and the turntable rise up un-
> der it. Bing Crosby's voice—golden. "Thanks for the
> memory, of sunburn at the shore—You might have been
> a headache, but you never were a bore—" And the truck
> driver sings for Mae's ears, you might have been a had-
> dock but you never was a whore—. (213)

True to one of the oldest and most widespread folksong impulses, the truck-driver engages in bawdy song-parody, and re-
leases into the folkloric stream of oral tradition another version
of well-known song. (Did Steinbeck *invent* the "haddock" variation or hear it from someone else? It is a natural variation, one
that seems remotely familiar to my ear, but since bawdy song-
parodies are the least collected of all varieties of folksong, I can
only suggest that this is probably one that Steinbeck heard
somewhere. In any case, its appropriateness to the song and the
situation is exact.) While the record plays, they talk, play the
slot, tell jokes and laugh, apparently paying little attention to the
song. Then, Steinbeck writes,

> Bing Crosby's voice stops. The turntable drops down
> and the record swings into its place in the pile. The

> purple light goes off. The nickel, which has caused all
> this mechanism to work, has caused Crosby to sing and
> an orchestra to play—this nickel drops from between
> the contact points into the box where the profits go.
> This nickel, unlike most money, has actually done a job
> of work, has been physically responsible for a reaction.
> (214)

It is a detailed, closely focused description of the jukebox. And, to underline the point about machines and the world of mechanism, Steinbeck follows immediately with an image of the steam which "spurts from the valve of the coffee urn"; and the "compressor of the ice machine chugs softly" while the electric fan sweeps and "waves," and "the cars whiz by" outside. This is followed by the narration of the wreck, the big Cadillac hitting the overloaded "cut-down" car of a migrant family; then the 1926 Nash sedan pulls "wearily" into the truck-stop and some members of yet another dispossessed migrant family come in to get some bread. Machines, then, and especially the jukebox, receive an extraordinary emphasis in this chapter, and Steinbeck's imagistic tactics underline the careful strategy of juxtaposition with the next intercalary chapter.

Chapter Seventeen, in contrast, focuses on a pre-machine world, a world that has little to do with "mechanism." Of course, the migrant families have cars to get them from one camp to the next, but these weary cars do not whiz "viciously," they creep, crawl, scuttle "like bugs to the westward" (264). In the migrant camps, no hamburgers hiss on griddles, no coffee urns spurt, no ice machines chug, and there are no slot machines. They gather firewood, carry water, cook pork or sidemeat on the open fire; they boil bitter tea in a can; there is no ice but the migrants remember their old homes, the old cool spring-houses, the "little cool-house."

All of these contrasts function deliberately in Steinbeck's design, but the most striking juxtaposition in the paired chapters comes through the imagery of song. Once again, as in Chapter Fifteen, the core image of this chapter is song, and here it is the singing circle around the campfire, the human family "welded to one thing" through folksong; the living voices and the guitar—"a gracious thing"—are counterpoised against the mechanism of the jukebox and a detached, unheeded Bing Crosby singing "Thanks for the Memory." At first glance, it seems that Steinbeck has shaped these two chapters around the master motif of the machine-in-the-garden and the pre-mechanization pastoral idyll. Yet the design is far more subtle. In fact, both chapters are concerned with dispossession and community, with deracination and memory. In Chapter Seventeen the people in the camps retain their old home places in the telling, through the old tales and talking, through *memory* that is more than a mawkish attenuated echo from a jukebox, and they keep their hold on their lives, on their traditions, on their sense of community, through the singing of folksongs and gospel songs around the campfire. However diminished by the machine community may be, in whatever fashion "mechanism" displaces tradition, regardless of how trivial and sentimental Bing Crosby's mechanized voice crooning "Thanks for the Memory" may be when compared to the "eerie" laments and shared songs around the fire, the point of the paired scenes is that a sense of decency persists, a sense of human community lingers, *even* at the truck-stop. It may be on the way out, it may soon be no more than the sentimental "memory" of Crosby's song, but, still, amidst the hissing, whizzing, spurting, chugging, purple-lit machines, kindness lingers, as seen in the actions of Al and Mae and the truck-drivers. Yet, ultimately, the sense is that it may be a passing thing, that human community may find its final thin dry asseveration by the vicious highway.

Since Chapter Seventeen contains the most effective folksong scene or passage in all of Steinbeck's work, we should examine it in some detail here. At the beginning of the chapter Steinbeck writes of the "strange thing" that happens in the camps in the evenings, how "twenty families became one family," the "loss of home . . . one loss," and the "golden time in the West" one dream. As the guitar is the sacramental agent ministering to the dream and to memory, so are the songs—"all *of* the *people*" (emphasis added)—the binding element in the communion of the reconstituted larger family, the new community of the road, the migration. At the end of the chapter Steinbeck renders in detail a picking-and-singing session:

> And perhaps a man brought out his guitar . . . and everyone in the camp moved slowly in toward him. Many men can chord a guitar, but perhaps this man was a picker. There you have something—the deep chords beating, beating, while the melody runs on the strings like little footsteps.

A guitar-player might wish to see the actual picking rendered more felicitously, but Steinbeck's description leads effectively toward the main point, the singing circle image:

> The man played and the people moved slowly in on him until the circle was closed and tight, and then he sang "Ten-Cent Cotton and Forty-Cent Meat." And the circle sang softly with him. And he sang "Why Do You Cut Your Hair, Girls?" and the circle sang. He wailed the song, "I'm Leaving Old Texas," that eerie song that was sung before the Spaniards came, only the words were Indian then. (272)

Speaking for the moment as a guitar-picker who has experienced the "singing circle" a thousand times, and as a writer who knows the difficulty of rendering such numinous moments in time, I would assert that Steinbeck handles the matter admirably. Yet, in order to gauge more exactly the effectiveness of this scene we should consider the provenance and appropriateness of the songs to which Steinbeck alludes, and the manner of presentation within the overall scene. The choices open to a novelist rendering such a singing scene are several: songs may simply be named, as here, or a few key lines may be included in the text, or the entire songs may be reproduced textually. Of the choices, the latter is almost always ineffective, since it hinders narrative and, more importantly, mixes modes, asks the reader to hear a song that is in fact not present, since songs do *not* exist—cannot be *present*—as a matter of text alone. Still, as in some of the novels which most skillfully employ folksong (such as William Faulkner's *Flags in the Dust* and Elizabeth Madox Roberts' *The Time of Man*), a few evocative lines of the song may well be included in the text, and this would seem to be the best choice, better than the mere list of titles which Steinbeck gives the reader. In fact, it is the business of allusion to arouse a curiosity that hungers for the larger frame of reference, and these song-titles function as allusions every bit as much as tags of poetry do in *The Waste Land*. Thus, since the songs mentioned (with the possible exception of "I'm Leaving Old Texas") are not well-known, Steinbeck owes the reader a key line or two, a core image from each song.

Having noted this as a minor flaw, however, I would insist that Steinbeck has aptly *selected* the songs which carry the scene. "Ten-Cent Cotton and Forty-Cent Meat" (also known as

"Seven-Cent Cotton and Forty Cent Meat") is a country blues song from the 1920s lamenting conditions for the cotton farmer, as in the first verse:

> Ten cent cotton and forty cent meat
> How in the world can a poor man eat?
> Flour up high, cotton down low,
> How in the world can we raise the dough?
> Clothes worn out, shoes run down,
> Old slouch hat with a hole in the crown;
> Back nearly broken and fingers all sore,
> Cotton gone down to rise no more.

The other verses continue in a similar vein, bemoaning the low prices the farmers get for everything they raise, and the high prices of everything they need to buy. The song is in the white country blues tradition of moderate protest, not in the radical left or Party-line or Popular Front tradition of protest songs which became predominant by c. 1940. That is to say, it is an exactly appropriate song for the people, the time, and the situation.

The next song that the circle sings, "Why Do You Cut Your Hair, Girls?", is a brush-arbor or camp-meeting song. Usually known as "Why Do You Bob Your Hair, Girls?", it was written in the 1920s and recorded by the West Virginia preacher Blind Alfred Reed (Victor 21350); it was a "hit" record and quickly entered oral tradition, especially in certain Fundamentalist circles, among the so-called "Holy Rollers." It is straightforwardly homiletic:

> Why do you bob your hair, girls?
> You're doing mighty wrong;
> God gave it for a glory
> And you should wear it long.
> You spoil your lovely hair, girls,
> You keep yourself in style;
> Before you bob your hair, girls
> Just stop and think a while.

Subsequent verses insist that "short hair belongs to men," and warn that bobbing the hair is "breaking God's command"; the girls better not do it or they won't "reach the glory land" (Randolph 442-43). Again, the song is precisely right for the scene; it defines—if the reader *knows* the song—exactly who these *people* are; moreover, there is a certain resonance of

California in that "glory land" which they may not "reach."
The third folksong is the "eerie" haunting old lament:

> I'm going to leave old Texas now
> They've got no use for the longhorn cow
> They've plowed and fenced my cattle range
> And the people now they're all so strange.

There are scores of versions and variants of this song in oral tradition and it is impossible to guess which version is sung in
Steinbeck's migrant camp; yet, since the constant emotional core
of the song is deracination, dispossession from a loved place
where new people have brought new strange ways, it is, once
again, a precisely apt song for the migrant camps. I stress the
aptness of the songs because it is very much to Steinbeck's credit
that he avoids the pitfalls of other "union" novels of the 1930s,
especially the worst kind of proletarian fiction that would have
us believe, say, that the migrants in these camps sat around fires
singing "Solidarity Forever," "Arise, You Workers," "The Internationale" or other so-called *Peoples* songs utterly inauthentic
for the place and the people involved. The importance of song
in *The Grapes of Wrath*, and the importance of having the *right*
song is underlined, of course, by the title allusion as by Steinbeck's insistence to his publisher that the novel's endpapers
print "*all all all* the verses of the Battle Hymn" as well as the
music (Benson 387-88). It is to be noted that Steinbeck has nothing to say about the version of the "Battle Hymn"—much more
frequently sung in 1930s leftist circles—known as "Solidarity
Forever." In *The Grapes of Wrath*, then, we get the real songs of
real people, made one in a singing circle:

> And now the group was welded to one thing, one unity,
> so that in the dark the eyes of the people were inward,
> and their minds played in other times, and their sad-
> ness was like rest, like sleep. He sang the "McAlester
> Blues" and then, to make up for it to the older people,
> he sang "Jesus Calls Me to His Side." The children
> drowsed with the music and went into the tents to
> sleep, and the singing came into their dreams. (272)

This is *not* proletarian or *peoples* propaganda, but real *folk* singing. Finally, the guitar-picker is tired, and they all bid each other
good night: "And each wished he could pick a guitar, because it
is a gracious thing." Thus Steinbeck concludes one of the more

effective scenes in the novel, one of the most challenging kinds of scene for a novelist to render. True folksong is here made to issue in the grace of community, a community of memory and desire, dispossession and destination. These "people," one feels, will be all right, and the image of their community lingers longer, for some readers at least, than any rhetoric about the "whole shebang," about the putative need to organize "One Big Solid Union." The entire scene is indeed "a gracious thing."

Steinbeck, then, seems to have known and understood folksong rather well, to judge from his use of it in such works as *In Dubious Battle* and *The Grapes of Wrath*. And there is evidence in Jackson J. Benson's biography of the role that folksong played in Steinbeck's life. For example, his second wife, Gwyn, was a singer who often performed folksongs and, through her, Steinbeck met other folksingers; and he knew Burl Ives. Ives recalls that Steinbeck especially liked ballads (i.e., story-songs). More generally, there are those who say that Steinbeck had a "good ear" and others who say that he "sang like a goat." (Of course, possessing a "good ear" for music is not necessarily tied to the ability to sing.) When I asked Elaine Steinbeck about her husband's knowledge of folksong, about his *singing* knowledge of ballads, she allowed that he wasn't much of a singer; she added, however, that he did know and love a good many folksongs.[1] It does seem that he had some remarkable blind or deaf spots when it came to music. One example would be his insistence to Eddie Condon, the legendary jazz guitarist, that he should play the banjo, the "only truly American instrument" (as Steinbeck maintained); but, as Condon knew, the banjo had long since become a corny cliché that "went out with button shoes" (Benson 579-80). Steinbeck's sentimental taste for the banjo may be evidence of a "bad ear" in some sense, just as his repeated, inaccurate citation of "Teen Age [sic] Angel" in *Travels with Charley* suggests another kind of defect. The song, of course, was "Teen Angel," one of the mammoth "hits" of that year. If, as Steinbeck writes, "in the course of a day you may hear 'Teen-Age Angel' thirty or forty times" (33), then surely with the aid of the insistent oft-repeated musical phrase ("teen angel") an even less-than-average ear would get the phrase right. One simply *cannot* say or sing the words "teen-age angel" to the key musical phrase of "Teen Angel" without destroying both rhythm and felicity of sound. It seems somehow laughable that an aging writer who so desperately wanted to be in touch once again with the country and the people would make such a mistake in hearing *the* story-song that millions were singing during his travels—laughable, were it not somehow so sad. Yet, more importantly, it should be noted that the song he singles out for commentary is in fact a ballad, a story-song which possesses strong elements of folk narrative.

Perhaps such evidence as we have of Steinbeck's faulty ear may suggest why some of the lines of songs included in *In Dubious Battle* are unsingable, i.e., not in the proper musical phrase. It may also explain why Steinbeck merely lists the names of half-a-dozen folksongs in *The Grapes of Wrath*, why he avoids giving words to songs, thus depicting the actual phrasing of the singing, especially if he was working from memory and oral tradition. All in all, Steinbeck's knowledge of folksong seems to be a mix of a rather good knowledge of it with a flawed musical feeling (or "bad ear"). For example, in a 1957 letter, he combines a musically egregious offhand reading of Elvis Presley with solid, informed commentary on folk music in general. Writing to Annie Laurie Williams (August 28, 1957) about "the Mice and Men music and plans" for the play, he talks about the "fake corn" in some songs and says: "I hate every pea-picking, Elvis Presley moment of them" (563). This is, of course, just plain silly, at best woefully inaccurate. Whatever one thought of Elvis Presley in 1957 his music was anything but the "country corn" evoked by the phrase "pea-picking." (That Steinbeck was apparently unable to *hear* the authentic power, the world-shifting force of early Presley, is another matter.) Yet in this same letter Steinbeck goes on to speak knowledgeably and effectively about what the music should do in the play:

> Now let me finally speak of music. I am pleased with the freshness and unhackneyed tone. I like the hint of the blues. Remember, please, though that music can pull the guts out of an audience. Consider then—hinting at the known—the square dance, the ballad, the ode, again the blues, even the Moody and Sankey hymn form. These are part of all of us and we rise like trout to mayflies to them. Hint at them—because after all this is a ranch. Let your audience *almost* recognize something familiar and out of that go to your freshness. (*SLL* 563)

This is well put and it suggests the range of Steinbeck's knowledge of and feeling for folksong—ballad, blues, country, and gospel—and his aesthetic sense of the uses of folksong. More head than ear, perhaps, but, above all—as it should be when it comes to folksong—mostly heart.

Given Steinbeck's extensive connections with folksong and folksingers, and his uses of folksong in his work, it is important to investigate his relationship with the figure often regarded as the greatest American folksinger: Woody Guthrie, the "Okie Bard." For indeed their paths did cross, and although the connections have been completely overlooked by Steinbeck scholars, the Guthrie-Steinbeck file is resonant, both aesthetically and politically.

III

> I just happen to believe in my soul that the rough people in this world are the best singers . . . the hard hit people, the hard hitting people.
>
> Woody Guthrie, liner notes, *Woody Guthrie Album* (Asch Records #432, 1945)

Since Woody Guthrie is one of the more mythicized figures in twentieth-century American lore—especially in the popular imagination—we had better ask, first, who was he exactly? Later appearances and legends to the contrary, he was *not* a dispossessed dustbowl farmer. Woodrow Wilson Guthrie was born on July 14, 1912, in Okemah, Oklahoma. His father, Charley, was a politician and real estate speculator, and a writer of sorts who contributed to the local newspaper his attacks on socialism, with titles like "Socialism Seeks to Destroy Christianity" and "Socialism Guards Secret Philosophy," and published his collected analyses of the comrades in a pamphlet called *Kumrids* (Klein 14-16). Although his family experienced tragedy and slipped into decline as he grew up, Woody Guthrie was never a poor dustbowl farmer. By the time he was seventeen, he was living in Pampa, Texas, where he began to play country or "cowboy" and popular music for local dances, to paint (signs and portraits), and to read everything available in the local library. A telling index to the sensibility of the future "folk bard" is provided by the fact that his paintings were "basic dime-store art," portraits of Jesus and imitations of Gainsborough's "Blue Boy," which he peddled in local bars; his favorite author was Kahlil Gibran; and his favorite songs included many sentimental popular "hits" such as "When You Wore A Tulip." That is to say, he

was no more grounded in the "folk tradition," no more au-
tochthonously connected to folk music than many eastern or urban counterparts of his generation. When the great dust storm
hit Pampa, Texas, on April 14, 1935, Woody's newspaper ad and
business card read: "Divine Healing and Consultation." As even
his sympathetic biographer Joe Klein notes, Woody "didn't seem
to notice" that the "rest of the country was suffering the Great
Depression"; in fact, "everyone seemed to be suffering in some
way. Except Woody" (66-71).

Eventually, Guthrie made his way to Los Angeles, where
he continued to sing wherever he could, finally landing a singing job (non-paying, at first) on KFVD, a small radio station
rather more concerned with politics than with "hillbilly" music.
A clear-headed view of Guthrie's musical career in these years
would need to take account of his very limited "commercial" potential as a country singer, of his slow evolution from a
"cowboy" singer (complete with phoney Western garb) to a self-
consciously folksy singer of old-time "hillbilly" songs and
hymns to, finally, a singer of leftist and protest songs, especially
those associated with the dustbowl and the Okies. This latter,
best-known phase of Guthrie's career, his ultimate persona,
seems to have had its inception around the time in late 1938
when Guthrie met Ed Robbin, the local correspondent for *People's World* (the west coast Communist Party newspaper), who
also had a radio show on Guthrie's station, KFVD. Robbin took
Guthrie to his first Communist Party rally, where Woody sang
his new song "Mr. Tom Mooney is Free"; then Robbin became
Woody's booking agent, handling the "steady stream of requests
to perform at fund-raising parties staged by the various Communist Party appendages and front groups," for which Woody
began to write political songs and from which he derived his income (Klein 123). By May, 1939, Guthrie had his own column
("Woody Sez") in *People's World*, where he was featured as "the
dustbowl refugee, songster and homespun philosopher."
Guthrie's country philosophizing and cartoons were mixed in
with party-line political harangues and feature articles about, for
example, the wonderful "progress" and "freedom" in the Soviet
Union. One of Guthrie's often-quoted sayings from his column
was: "I ain't a communist necessarily, but I been in the red all
my life." But, of course, he was a Party member.

I have heard it argued that Guthrie, his songs, his persona
as "Okie Bard" and his views about the plight of the migrants

and the need for "one big Union" must have influenced Steinbeck during the writing of *The Grapes of Wrath* and afterwards.
This is a notion that needs close examination. Steinbeck *may*
have heard Guthrie's radio show while he was writing the
novel, and he probably read Guthrie's column "Woody Sez"
shortly *after* the publication of *The Grapes of Wrath* since, as
Benson notes, Steinbeck apparently did subscribe to *People's
World* in 1939 (513). Yet the songs Guthrie sang on the radio
were quite different from the songs he sang at Party fund-raising
rallies and, for the most part, had nothing to do with "Okie consciousness." In fact, in arguing Guthrie-Steinbeck influences, I
would insist that there is a seminal influence, and that it flows
in one direction only—*from* Steinbeck *to* Guthrie. Consider
carefully Joe Klein's sympathetic assessment of Guthrie in mid-
1939, when

> Woody was allowing his class consciousness to seem a
> bit more "native" than might normally have been the
> case. He sensed that the more proletarian he ap-
> peared, the more successful he'd be with his new fans.
> He had played the rube rather shamelessly on the ra-
> dio . . . and now that tendency became more pronounced
> . . . especially after John Steinbeck's *The Grapes of
> Wrath* was published that April and the Okies
> achieved a new celebrity status in the party's martyr-
> ology of the oppressed. (124)

Indeed, *The Grapes of Wrath*, far more than Klein suspects, has
everything to do with the persona which Guthrie forged, the
new identity which finally carried him into the mainstream of
American myth and the popular imagination.

There is more to say on that score but, for the moment, let
us attempt to set the record straight on Guthrie-Steinbeck meetings. Unfortunately, since Benson's biography does not mention
Guthrie, we must rely on Guthrie "scholarship," such as it is, all
too often vague and contradictory regarding dates and events
and significance. Klein, the most reliable source on Guthrie,
gives an account of only one meeting between Guthrie and
Steinbeck, sometime in the summer of 1939, when Will Geer
("closely associated with the Communist Party") was

> starting to bring Woody to fancy Hollywood parties—
> they played for Eddie Albert, for the gang at the Hal
> Roach studios, for John Garfield and the Group Theater

> refugees from New York, and even for John Steinbeck
> one night. It looked to Mary [Guthrie's wife] as if
> Woody was finally hitting the big time . . . Mary didn't
> even mind the left-wing business so much when it was
> glamorous (although it still tended to frighten her:
> these people were talking against America). (127-28)

Other accounts of Guthrie-Steinbeck meetings are mentioned in
an interview in Ed Robbin's *Woody Guthrie and Me*, where
Will Geer recalls: "after Woody's songs had begun to be sung
around, I introduced Woody to Steinbeck and he said: 'Took me
years to do Grapes of Wrath and that little squirt tells the whole
story in just a few stanzas.' We all had a good laugh over that"
(108). Maybe *Geer* had a good laugh when he invented this
tale—unless it actually did happen much later—but Steinbeck
most certainly did not say this about Guthrie's ballad "Tom
Joad" in the summer of 1939, Geer's date for this meeting, since
Guthrie did not write "Tom Joad" until 1940, in New York,
sometime after the movie came out. (Guthrie said he had not
read the book—he saw the movie.) Geer recounts another
Guthrie-Steinbeck meeting, during the making of the film *Fight
For Life* in 1939. Geer played the doctor in this public health
documentary, Guthrie and his wife apparently appeared briefly
("I got Woody into that picture, I suppose because his wife was
pregnant"), and of course, Steinbeck was much involved in the
making of the film. Geer writes:

> John lived just a couple of blocks away, at the Garden of
> Allah Apartments. I remember walking over to John's
> with Woody one time. We picked up John and we
> walked right up to the drugstore just about a block
> away. John stopped on the corner and picked up a copy
> of the *People's World* at the newstand and a copy of
> Hearst's *Examiner*. Glen Gordon, one of the actors in
> the picture, had joined us. He said, "How in the hell
> can you read that paper knowing the things you know?"
> And Steinbeck said, "Well, a writer has to know all
> sides of a question. I have to know what that old buz-
> zard Hearst is thinking and writing." And Woody was
> impressed with that. It really made a great impression
> on him . . . So later on in New York when I'd take him to
> whorehouses, he'd say, "Well, Walt Whitman used to
> go to whorehouses to study." And he'd say, "John
> Steinbeck said you gotta study all sides of a thing."
> (Robbin 109)

(Since Steinbeck moved out of the Garden of Allah in early August 1939 [Benson 414] this meeting must have taken place in July 1939.)

These three accounts, then, are the only published record I have been able to find of Guthrie-Steinbeck meetings. They may have met at other Hollywood parties and on other occasions, especially since they were both involved in the making of *Fight for Life*. Or they may have met at the studios during the filming of *The Grapes of Wrath* since, according to Guthrie, Twentieth Century Fox used him as a kind of music "consultant," asking him to sing typical Okie songs, one of which—"I'm Goin' Down That Road Feeling Bad"—did end up in the film. (The only source for this appears to be Guthrie himself, in *Hard-Hitting Songs* [215]). Also, there *may* have been some Guthrie-Steinbeck correspondence. On April 21, 1940, Guthrie performed on the CBS radio variety show called "The Pursuit of Happiness," and was introduced by Burgess Meredith:

> Our next guest really has traveled. He is Woody Guthrie of Oklahoma, one of those Okies who, dispossessed from their farms, journeyed in jalopies to California. There, Woody . . . managed to get some work performing at a small radio station. He got a lot of fan letters, one of which was from John Steinbeck, who wrote the saga of the Okies. Not long ago, he set out for New York and rode the freights to get here. (Klein 156)

There seems no real reason to believe that Steinbeck did write a "fan letter" to Guthrie, since almost everything else in Meredith's introduction is fabricated, distorted or slanted toward the creation of Guthrie's new mythic persona, his born-again leftist identity as the dispossessed proletarian Okie Bard. Since, after coming to New York in 1940, Guthrie was increasingly and publicly identified with the party and with Popular Front causes, and given Steinbeck's anti-Marxism, it seems unlikely that Steinbeck and Guthrie ever met again. Guthrie's subsequent career in New York as the ultimate proletarian, the ultimate Okie, and his work as singer and writer (e.g., his autobiography *Bound for Glory*), his minimal "folksinger" celebrity in left-wing circles through the 1940s and into the 50s, the shabby chronicle of Guthrie's life as he deteriorated mentally and physically (Klein deals, for example, with his "megalomania" and his alcoholism), his federal conviction for sending obscene material through the mail (for which he was sentenced to 180 days in jail in 1948), then his tragic bout with Huntington's chorea, and finally his canonization, first as a saint of the left but ultimately through the slick, shapeshifting avatars of the 1960s as the apotheosis of the "true American folksinger"—all of this, fascinating and convoluted as it was, and owing ever so much to Steinbeck's saga of the Okies as it did, was apparently of no interest to Steinbeck after the early 1940s when he recorded his only published commentary on Guthrie (see below). Yet one wishes Steinbeck had followed the Guthrie story, had said something final about this instructive parable, for one of the most startling and unanticipated conclusions of my research on the Guthrie-Steinbeck relationship is this: Woody Guthrie, the mythic Woody who seems to stand at the center of the American "folk experience," is an unacknowledged Steinbeck creation, is in some very real sense a by-product of *The Grapes of Wrath*.

If the case is not yet proved, let us take a hard look at the facts about Guthrie: 1) a very small-time, unknown country singer, with a very modest talent (even his fans found his guitar-work minimal and his voice monotonous), comes to California, finds he is unable to make a living as a "hillbilly" singer although he "shamelessly" plays "the rube," finds that he can make money at party and left-wing fundraising rallies, discovers that the role of the rural proletarian bard works well with these audiences then shamelessly plays that role, especially in the wake of *The Grapes of Wrath* when the Okies become saints in the party's "martyrology"; 2) the son of that middle-class, small-town real estate speculator, caught up in the world of entertainment and politics, adapts from Steinbeck the role of dispossessed dustbowl farmer and plays it to the hilt for the rest of his life, even though Guthrie is more of an urban leftist intellectual than he is a rural proletarian bard—is, at best, a poet who never farmed a day in his life, a writer who loved to flaunt his "authenticity" as a "worker" yet never truly labored in his life, a New Yorker or bi-coastal radical who left Oklahoma in his mid-teens yet built everything he ever did on a Steinbeck-derived sensibility which he manipulated for leftist audiences; 3) a clever opportunist, he seizes every chance to identify himself with *The Grapes of Wrath*, from the story that he served as music consultant for the film, to his 1940 movie review in which he says the film is "about us a pullin' out of Oklahoma . . . busted, disgusted, down and out," to the composition of one of his best-known bal-

lads "Tom Joad" (commissioned by Victor records and first published in *The Daily Worker* in 1940), to the tone and imagery of
introductions used at rallies and promulgated in the party press,
to his first important concert appearance in New York City. Everything about Guthrie's *career* is inextricably bound up with the
vogue of *The Grapes of Wrath*, has more to do with Steinbeck's
fiction than with any actual experience Guthrie ever had.

Consider Guthrie's first big show in New York:

> Will Geer organized a "Grapes of Wrath Evening" to
> benefit the "John Steinbeck Committee for Agricultural
> Workers," a show that changed the course of Woody's
> career and, perhaps, of American music as well. It was
> held at the Forrest Theater, home of *Tobacco Road* . . .
> Several days before the show, Woody was promoted in
> a *Daily Worker* blurb as "a real dust bowl refugee" . . .
> Along with the story was a photo of a rather stern-
> looking Woody in the *Daily Worker* offices . . . a west-
> ern hat pushed back on his head, and the caption:
> "'Woody'—that's the name, straight out of Steinbeck's
> 'The Grapes of Wrath'—sings People's Ballads."
> (Klein 143)

Apparently unaware of the ironies involved and the implicit
Steinbeck-Guthrie thesis herein demonstrated, Klein continues
his account of that March, 1940 concert, that "Grapes of Wrath
Evening" at the Forrest:

> [Woody] stood alone, fixed by a spotlight slanting down
> from the balcony, and seemed to fit in perfectly with
> Jeeter Lester's tarpaper shack on the *Tobacco Road* set
> behind him. He scratched his head with a guitar pick
> and said, "Howdy" . . . Muttering something about how
> pleased he was to perform in a "Rapes of Graft" show,
> he tilted up his chin, leaned into his guitar, and began
> to sing. (143)

That's Show Biz. Or, depending on the angle of vision, that's
politics. Or that's kitsch. Indeed this "Grapes of Woody" inven-
tory could go on indefinitely.

One of the most telling pieces of written evidence is the
first book that Guthrie worked on, *Hard Hitting Songs for Hard-
Hit People*. Compiled in 1940 by Alan Lomax, with Pete Seeger
as music editor, the book features Guthrie's notes on the songs
and running commentary with frequent allusions to *The Grapes*

of Wrath. In the autobiographical essay entitled "About Woody" at the beginning of the songbook these are the first words: "You know I been in every town mentioned in John's book 'Grapes of Wrath,' and in the picture show too. All I know how to write is just sort of what I seen up and down the road" (21). Such a beginning to his autobiography declares, unwittingly perhaps, that Guthrie was somehow born "in John's book," that he sprang full-blown from Steinbeck's conception of the Okie experience. In his notes to songs, even the songs written by others, Guthrie contrives to identify himself with Steinbeck, as when he introduces "The Farmer is the Man": "I believe the best I ever heard this song sung was out there in the cotton strikes in California, around the country mentioned in John Steinbeck's 'Grapes of Wrath'" (32). And in his introduction to "The Okie Section," where all thirteen of the songs are Guthrie's (or versions of songs from oral tradition with a Guthrie copyright), he writes: "Almost everybody is a Okie nowadays . . . Some politicians throwed mud at John Steinbeck for coining the word, Okie. I want to put my nickel in. He ain't the guy that made up that word . . . I heard that word long time before the Grapes come out" (213). Everything, even Guthrie's prose style, with its calculated solecisms and phoney local color "folk-speech," pivots on Guthrie's "Grapes" persona. Almost all of his "dustbowl" and "Okie" songs—especially the *political* ones—date from after *The Grapes of Wrath*. Presenting his song "When You're Down and Out," he writes: "I walked the highways of California. I been in every town mentioned in 'Grapes of Wrath'—every single town the Joads come through . . . Thousands of us Okies . . . All of us that was hit by hard times, dry weather, the banks, the dust, and the tractor" (232). But this is *not* Guthrie's experience; perhaps the most charitable reflection on the matter would point to the intensity with which Guthrie responded to the novel (or the film), the profound effect on him of Steinbeck's vision, so thoroughly assimilated that maybe he *thought* he had lived it. Regarded in another light, Guthrie's work may amount to one of the major tributes paid to Steinbeck.

If that is the case then the pièce de résistance is, of course, "Tom Joad," Guthrie's long ballad which retells the novel. After "This Land is Your Land," it is probably Guthrie's best-known song. It is a well-made, effective ballad and Pete Seeger's judgment that it is one of Guthrie's masterpieces is on target. And it is not the only Guthrie song which refers directly to *The Grapes of Wrath*. His little-known "Vigilante Man," for example, contains this verse:

> Preacher Casey was just a working man,
> And he said, "Unite the working man."
> He was killed in the river by a deputy sheriff.
> Was that a Vigilante man?

Clearly, Guthrie owes a tremendous debt to Steinbeck, and his "Grape-redolent" prose and songs in *Hard Hitting Songs* underline the beholdenness. (Guthrie acknowledged the debt in another fashion in 1948 when he named his son Joady.) Thus it is most appropriate that the "Foreword" to this volume is provided by Steinbeck. The primary question remains: without *The Grapes of Wrath* would there have been a Woody Guthrie? Perhaps a Woody Guthrie who would be a footnote in some scholarly dissertation on early and commercially non-viable "hillbilly" singers in California, but not, certainly, the Woody who has entered the mainstream of American lore and legend. And we must add to the vast implicit debt the explicit contribution made by Steinbeck to the myth of Woody.

> IV
> Woody is just Woody. Thousands of people
> do not know he has any other name. He is just a
> voice and a guitar. He sings the songs of a peo-
> ple and I suspect that he is, in a way, that peo-
> ple. Harsh voiced and nasal, his guitar hang-
> ing like a tire iron on a rust rim, there is nothing
> sweet about Woody, and there is nothing sweet
> about the songs he sings. But there is something
> more important for those who will listen.
> There is the will of the people to endure and
> fight against oppression. I think we call this
> the American spirit.
> John Steinbeck, "Foreword," *Hard Hitting
> Songs*

This brief paragraph seems to be the only commentary Steinbeck ever made, or ever published, about Guthrie. It may prove to be the most enduring image of Woody; it is, certainly, the highest praise he received from a major American writer. Guthrie was fond of citing Steinbeck's words and he featured them in one of his self-celebrations which he composed in 1947, entitled "Things They Said About Woody Guthrie All Along" (Klein

345). Although some Guthrie enthusiasts are aware of Steinbeck's observations, they seem to have escaped the attention of Steinbeck scholars, a neglect that may be accounted for by the circuitous path that led to the eventual publication of Steinbeck's "Foreword."

In the late 1930s, Alan Lomax began to pull together the collection of songs that would become *Hard Hitting Songs*. Then, after he heard Guthrie sing at the Forrest Theater "Grapes of Wrath Evening" in 1940, Lomax involved Guthrie in the book project. Irwin Silber, in his "Publisher's Foreword," says that when the book was finished "John Steinbeck, who had met Woody in the 'Grapes of Wrath' days, was asked to write a foreword, which he did" (12). The chronology of all this is quite vague, although Silber seems to say that Steinbeck wrote his foreword in 1940; yet what was 1940 if it was not those "'Grapes of Wrath' days" that Silber mentions as if long past? In any case, Silber, writing in 1966, says that the book was rejected by "every publisher in town," because it was too angry, "too hot" politically, and the project was shelved. The manuscript gathered dust in the file of the "People's Song Library," and was eventually scattered, lost, separated, as individual songs were removed and refiled under other headings. Many years later, a second intact manuscript turned up and the book was finally published in 1967.

There are several oddities in the process. The 1967 edition of *Hard Hitting Songs* inaccurately claims to be the first publication of the material. In fact, Steinbeck's ostensible "Foreword" to the book had been published in 1945 as liner notes to an obscure Guthrie recording, *The Woody Guthrie Album*. Is it possible that Steinbeck initially wrote his brief essay on folksong and Guthrie for this 1945 album? Neither Guthrie nor Steinbeck studies shed any light on the question and the definitive answer, the precise date of Steinbeck's composition (and disposition) of the piece will have to be sought out in his unpublished papers. Yet, given the fact that Steinbeck's notes on folksong do not address the specific songs in the Guthrie album it would appear that Silber's chronologically vague statement may be correct.

There are, however, even more vexing questions: why did Steinbeck permit his two-page essay on folksong and Guthrie to appear in a radical leftist volume in 1967? Was he aware of its appearance? Would he have approved of its publication in an anti-capitalist, anti-imperialist demonstrator's hymnbook, given

his general contempt for most elements of the "movement"—
especially the antiwar protestors—of the 1960s? For that matter,
given what Benson sees as Steinbeck's lifelong anti-Marxism
and apolitical stance, did Steinbeck even know about the appearance of his "essay" on the 1945 album of a publicly identified
Communist, a "folksinger" or coterie "protest" singer who was
the darling of New York radical circles? These are bibliographi-
cally complex and politically resonant questions which I have
addressed elsewhere,[2] and the final answers may not reside in
Steinbeck's papers. Since Steinbeck criticism and scholarship has
not even noted the existence of his brief essay on folksong and
Guthrie—for the good reason, I suppose, that both the 1945 and
the 1967 publications occurred in very obscure places, far outside
the literary mainstream—it must suffice here to call attention to
the questions.

The important thing is that we do have the piece and
there are a few more important things to be said about it, based
on its 1945 album appearance. Steinbeck demonstrates his familiarity with folksong in his general discussion of the songs of the
"working people," of spirituals, of cowboy songs. He celebrates
the "great race," the refugees from the dustbowl whose songs he
listened to in the migrant camps, songs of "anger and survival"
which proclaimed their "will to fight." Although his remarks,
judged from the vantage point of a folksong scholar, possess no
special perspicacity, they are pointed observations, significant
and vintage Steinbeck. He finds in the angry songs, as he finds
in Guthrie, "the American spirit." Juxtaposed with Steinbeck's
comments are Guthrie's album notes. He reflects on his songs
(e. g., "Jesus Christ," who was "nothing more than a union
man," "a union organizer"); and he urges solidarity both in the
war effort and in the work toward the "union world," the "real
dawn of the new world that we are already on our way to building." He makes no great claim for his picking and singing: "I
won't say that the guitar playing nor the singing is anything
fancy on the stick." He would rather sound like a cursing cab-
driver, a whooping cowhand or "the lone wolf barking, like anything in this world than to sound slick, smooth tongue [sic], oily
lipped. You will just find me here and not a real slick singer."
Then he gives his basic credo:

> I just happen to believe in my soul that the rough peo-
> ple in this world are the best singers for my money, the
> hard hit people, the hard hitting people [e.g., miners,

> soldiers, farmers] . . . We don't hate you on account of
> your smooth voice, but we do hate you if [for?] the
> phoney champaign [sic] hangovers and headaches of a
> handful of idle playboys and play gals in their wasted
> and rotten lives of jerks and dopes and sexual fits. If
> your words are not about our fight for our union and our
> war, to pay the highest tribute and the highest honor
> to the workers and the fighters, then, of course, you are
> screwball and we mark you off our list.

Guthrie's prose here is restrained—perhaps by a sense of the occasion, or by commercial instincts, or by the decorum of the shared war effort—when compared to his party-line revolutionary rhetoric on other occasions; in addition, the songs included on the album are hardly his most radical material. Still, there is enough between the lines to elicit what is probably a note of political reservation in Steinbeck's image of Woody: "He sings the songs of a people and I *suspect* that he is, *in a way, that people*" (emphasis added). What people? The people as in the party songbooks, in the "People's Songs?" Steinbeck, whether he wrote this in 1940 or 1945, knew enough about Guthrie to be suspicious about the "ways" that Guthrie might be the voice of "the people."

It may be, given the drift and the curious shifts of history, given, too, the inexorable processes of myth, that none of this matters, that Steinbeck truly heard in Guthrie, in spite of political reservations, what the popular imagination much later found—when the politics were forgotten or given another name—in the exemplary folk figure of "just Woody." To attempt to say more precisely what Steinbeck may have heard in Guthrie it is necessary here to relinquish the detached scholarly voice and to speak as a "folksinger." For many years, in the 1950s and 1960s, I made a living as a "folksinger" on the road, Guthrie's roads and Steinbeck's roads, although I didn't know that they were, or *how* they were, Guthrie's and Steinbeck's roads for a long time, for a million miles. I sang songs like "Goin' Down the Road Feeling Bad" and "Tom Joad," and for a while at least, I didn't know what they had to do with Guthrie or Steinbeck, whom I had barely heard of. Once, hitchhiking in Texas, a farmer picked me up and taught me some new verses of "Tom Joad," and he told me "that Steinbeck writer-feller stole that story from ol' Woody." But that didn't matter, since it was a good song, a good *story song*, and anyway it would be years before I would read *The Grapes of Wrath* or know anything about Guthrie or Steinbeck. Yet, somehow, in our curious hungry innocence we did absorb them on the road. We knew we had to be "rough," and if our lives, our voices, were not naturally "rough" enough, we made them rougher. Nothing slick or sweet or smooth for us. We did not know what Steinbeck and Guthrie had said about harsh, rough people and singers—we just *knew* it. And if we sometimes thought that not only were rough people the best singers, but rough singers the best people—well, we were very young and in our hearts we were already learning the larger truth. For somewhere on the road—and in odd jobs, steel mills, factories and fields in between songs—somehow all of it with the road and the roughness, insofar as it was authentic, taught us something about suffering and compassion, taught us humility. We did not know where or how we had attained humility, and we would never name it to each other. But we knew—and we learned more about it as we went along—that the guitar is "a gracious thing" and a true song was a gift that you gave freely, not an occasion for glory or dollars or self-aggrandizement. Oh yes, we knew that we had to do Route 66 through Oklahoma and on West, even if we hadn't read Steinbeck; and we all hopped freights and sang "This Land is Your Land" as we "roamed and rambled" through the country we loved and had to see. We didn't know then that Woody was a Communist, that "This Land" was at first a bitter satirical parody of "God Bless America," that it had other more radical verses questioning—in the original key line—"if God blessed America for me" (later changed to "this land was made for you and me"). And if we had known, maybe we wouldn't have believed it, or we wouldn't have known what to make of it, or maybe it just wouldn't have mattered anyway because we were *moving*, we were *singing*.

Yet perhaps my communal "we," speaking for some teenaged folksingers hitchhiking around the country in the 1950s, had better be qualified. In the cities, in Greenwich Village, on the urban coffee-house "folksong" circuit it was different and many of them already knew about Woody, knew what we eventually learned. Pete Seeger knew, had long known, ever since he attached himself to Woody in 1940; Seeger, of the East Coast Brahmin Caste, Harvard student, party member, who, after he met Woody, became one of the first of many who mythologized themselves in Woody's image, reinvented themselves like in-

verted Gatsbys, fabricated southern rural proletarian backgrounds, faked southern drawls and dressed like "downtrodden
workers" (Klein 196). Some of us sensed this early on and, as it
grew clearer in each narrow, rigid, dogmatic coffeehouse we sang
in, some of us who were trying to make a living as "folksingers"
fled New York and the East Coast, dismissing all of it with one
word: "phoney." We fled for the South, a place more ample and
authentic, our true home where the songs came more naturally,
and we began calling ourselves "country singers." Maybe, insofar as we understood the intricacy of it all, we didn't like the politics of the professional "folksonger's" world, but what we resisted most was what we saw as the phoniness. And, of course,
we found plenty of phoniness in country music, too, almost as
much in Nashville as in New York, and we finally learned that
authenticity was no more a matter of *place* than it was a question
of *politics*. But there were the others, like Elliot Adnopoz, Jewish doctor's son from Brooklyn, who came along in the 1950s
and perfectly mimicked Woody's voice, dress, speech, walk,
mannerisms, and music, and became well-known in urban folk
music circles as Ramblin' Jack Elliot. Until I met him, I thought,
as did thousands of his fans, that Elliot was a country boy from
Oklahoma. And still others, above all Robert Zimmerman, son
of a Jewish storekeeper in Hibbing, Minnesota, who swallowed
the Guthrie Myth whole, changed his name to Bob Dylan,
Woody-ed his image, southernized his being, made the requisite
pilgrimage east to visit Guthrie in the hospital, cultivated his
persona in his prelapsarian Garden of the Village (and later,
Woodstock) but, because his spirit was sufficiently ample and
open to change, his intelligence keen to puncture myths, he
changed forever the landscape of "folk" and "rock" and "popular" and "gospel" music in America. Still others, kids from
small-town upstate New York, changed names and identities,
reinvented themselves as postmodern Woodys, and became
famous as Texas redneck rockers, teaching Texans—if there were
any left—how to be Texans; and so on down the line, all down
the years. In the lucid dance of options, the play of will was im-
perfectly free, for we were compelled, and image became destiny:
vaga-bondage. Changed names, changed provenance, changed
identities, changed speech and dress—the migrant change moving almost always in a south-southwesterly direction—and the
archetypal exemplar and shapeshifter behind all of it was Woody
Guthrie. But none of us really knew that Woody himself had

changed, had by an act of volition created his public persona, compounded of one part Steinbeck, one part politics (party-line) one part show biz, and a dash of middle-class Oklahoma. So, in the end, we are all in Steinbeck's debt, we are all heirs to *The Grapes of Wrath*, children of the road, of the tribe of Joad, in ways which are so mysterious, which reverberate so far beyond exact knowledge that we will never comprehend the resonance and the reach of it all. This luminous web, this numinous force—I finally realized as I sang the ballad of "Tom Joad" to a gathering of Steinbeck scholars at the University of Alabama in 1989—this was Steinbeck's great contribution to folksong, his tangled flame and legacy passed on to all of us who were "rough" singers on the roads of an America which we were determined to love, to discover. And no matter what the turning of the road—east, west, north, south—no matter what the wearying infinitives of the highways, the revivifying byways, of Europe, of Asia, we could not utterly abjure the rough magic— we were doomed to sing, and what we sang was always, somehow, what Steinbeck called "the American spirit." Yes, somewhere behind it all, in ways even he couldn't have imagined, there was Steinbeck and John was just John, another rough singer.

Notes

[1] "Interview," i. e., in conversation at the 21 Club, New York, April, 1989.

[2] "Songs of Anger and Survival: John Steinbeck on Woody Guthrie," *Steinbeck Quarterly*, 1990.

Works Cited

Benson, Jackson J. *The True Adventures of John Steinbeck, Writer*. New York: Viking Press, 1984.

Guthrie, Woody. *Woody Guthrie Album*. New York: Asch Records #432, 1945.

Klein, Joe. *Woody Guthrie: A Life*. New York: Alfred A. Knopf, 1980.

Lomax, Alan, Comp. *Hard Hitting Songs for Hard-Hit People*. New York: Oak Publications, 1967.

Randolph, Vance. *Ozark Folksongs*. Urbana: University of Illinois Press, 1982.

Robbin, Ed. *Woody Guthrie and Me*. Berkeley: Lancaster-Miller Publishers, 1979.

Steinbeck, Elaine, and Wallsten, Robert. *A Life in Letters*. New York: Viking
      Press, 1975.
Steinbeck, John. *Cup of Gold*. New York: Penguin Books, 1976.
—. *The Forgotten Village*. New York: Viking Press: 1941.
—. *The Grapes of Wrath*. New York: Viking Press, 1939.
—. *In Dubious Battle*. New York: Covici-Friede, 1936.
—. *Travels with Charley in Search of America*. New York: Viking Press, 1962.
Yurchenco, Henrietta. *A Mighty Hard Road: The Woody Guthrie Story*. New
      York: McGraw-Hill, 1970.

Patterns of Reality and Barrels of Worms:
From *Western Flyer* to *Rocinante*
in Steinbeck's Nonfiction

Louis Owens

"The design of a book is the pattern of a reality controlled and shaped by the mind of a writer," John Steinbeck wrote in the first line of *Sea of Cortez* in 1941. Twenty years later, attempting to find a pattern in the work that would become *Travels with Charley*, Steinbeck wrote to his friend and editor Pat Covici to say, "And the little book of ambulatory memoirs staggers along, takes a spurt and lags. It's a formless, shapeless, aimless thing and it is even pointless . . . Somewhere there must be design if I can only find it" (*SLL* 702). Later, in *Travels with Charley*, he would add, "I wanted to give the journey a design, and everything in the world must have design or the human mind rejects it" (*Travels* 63).

As everyone who has read his work with care will have recognized, Steinbeck was always interested foremost in the larger picture, the design or pattern of thought underlying the actual plot and characters of a work, what in reference to *East of Eden* he called "the great covered thing" and in his short fiction he referred to as "the stream underneath." Steinbeck's method was invariably to conceive his plots and characters—"symbol people" as he called them in *East of Eden*—as devices through which he could illustrate and animate his philosophical interests. (Never particularly fond of nor interested in the approaches familiar to fiction usually termed "realistic," in a letter to a friend, written in 1933, Steinbeck confessed: "I don't think you will like my later work. It leaves realism farther and farther behind. I never had much ability for nor faith nor belief in realism" (*SLL* 87). Steinbeck's primary obsession with underlying and unifying concepts is evident in the nonteleology of *To a God Unknown* and *The Pastures of Heaven*, in the group-man theme of *In Dubious Battle* and *The Grapes of Wrath*, and in the treatment of the American Myth in *The Pastures of Heaven*, *The Grapes of Wrath*, *East of Eden* and elsewhere.

In Steinbeck's major nonfiction, with rare exceptions such as the essays collected in *The Harvest Gypsies* and, perhaps, *A Russian Journal*, the same habit of creation holds true. Operating *a priori*, Steinbeck brings to his work the pattern of thought according to which observed reality will be shaped. Perhaps the most astounding example of such *a priori* patterning is found in the dispatches collected in *Once There Was a War*, pieces written over a period of six months, often under great stress, and yet unified to a remarkable degree through the use of Jungian imagery to explore the experience of war on the level of the unconscious.

It is interesting to examine Steinbeck's two most successful non-fiction works—*The Log from the Sea of Cortez* and *Travels with Charley*—in this light. For between these two books—his most critically successful and his most commercially successful non-fiction works respectively—there is considerable falling away in significance and quality. Perhaps the primary cause for this decline may be found in precisely Steinbeck's habit of beginning with a controlling pattern of thought to which observed reality will be shaped and fitted.

The Log from the Sea of Cortez appeared originally in 1941 as *Sea of Cortez: A Leisurely Journal of Travel and Research, With a Scientific Appendix Comprising Materials for a Source Book on the Marine Animals of the Panamic Faunal Province*, by John Steinbeck and Edward F. Ricketts. Refusing Viking Press editor Pat Covici's suggestion that Steinbeck alone be credited with authorship of the narrative portion of the *Log*, Steinbeck and Ricketts wrote to Covici to say,

> Originally a journal of the trip was to have been kept
> by both of us, but this record was found to be a natural
> expression of only one of us. This journal was subse-
> quently used by the other chiefly as a reminder of what
> actually had taken place, but in several cases parts of
> the original field notes were incorporated into the final
> narrative, and in one case a large section was lifted
> verbatim from other unpublished work. (Benson 481)

As Richard Astro has pointed out, the large section "lifted verbatum" is the "Easter Sermon" on nonteleological thinking taken from Ed Rickett's notebooks written prior to the journey recorded in *Sea of Cortez* (Astro 14).

The narrative portion of *Sea of Cortez*, published separately in 1951 as *The Log from the Sea of Cortez*, is justly Steinbeck's most critically celebrated nonfiction work. However, as the letter from Steinbeck and Ricketts to Covici makes clear, and as Astro has convincingly shown in his study, *John Steinbeck and Edward F. Ricketts: The Shaping of a Novelist*, the pattern of reality found in the *Log* is shaped and controlled not by the mind of a writer but by the combined minds of two writers and thinkers, Steinbeck and the author's close friend, marine biologist Ed Ricketts.

And as the sermon on nonteleological thinking illustrates, a significant portion of the philosophical shape of the *Log* had been determined before Steinbeck and Ricketts set out to explore the Gulf of California in 1940. That Steinbeck already shared Ricketts's fascination with this pattern of thought is evident in the nonteleology at the center of Steinbeck's 1933 novel *To a God Unknown*. Astro illuminated Ricketts's indebtedness to the ecological theories of W. C. Allee at the University of Chicago, where Ricketts studied, theories which are echoed in *The Log from the Sea of Cortez*, and Astro has further pointed out Steinbeck's interest in the holistic philosophy of William Emerson Ritter's "organismal conception of life." Astro suggests convincingly that the influence of Ritter, absorbed by Steinbeck as early as 1923, long before the author's first meeting with Ricketts, informs the *Log's* discussion of what Steinbeck calls "colonial animals" such as the colonies of pelagic tunicates (Astro 45). As Steinbeck writes, each "member of the colony is an individual animal, but the colony is another individual animal, not at all like the sum of its individuals" (*Log* 167). It is obvious that while Steinbeck scrupulously allowed Ed Ricketts his say in the *Log*, it was Steinbeck who brought this pattern of thought to the Sea of Cortez journey, and that, like Ricketts's concept of nonteleological thinking, this particular hypothesis preceded the observation and speculation that would support it. Steinbeck's obsession with the theme of "group man" in *In Dubious Battle* and *The Grapes of Wrath*, works published in 1936 and 1939 respectively, indicates the author's fascination with this line of thinking before the trip to the Sea of Cortez, as does the fact that, as Astro points out, these reflections on colonial animals do not appear in the journal by Ricketts from which Steinbeck worked in compiling the narrative published as the *Log* (Astro 45).

In his preface to the third edition of Ricketts's and Calvin's *Between Pacific Tides* in 1952, Steinbeck wrote:

> There are good things to see in the tidepools and there are exciting and interesting thoughts to be generated from the seeing. Every new eye applied to the peep hole which looks out at the world may fish in some new beauty and some new pattern, and the world of the human mind must be enriched by such fishing. (vi)

Of Ricketts's and Calvin's method of proceeding "from observation to speculation and ultimately to hypothesis," Steinbeck declared that "it is the creative process, probably the highest and most satisfactory we know" (Astro 8). When it fell to him to give final form to the *Log*, Steinbeck found a balance between the preconceived patterns of thought that shape reality and this "creative process," and it is in this balance that much of the success of the *Log* lies. Though the pattern of reality recorded in the *Log* may well be controlled and shaped to a large extent by the authors' philosophic preconceptions, the *Log* nonetheless records the creative excitement of fishing in new beauty and new patterns as the authors plunge into the tidepools in search of discoveries.

The effective balance between these two impulses in the *Log* may have been made more attainable for Steinbeck because the discoveries of the journey and the patterns into which the discoveries are to be neatly fitted cannot be Steinbeck's alone. In composing the narrative portion of the *Log* Steinbeck was forced to contend with a number of peep holes serving different visions—not only his and Ricketts's but Tiny's and Sparky's and Tex's and Tony's as well. The rocks turned over in the tide pools offer up new worlds to other eyes than the author's own, and to make room for this multiplicity of perspectives Steinbeck must diminish his own role in the narrative. Thus, the discoveries could not be merely self-reflexive—the patterned reality of the *Log* cannot merely give Steinbeck back his own reflection as will be the case when, in *Travels with Charley*, the shaping consciousness will be Steinbeck's alone.

Perhaps equally critical to the success of the *Log* is the fact that it is a work conceived at the zenith of both authors' careers, a patterned reality informed by an exuberant and confident celebration of life. When they set out to explore the Gulf of California in 1940, Steinbeck was at the apex of his career, having published *The Grapes of Wrath* the year before to tremendous popular and critical response, while Ricketts was enthusiastically engrossed in his own attempts not only to document the marine biology of the Pacific tidal zone but also to chart the course of his developing philosophy. And by the time he sat down to begin the actual writing of the narrative portion of the *Log* in January of 1941, Steinbeck had won a Pulitzer Prize for *The Grapes of Wrath*. The vitality and confidence of the *Log* reflect the conditions of its authors.

In sharp contrast to the *Log*, the discouragement of *Travels with Charley* arises out of an unavoidable sense that the author is looking through a tired peep hole at a too-familiar pattern formed out of personal disappointment and despair. Steinbeck was deluding himself when he wrote to Covici of desperately searching for a pattern in *Travels with Charley*, for the pattern was already there, locked into the author's consciousness long before the trip began. In *Travels with Charley* Steinbeck appears to proceed almost exclusively from *a priori* judgment toward observation and speculation carefully selected to confirm previously established hypotheses. In this, the penultimate work of his lifetime, the author sets out to find what he knows is already there; what Steinbeck celebrated as the "creative process" in *Between Pacific Tides* is reversed.

Throughout his career, Steinbeck's fiction formed itself around two primary myths. The first of these, a structure that informs Steinbeck's work from *The Pastures of Heaven* in 1932 to *The Winter of Our Discontent* in 1961, is the so-called American Myth, the pattern of thought originating with the English colonies and focusing upon the figure of the American Adam in a struggle to reclaim the new Garden. Central to Steinbeck's conception of this myth is the westering impulse articulated powerfully in Jody's grandfather in *The Red Pony* and again in the movements of the migrants in *The Grapes of Wrath*. The second mythological structure that dominates Steinbeck's fiction from his first novel, *Cup of Gold*, in 1929 to his last, unfinished work, *The Acts of King Arthur*, is that of the Arthurian legends of Malory, particularly the grail quest, the mythic tale of man's quest for impossible innocence and of flawed man's inevitable failure in that quest. In each of these mythic patterns—the American Myth and the Arthurian quest —man rides off in search of an impossibility, carrying the pattern within him to which he will fit reality as he finds it.

It is a wonderful coincidence that the vehicle for Steinbeck's first non-fiction quest recorded in *The Log from the Sea of Cortez* was a sturdy little purse-seiner from Monterey called the *Western Flyer*. Evoking as it does Steinbeck's fascination with the Westering pattern that shaped the American consciousness, complete with the romantic image of flight, the *Western Flyer* suggests the arc of Steinbeck's career as he soared along the path of the American westering archetype in search of big, broad, relational truths.

When, two decades later, it came time for Steinbeck to set out alone on a journey he labeled "Operation Windmills," his vehicle was a truck even more aptly named *Rocinante*. Recalling the most famous romance in western literature, and a protagonist awash in a distorting sea of chivalry, *Rocinante* illuminates the real quixotic nature of Steinbeck's journey recorded in *Travels with Charley*. Just as Don Quixote set out with preformulated patterns into which such reality as windmills and flocks of sheep would be required to fit, Steinbeck set out in *Travels with Charley* with an image of his country that he would not allow to be altered. Looking for moral windmills and required neither to share scientific peep holes nor to fish in new waters, in *Charley* Steinbeck tilted rather hastily across the continent, finding what he carried inside himself and recording that internal landscape. Glaringly missing in *Travels with Charley* is the exuberant celebration of life which Ed Ricketts, even more than the younger Steinbeck, brought to the Sea of Cortez.

In both *The Log from the Sea of Cortez* and *Travels with Charley*, Steinbeck is careful to declare very early, "We had no urge toward adventure . . . none of us was possessed of the curious boredom within ourselves which makes adventurers or bridge-players" (*Log* 6). In *Travels with Charley*, however, Steinbeck sets out very clearly as just such an adventurer. To accomplish this end, the author fixes himself firmly in the role of hero before his journey begins when he recounts the exciting story of his battle to save his boat, the *Fayre Eleyne* from a hurricane, leaping courageously into the storm-tossed sea and saving the fair maiden boat. This vignette, lacking clear relation to the journey recorded in the book, nonetheless informs the entire work. With this story, Steinbeck is saying to his reader at the outset, "Look, this is the kind of man I am. Now let me see what kind of men the rest of you may be." Immediately, the narrator is established as heroic and the journey becomes a quest as internalized as Quixote's. A quester after truths he already carries inside, the author, like Hawthorne's Ethan Brand, can travel only a circular journey.

In both the *Log* and *Travels with Charley*, Steinbeck is careful to define his purpose. "We were curious," he writes in the *Log*. "We wanted to see everything our eyes would accommodate, to think what we could, and, out of our seeing and thinking, to build some kind of structure in modeled imitation of the observed reality" (*Log* 2). In *Travels with Charley*, he writes: "My plan was clear, concise, and reasonable . . . I discovered that I did not know my own country. I, an American writer, writing about America, was working from memory, and the memory is at best a faulty, warpy reservoir . . . So it was that I determined to look again, to try to rediscover this monster land. Otherwise, in writing, I could not tell the small diagnostic truths which are the foundations of the larger truths" (*Travels* 5). In *Travels with Charley*, however, Steinbeck isn't really interested in "the small diagnostic truths"—the truths of the tide pool—for he knows the truths before he asks the questions. Peter Lisca has argued that "Ironically, there is very little in the 245 pages of *Travels with Charley* that Steinbeck could not have written without ever leaving New York. For he had not really lost touch with his country, but had purposefully insulated himself from a reality with which he felt increasingly uncomfortable . . ." (Lisca 232). Steinbeck, himself, wrote in *Travels with Charley*, ". . . I cannot commend this account as an America that you will find. So much there is to see, but our morning eyes describe a different world than do our afternoon eyes, and surely our wearied evening eyes can report only a weary evening world" (*Travels* 77).

Travels with Charley is a report of a weary evening world. The smug, aging hero who climbs from the sea after saving the *Fayre Eleyne* has lost the morning, or perhaps mid-day, eyes of the *Log*. Steinbeck had been shaping this dark pattern of thought for some time before setting out in search of America in 1960. As the cynical indictment of American materialism in *The Short Reign of Pippin IV*, published in 1957, indicates, the failures illuminated in *Travels with Charley* were much on Steinbeck's mind throughout the fifties, culminating not only in *Travels With Charley* but more bitterly yet in *The Winter of Our Discontent*, the novel Steinbeck completed just before setting out on his adventure with a poodle named Charley.

In his first conversation of the journey, with a young crew member of a submarine, Steinbeck feels deeply his own alienation, responding to the young man's enthusiasm by thinking back to his private experience as a correspondent in World War II: "And I remember too well crossing the Atlantic on a troop ship and knowing that somewhere on the way the dark things lurked searching for us with their single-stalk eyes" (*Travels* 21). Soon after this dark memory he records a conversation with a Yankee farmer. "Do you think people are scared to have an opinion?" Steinbeck asks the farmer, and the farmer, after despairingly comparing his own world of uncertainty with the certain world of his ancestors, says, "Nobody knows . . . We've got nothing to go on—got no way to think about things" (31-32). Soon Steinbeck is writing, "A desolate loneliness settled on me —almost a frightening loneliness" (60). And when he attempts to condense what he's learned midway through the journey, his questions have a bleakly rhetorical air about them as he asks, "If this people had so atrophied its taste buds as to find tasteless food not only acceptable but desirable, what of the emotional life of the nation? Do they find their emotional fare so bland that it must be spiced with sex and sadism through the medium of the paperback?" (141-42). A few pages after this grim query, Steinbeck enters the nadir of his trip from east to west as he plunges into the Badlands of North Dakota where, he reports, "I went into a state of flight, running to get away from that unearthly landscape" (156). What he is really running from in this episode is a solitary Badlands hunter who would not speak and a desperately lonely Badlands wife who cannot stop speaking. These two examples of isolate humanity seem both to depress and terrify Steinbeck. Only when he is alone does the terrain grow friendlier, and he writes: "And then the late afternoon changed everything. As the sun angled, the buttes and coulees, the cliffs and sculptured hills and ravines lost their burned and dreadful look and glowed with yellow and rich browns and a hundred variations of red and silver gray, all picked out by streaks of coal black. It was . . . beautiful . . . In the night the Bad Lands had become Good Lands" (156-57). Just as the eastern and western mountains reflect back the author's own myth-making consciousness in the opening paragraphs of *East of Eden*, here the Badlands seem to reflect Steinbeck's state of mind. And there is the suggestion in this passage that Steinbeck may be disturbed by the too-clear light of day, that he prefers the enriching and obscuring shadows of evening that Hawthorne claimed as the property of the romancer in the preface to *The House of Seven Gables*.

Shortly after the Badlands experience, Steinbeck again attempts to take stock, writing: "I tried to reconstruct my trip as a single piece and not as a series of incidents. What was I doing wrong?" And he remembers advice from a friend whom he refers to rather ostentatiously as "a well-known and highly respected political reporter" who "was not happy, because he loves his country, and he felt a complete sickness in it" (*Travels* 168). Finally, when Steinbeck arrives at his home in Northern California, he visits his old haunt, Johnny Garcia's bar, only, in an echo of Thomas Wolfe, to discover that you can't go home again. "Let us not fool ourselves," he tells his friend. "What we knew is dead. What's out there is new and perhaps good, but it's nothing we know." Steinbeck concludes his visit with a litany that reverberates with the melancholy found in the opening paragraphs of *Tortilla Flat* and the sadness in the beginning of *Sweet Thursday*:

> "Where are the great ones? Tell me, where's Willie Trip?
> "Dead," Johnny said hollowly.
> "Where is Pilon, Johnny, Pom Pom, Miz Gragg, Stevie Field?"
> "Dead, dead, dead," he echoed.
> "Ed Ricketts, Whitey's Number One and Two, where's Sonny Bo, Ankle Varney, Jesus Maria Corcoran, Joe Portagee, Shorty Lee, Flora Wood, and that girl who kept spiders in her hat?"
> "Dead—all dead," Johnny moaned. (*Travels* 202)

The passing of these friends signifies the inexorable loss of the past, just as the lost Arthur Morales in *Tortilla Flat* had signified the death of an old order and just as the death and change emphasized at the beginning of *Sweet Thursday* signals the dramatic shift between *Cannery Row* and the later novel. And Steinbeck flees from his lost past and the place of his greatest fiction, racing away from California toward the racial ugliness he knows he will find in the demonstrations in New Orleans.

Steinbeck, himself, defines the failure of this quest. "It would be pleasant, " he writes, "to be able to say of my travels with Charley, 'I went out to find the truth about my country and I found it.'. . . But what I carried in my head and deeper in my perceptions was a barrel of worms. I discovered long ago in collecting and classifying marine animals that what I found was closely intermeshed with how I felt at the moment. External reality has a way of being not so external after all" (*Travels* 207).

Steinbeck headed for New Orleans determined to observe first-hand the sordid racism of the "Cheerleaders," those housewives who gathered daily to taunt a small black child—knowing precisely what he would find before he set out—and after the sad experience of New Orleans he turns wearily homeward, arriving in New York City only to become befuddled in traffic. "And now I'm back in my own town, where I live" he tells a traffic cop, "and I'm lost" (*Travels* 275). This statement, virtually Steinbeck's last in the book, underscores a profound dislocation for the author. He had tried to go home again, home to an understanding of his country, and home to the place of his birth and greatest fiction in Northern California. By the end of the book it is clear his quest has failed and when he returns to New York he is pathetically lost, having confirmed the idea of America he began with but having discovered no "new beauty" or "new pattern."

Just as the two vehicles, the *Western Flyer* and *Rocinante*, hint neatly at the mythic underpinnings of Steinbeck's life's work, two other interesting metaphors illuminate key distinctions between *The Log from the Sea of Cortez* and *Travels with Charley*. In the *Log*, Steinbeck describes a library cabinet constructed for the journey, "a strong, steel-reinforced wooden case" which held "twenty large volumes," had filing cases, boxes for "pens, pencils, erasers, clips, steel tape, scissors, labels, pins, rubber bands" as well as compartments for index cards and cubby holes for envelopes, separates, typewriter paper, carbon, ink and glue. Ponderous and filled with weighty treatises and materials, the wooden case proved impractical and ended up "lashed to the rail on top of the deckhouse, covered with several layers of tarpaulin and roped on." Steinbeck and Ricketts wisely refused to let the ponderous case overburden their journey, just as they did not allow the philosophical preconceptions each carried onto the boat to interfere with the excitement of discovery (*Log* 10-11).

An image in sharp contrast to the slighted library case of the *Log* is that of *Rocinante* in *Travels with Charley*, weighted with, in Steinbeck's words, "too much of everything—too much food, too many books, tools enough to assemble a submarine" (*Travels* 183), waddling along the Oregon coast highway with tires ready to burst and, in fact, bursting. Undertaking an undeniably courageous quest but sadly over-burdened with preconceptions and pre-established patterns, on this journey Steinbeck found only his own barrel of worms.

Describing the process of collecting marine specimens in the *Log*, Steinbeck wrote:

> At first the rocks are bright and every moving animal makes his mark on the attention. The picture is wide and colored and beautiful. But after an hour and a half the attention centers weary, the colors fade, and the field is likely to narrow to an individual animal. Here one may observe his own world narrowed down until interest and, with it, observation, flicker and go out. And what if with age this weariness become permanent and observation dim out and not recover? Can this be what happens to so many men of science? Enthusiasm, interest, sharpness, dulled with a weariness until finally they retire into easy didacticism? (*Log* 87)

In *The Log from the Sea of Cortez* the rocks are bright, the picture "wide and colored and beautiful," but by the time he came to write *Travels with Charley*, Steinbeck's world had narrowed, his enthusiasm and interest dulled with age as he predicted until, finally, he did indeed retire into easy didacticism.

Steinbeck's "weary evening world" was not to lighten again in his lifetime, as his next and final nonfiction work, *America and Americans*, makes clear. Published in 1966, two years before the author's death, *America and Americans* borrows heavily from Steinbeck's previous works and, in spite of Steinbeck's attempts at occasional optimism, documents didactically a darkly patterned reality. "Is that what we are becoming," Steinbeck asks in this final book, "a kennel of animals with no purpose and no direction?" (172). Declaring that "we are poisoned with things," Steinbeck laments: "Why are we on this verge of moral and hence nervous collapse?" (173). External realities had become almost solipsistically internalized; the shaping and controlling mind had patterned a weary world.

Works Cited

Astro, Richard. *John Steinbeck and Edward F. Ricketts: The Shaping of a Novelist*. Minneapolis: University of Minnesota Press, 1973.

Benson, Jackson J. *The True Adventures of John Steinbeck, Writer*. New York: Viking Press, 1984.

Lisca, Peter. *John Steinbeck: Nature and Myth*. New York: T. Y. Crowell, 1978.

Steinbeck, Elaine, and Robert Wallsten, eds. *Steinbeck: A Life in Letters*. New York: Viking Press, 1975.

Steinbeck, John. *America and Americans*. New York: Bantam Books, 1968.

—. "Foreword." *Between Pacific Tides*, 3rd ed. By Edward F. Ricketts and Jack Calvin, revised by Joel W. Hedgpeth. Stanford: Stanford University Press, 1952.

—. *The Log from the Sea of Cortez*. New York: Penguin Books, 1976.

—. *Travels with Charley in Search of America*. New York: Bantam Books, 1963.

Steinbeck's War

Robert E. Morsberger

Mention war and modern writers, and it is Hemingway rather than Steinbeck who comes to mind. We tend to associate Steinbeck with migrant farm workers or happy-go-lucky bums around the Monterey peninsula or with the Salinas valley. When the United States entered World War II, Hemingway had already been in just about every war of the century; three of his four novels, many of his short stories, and his one play dealt with war, and he was the natural choice to edit an anthology of *Men at War*. We therefore expected that Hemingway would write the major novel about World War II. Instead, he wrote nothing for ten years but a minimal amount of war reporting, got sidetracked into his androgynous and unwieldy *Garden of Eden*, and his war novel, when it finally appeared, was his weakest, *Across the River and into the Trees*, which deals more with love and death in Venice than it does with the war. On the other hand, the war galvanized Steinbeck into action; before we even entered the war, he wrote a novel/play, *The Moon is Down*, and within the next nine months he wrote *Bombs Away*, a book for the Army Air Force on the training of a bomber crew. The next year he wrote in the form of a novel a treatment for a film about the merchant marine that Alfred Hitchcock filmed as *Lifeboat*. Another film, *A Medal for Benny*, based upon a story by Steinbeck and Jack Wagner, shows the war from the Chicano perspective on the home front. As a war correspondent, Steinbeck wrote enough dispatches to be collected in a substantial book, *Once There Was a War*. Thus by contrast to Hemingway's one disappointing novel, a bit of war correspondence included in *By-Line*, and one episode of *Islands in the Stream*, Steinbeck's war writing consists of one novel, a play, three movies, two complete books of nonfiction, and parts of *The Wayward Bus* and *A Russian Journal*. No major American author wrote as much about the war.

Let us now examine what he had to say about the war and how he said it. Steinbeck became involved even before Pearl Harbor. In the fall of 1941, he was writing broadcasts for what became the Office of War Information (*SLL* 237). He did not broadcast himself; he wrote to Webster F. Street that his voice tested badly: "My enunciation is so bad and the boom in my voice is so bad that I can't be understood. I am glad too because now they will never ask me again" (243-44).

That fall 1941, he began writing *The Moon Is Down* at the request of William J. Donovan's Coordinator of Information office that shortly became the Office of Strategic Services (OSS). Outraged at the Nazi invasion and occupation of Norway and punitive acts against patriots who resisted, Steinbeck had already become involved with resistance movements and with fugitives from occupied countries attempting to aid the underground at home. Thus when Donovan asked him to write something that would encourage such resistance movements, he had his subject ready at hand. To prevent "each separate people" from having "to learn an identical lesson, each for itself and starting from scratch," he thought that ". . . if I could write the experiences of the occupied . . . such an account might even be a blueprint, setting forth what might be expected and what could be done about it" ("Reflections on a Lunar Eclipse" 3).

He started the work as a play, set at first in an American town to show, as in Sinclair Lewis's *It Can't Happen Here*, that it can happen here. But the Foreign Information Service rejected this premise, arguing that even a fictional story of our possible invasion and occupation might harm morale (Benson 489-90). Steinbeck therefore "placed the story in an unnamed country, cold and stern like Norway, cunning and implacable like Denmark, reasonable like France" ("Reflections" 3). He made the names of the characters as international as he could and did not even identify the invaders, though from the fact that they are fighting England and Russia, there is no doubt that they are Germans. The play might be set in any country, but the novel version, with much more detail about terrain and weather, clearly takes place in Norway. The film throws aside any ambiguity by opening with a shot of Hitler's hands moving possessively over a map of Norway.

To Webster F. Street, Steinbeck wrote about the play that "It isn't any country and there is no dialect and it's about how the invaders feel about it too" (*SLL* 237). On December 7, Pearl Harbor Day, he completed the play and titled it *The Moon Is Down*. Then, reversing his procedure with *Of Mice and Men*, he quickly turned it into a novel, which was rushed into print by March, 1942. On April 8, the play opened in New York, under the direction of Chester Erskin, with Otto Kruger as Colonel Lanser, Ralph Morgan as Mayor Orden, and Whitford Kane as Dr. Winter. As the novel was initially outselling *The Grapes of Wrath* by two to one, hopes for the play ran high, but Steinbeck was prophetic when he wrote to Webster Street that "the critics will crack down on the play" (243). Two days later, he informed Street that the reviews were "almost uniformly bad," that the play was in fact dull (244). But critics of both the play and the novel objected not to the dullness but to the way in which Steinbeck dealt with the feelings of the invaders. Dorothy Thompson and James Thurber (then undergoing a series of eye operations for oncoming blindness) were intensely hostile, going almost so far as to accuse Steinbeck of treason because he treated the Nazis as human beings, capable of lethal brutality but also lonely and homesick. When the widow of an executed villager kills a basically decent German who was lonely enough to seek her companionship in a Platonic way, our sympathies are certainly mixed. Critics also charged that Steinbeck's thesis that a people cannot be conquered unless they want to be and that the resistance movement will inevitably triumph was bland and wishful thinking. Later, Alfred Kazin and Stanley Edgar Hyman complained of Steinbeck's propaganda and used *The Moon Is Down* as a reason to dismiss Steinbeck as a serious writer (Kazin 1; Hyman 10). But such sweeping judgments must be challenged. Of course, *The Moon Is Down* is not in the same league with *The Grapes of Wrath*. Steinbeck did not intend it to be. He wrote it quickly, on assignment, and it fulfilled his objective—to encourage underground resistance and to show how it can demoralize and ultimately destroy the invaders. The resistance movements applauded the novel, and the underground distributed mimeographed copies (Benson 499). I would argue that it is the best novel about the war written during the war. But putting aside aesthetic considerations and focusing only on the war, one factor that hostile critics overlook is that while Steinbeck was writing the play, we were not even in the war, and when the novel and play appeared in the spring of 1942, the Axis powers still seemed to be winning everywhere. Yet Steinbeck was prophetically accurate in picturing the nature of the ultimate defeat. In his portrayal of the supposed conquerors admitting that in essence they have already been defeated by the relentless resistance of the supposedly conquered, there is considerable subtlety. Scene/Chapter 5 is particularly effective as Steinbeck shows the invasion force terrified "by death in the air, hovering and waiting" (*Moon* 101), by the persistent sabotage, assassinations, the sullen hatred of the villagers, by their inability to relax and lower their guard for a moment, by the nervous tension growing uncontrollably, intensified by homesickness and loneliness, by their suspicion that everywhere else where victory has been officially proclaimed, a similar sense of hopeless futility prevails, by the knowledge that if given the chance, the conquered will kill them all and that punitive measures bring not submission but only more hatred and defiance.

With the hysteria of war long passed, we can now see that *The Moon Is Down* is unquestionably anti-Nazi. Steinbeck deserves credit for the very quality that caused him to be denounced in 1943—for his awareness that not all members of the Wehrmacht were intrinsically evil, that some may have been decent people deceived by their own propaganda or forced by military discipline to participate in actions that they too found revolting. But while Colonel Lanser realizes that the Führer is a madman and that his orders to execute more hostages only intensify the hatred and resistence, he carries out those orders nevertheless, starving the families of miners who refuse to cooperate and shooting hostages. Richard Lockridge's protest that Steinbeck's invaders are "more sinned against than sinning" (Mantle 72) is wholly unjustified. Lanser prides himself on being a civilized man who wants to minimize casualties, but he commits the fatal error of war criminals, trying to exonerate himself by just obeying orders, rather than engaging in civil disobedience. He admits he has no faith in those orders, but he says that they are unambiguous and that he will carry them out "no matter what they are" (*Moon* 186). In the play he adds, "I can act apart from my knowledge. I will shoot the Mayor . . . I will not break the rules. I will shoot the doctor. I will help tear and burn the world" (Mantle 104-05). Steinbeck's characterization of the Germans is, however, far subtler than those in wartime movies, which generally portrayed them all as sadistic butchers. Obviously some, perpetrating the atrocities of the death camps, were so, but the worst of these horrors had not yet happened in 1941 or had not yet come to light. In any case, with his belief that people are not "very different in essentials" ("Reflections" 3), Steinbeck portrayed even the Nazis as human beings. It was this portrayal that caused hostile critics to call Steinbeck's humane approach sentimental at best, at worst, close to treasonable. To Webster Street, Steinbeck observed, "The controversy that has started as to whether we should not hate blindly is all to the good and is doing no harm. What does the harm is that it is not a dramatically interesting play" (*SLL* 244).

Though the play ran only nine weeks in New York, it had a successful tour on the road, came in second in the New York Drama Critics' vote for the best play of the year, and was a smash hit in London and Stockholm. While Steinbeck was in Moscow in 1963, the play was revived there and reviewed favorably in *Tass* (Tuttleton 89). As for the novel, Steinbeck noted that "The little book was smuggled into the occupied countries. It was copied, mimeographed, printed on hand presses in cellars, and I have seen a copy laboriously hand written on scrap paper and tied together with twine. The Germans did not consider it unrealistic optimism. They made it a capital crime to possess it, and sadly to my knowledge this sentence was carried out a number of times. It seemed that the closer it got to action, the less romantic it seemed" ("Reflections" 3). In 1957 Steinbeck wrote to Covici: "At a cocktail party I met an Italian man from the underground, a fugitive not only from Mussolini but Hitler. He told me that during the war he came on a little thin book printed on onion skin paper which so exactly described Italy that he translated and ran off five hundred copies on a mimeograph. It was The Moon Is Down. He said it went everywhere in the resistance and requests came in for it from all over even though possession was an automatic death sentence. And do you remember the attacks on it at home from our bellicose critics?" (*SLL* 590). Thus, while *The Moon Is Down* may have fewer intellectual and aesthetic complexities than fiction and drama more admired in graduate schools, it made more of an impact in real life and fulfilled the purpose for which Donovan requested it. Certainly Norway appreciated Steinbeck's work, awarding him the Haakon VII cross for the support he gave in *The Moon Is Down* (*SLL* 767).

Despite the play's brief run in New York, the novel's sale of nearly a million copies in its first year (*Time* 41: 54) encouraged Twentieth Century-Fox to pay an unprecedented $300,000 for the film rights, by comparison to $75,000 for *The Grapes of Wrath* (*Time* 39: 84). The book was the most expensive aspect of the film. To economize on the production, Fox used no big-name players and redressed the sets from the Welsh mining village of *How Green Was My Valley* to use for Norway. Nunnally Johnson, who had scripted *The Grapes of Wrath*, wrote an adaptation and produced the film. When he asked Steinbeck for suggestions, the novelist replied, "Tamper with it." Actually, Johnson did very little tampering, retaining much of Steinbeck's dialogue and remaining faithful to the plot. His chief contribution was to open up the action and dramatize episodes that are offstage in the play and only summarized in the novel. The movie shows the Nazi capture of the town, the storm troopers massacring a handful of Norwegian soldiers, the details of German brutality that (as in *The Grapes of Wrath* and later in *Viva Zapata!*) provokes the spontaneous anger of the oppressed and turns resentment into resistance. *Time*'s reviewer found the Nazis much harsher in the film and the story more effective as it used "the sharp language of action rather than introspective comment" to "describe the villagers' growing hatred and resentment, the Nazis' growing fear" (*Time* 41: 54). Steinbeck acknowledged, "There is no question that pictures are a better medium for this story than the stage ever was. It was impossible to bring the whole countryside and the feeling of it onto the stage, with the result that the audience saw only one side of the picture" ("Brighter Moon" 86).

With controversy over the book still fresh, reviewers were primed to see whether the film made the Nazis in any way sympathetic. Bosley Crowther was gratified to find that Nunnally Johnson "has carefully corrected the most censurable features of the work" by making Colonel Lanser "a cold and ruthless tyrant . . . He has wrung out such traces of defeatism as were apparent in the book and has sharpened with vivid incidents the horror of being enslaved" ("The Moon is Down" 8). (Actually the book's resistance thesis is a denial of defeatism.) According to Crowther, Sir Cedric Hardwicke turned Lanser into a cold contemptuous intellectual. Likewise, *Newsweek*'s reviewer praised the "cold, impersonal intelligence" that Hardwicke gave Lanser ("Brighter Moon" 86). Yet the scenario is faithful to Steinbeck's characterization of the Nazi commander; calling Hardwicke's performance "magnificent," Philip T. Hartung described the film's Lanser as "a wise, experienced officer who learned in the last war not only how a conquered people behaves but also the futility of expecting a complete vanquishment" (Hartung 617). Above all, the film retained Steinbeck's psychology; and while *Time*'s reviewer considered this "an extraordinarily naive view of the facts of Nazi life" (*Time* 41: 54), Hermine Rich Isaacs wrote in *Theatre Arts* that Johnson's adaptation was "faithful to the author's almost revolutionary concept of the Nazis as credible human beings, invested with intelligence as well as sheer brute strength and subject to the fallibility of mortals. They have a three-dimensional quality that stands out in bold relief against the usual run of Nazi villain, Hollywood style . . . In Lanser's sense of the futility of the Nazi brutalities is the most convincing promise of their eventual nemesis" (Isaacs 289-90).

Two other films on the Norwegian resistance movement were released at the same time as *The Moon Is Down*: Columbia's *The Commandos Strike at Dawn*, with Paul Muni, directed by John Farrow, and Warners' *The Edge of Darkness*, starring Errol Flynn, Ann Sheridan, and Walter Huston, directed by Lewis Milestone from a screenplay by Robert Rossen. All three had a positive reception, but critics were unanimous in preferring the low-budget *The Moon Is Down*, observing that even the lack of star performers was an asset because the unfamiliar faces aided the film's realism. Irving Pichel's direction received universal acclaim. Above all, *The Moon Is Down* stood out from the usual war films of violent adventure as "essentially a conflict of ideas" (Isaacs 289). Bosley Crowther found it too Socratic and dispassionately intellectual yet concluded that it is the "most persuasive philosophical indictment of the 'new order' that the screen is ever likely to contain" ("Moon" 8). If it had more words than action, Hermine Rich Isaacs found that "the speeches that rang out most gloriously from the pages of the novel sound a clarion call once more upon the screen . . . eloquent reminders that in talking pictures there is a seat up near the throne for talk that is worth hearing" (Isaacs 289). It seems that as a movie *The Moon Is Down* found the proper medium for its message.

During the spring of 1942, Steinbeck did some temporary

and unpaid work for Robert E. Sherwood's Foreign Information
Service. When it was to be moved into the Office of War Information, the O. W. I. offered Steinbeck a job, which he declined
because he would have to have a security check, and his friends
wanted to use him as a test case for all those who had been accused of subversion because of their liberal sympathies, and he
did not want to be a "clay pigeon" (Benson 503).

Instead, General "Hap" Arnold, of the Army Air Force,
proposed that Steinbeck write a book about the selection and
training of bomber crews. Steinbeck was reluctant at first, not because he objected to writing journalism but because he did not
want the responsibility for anyone's being injured or killed
(Benson 504). But when President Roosevelt invited him to the
White House and asked him to take on the project, he was unable to refuse. Having agreed, he entered wholeheartedly into
the project, writing to Gwyndolyne Conger, "It's a tremendous
job I've taken on and I have to do it well" (Benson 504). At a
briefing in Washington, he was told that he would spend about a
month visiting twenty air fields in nine states, where he would
study every aspect of the flying fortress. Though some kinds of
bomber crew members had three or four months of intense
training, Steinbeck had to cram all of their various experiences
into thirty days, during which he sampled their classes and
exercises, took some of their tests, practised with some of their
equipment, crawled into their positions in the bombers to
experience their hands-on operations and their viewpoint, and
relaxed with them after work at diners, bars, and dance halls.
This first-hand experience was supplemented by material sent to
him by the Air Force, which was not provided on time, though
the Air Force was pressuring him to meet his deadline. By June,
he was dictating about 4000 words a day and was worried that he
was writing too rapidly (Benson 506). Late in the month, he sent
some introductory pages to Pascal Covici with the complaint that
the promised material had not yet come from Washington and
expressed frustration with "the army game of doing nothing and
passing the buck" (Fensch 33). When prodded to hurry with the
project, he insisted that he would not do slipshod work. Though
he missed his August 1 deadline, he finished the manuscript by
the end of the summer. A few weeks later, Covici informed him
that the Air Force wanted him to add a final chapter describing a
bomber crew on a real combat mission. But Steinbeck had not
gone on such a mission and refused to write something not au-

thentic (Benson 506-07). Viking rushed to publish a first print-
ing of 20,000 copies on November 27, 1942 (Fensch 33). *Bombs
Away* was a book of 185 pages, roughly 43 of them taken up with
sixty photographs by John Swope to accompany 130 pages of
closely detailed text by Steinbeck.

Though written on assignment and under pressure,
Bombs Away is by no means a piece of hackwork journalism.
Perhaps Steinbeck's most neglected book today, and one of the
few out of print, it is well worth reading and has a number of
elements significant to Steinbeck studies. In particular, it is the
most elaborate treatment of Steinbeck's so-called phalanx theory,
his interest in what happens when people work together as a
group. The focus of *Bombs Away* is "the training of the individual members of the bomber crew and its final assembling
into a close-knit team" (*Bombs* 32). Repeatedly, Steinbeck
stresses the point that the successful operation of a bomber does
not depend just on a hot-shot pilot but on a bomber team
functioning as a unit in which each member is essential and all
are dependent on the others. He even cites the motto of Dumas'
three musketeers, "All for one, and one for all." He writes at
length about the advantages American boys enjoy in having
played team sports, in which fullbacks, quarterbacks, and block-
ers, pitchers, catchers, infielders and outfielders all make
essential contributions to the team. Writing in part to encourage
qualified young men to apply for bomber crew training,
Steinbeck stresses the indispensibility of each member and the
fact that each must command as well as obey. Though the pilots
seem in control, they must take directions from the navigator
and, once over the target, from the bombardier, while the radio
man keeps the plane in contact with its squadron and home
base, the engineer keeps things functioning, and the gunners defend them from enemy fighter planes. "Here is no commander
with subordinates, but a group of responsible individuals functioning as a unit while each member exercises individual judgment and foresight and care" (23). Steinbeck found such a team
exciting, a genuinely democratic organization in which each person plays the role for which he is best suited after undergoing
elaborate testing to determine his qualifications. In his chapters
on the training of each member, Steinbeck tried to make them
no longer frustrated that they are not all pilots and to help them
take pride in their roles and in the team as a whole. Identifying
himself with the raw recruits, tired, disheveled, apprehensive,

lonely, and homesick, Steinbeck wrote his book in part to brief them on each step that they would experience in training that would turn them into effective members of the bomber crew.

Steinbeck was never a gung-ho military type, and he contrasts the responsibility that each member of the Air Force must take to the "old iron discipline" of the regular army, with its too frequent martinets (153). Ridiculing the old-time soldier's argument that discipline can be maintained only through blind obedience, Steinbeck admired the concept that in the Air Force, discipline comes from respect and trust, that "the Air Force cannot have bad officers or the ships do not fly" (153). One thing that appealed to him about the bomber crews was the fact that the success of their operations depends on individual judgment, that each crew member develops leadership instead of being subordinated by fear or "stultified by unquestioned orders and commands. For it is the principle of the Air Force that men shall know the reasons for orders rather than that they shall obey blindly and perhaps stupidly. Discipline is in no way injured by such an approach. In fact, it is made more complete, for a man can eventually trust orders he understands" (46). In this way, *Bombs Away* relates not only to Steinbeck's studies of group man but also to his studies of leadership in *In Dubious Battle*, *The Leader of the People*, *The Grapes of Wrath*, *The Moon is Down*, and *Viva Zapata!*

Steinbeck found that as the men got to know, like, and trust each other, they developed a good feeling about the "concerted action of a group of men," even taking pride in the precise unison of close-order drill (49). The effective teamwork of a bomber crew contrasts to the near-fatal disunity of the survivors in Steinbeck's script for *Lifeboat*, an allegory about the need for the quarrelsome Allies to put aside their differences and pull together. Repeatedly Steinbeck stresses the point that "Air Force tactics have definitely become group tactics where men and machines work together toward an objective" and in which the pilot, instead of being the knight errant of World War I dogfights, "is only one part of the functioning unit . . . " (114).

Besides aiming at building morale and esprit de corps for potential members of a bombing crew, *Bombs Away* has something of the quality of Studs Terkel's *Working*, as it helps the reader experience vicariously the various roles of the bombardier, aerial gunner, navigator, pilot, engineer or crew chief, and radio engineer. Devoting a chapter to each, in that order

(note that the pilot comes not first but fourth), Steinbeck introduces us to a representative cross-section of American life: Bill
the bombardier was a trumpet player from Idaho; Al the gunner
was a tough little man from a Midwestern small town where he
was an amateur boxer, a hunter, and a soda jerk until the war;
Allan the navigator, from central Indiana, had a degree in civil
engineering; Joe the pilot was a farm boy from South Carolina;
Abner the engineer or crew chief was a wizard car mechanic
from a small town in California; Harris the radio engineer was a
ham radio operator who worked in a chain grocery store. In
keeping with Steinbeck's interest in proletarian protagonists,
most of them are blue-collar types. Steinbeck gives idealized
portraits of them but at the same time presents realistic details
about their backgrounds and makes them well-rounded
character studies, getting into their minds, providing dialogue
for dramatized episodes, and considering the way in which the
Air Force will help them in their postwar careers. We do not
know if they are actual individuals or imaginary composite
figures. But in describing the training that welds them together
as a team, in as much precise detail as wartime security could
permit, Steinbeck imparts the flavor of an epic, like the recruiting of the Argonauts, the knights of the Round Table, Robin
Hood's band, or the Seven Samurai.

In giving their backgrounds, Steinbeck dwells at length on
the advantages American boys have in experience with team
sports, their love of tinkering with jalopies and other machinery, and their familiarity with guns. In 1942, the latter would not
have seemed controversial, but in today's era of violence, murder, and random shootings, he sounds like a zealous lobbyist for
the NRA, as he writes that "we may be thankful that frightened
civil authorities and specific Ladies Clubs have not managed to
eradicate from the country the tradition of the possession and
use of firearms, that profound and almost instinctive tradition
of Americans" (29). Steinbeck's picture of the supposedly typical
American boy's experience with guns sounds like the boyhood
of Ernest Hemingway. He concludes that "Luckily for us, our
tradition of bearing arms has not gone from the country, and the
tradition is so deep and so dear to us that it is one of the most
treasured parts of the Bill of Rights—the right of all Americans
to bear arms, with the implication that they will know how to
use them" (30). Perhaps echoing the movie *Sergeant York*, for
which Gary Cooper won the Oscar in 1941 as a twentieth-century

Daniel Boone, Steinbeck portrays the aerial gunners as natural descendents of frontier marksmen.

Although dedicated to helping us win the war, Steinbeck was no hawk or militarist. Criticizing the tradition of blind obedience—whereby the men in arms are not to reason why but only to do and die—he insists that the Air Force recruit "should not enter the Service with any martyrish complex about dying for his country. . . . The best soldier in the world is not the one who anticipates death with pleasure or with the ecstatic anticipation of Valhalla, honor, and glory, but the one who fights to win and to survive" (32). Just as *The Moon Is Down* presents the Germans as human beings, misled by a murderous führer, Steinbeck argues in *Bombs Away* against flag-waving propaganda that encourages "frothy hatred"; "There is only time for hatred among civilians. Hatred does not operate a bombsight" (66). Yet Steinbeck once indulges in racial stereotypes, writing about "the dark Aryans of Italy and the yellow Aryans of Japan" (20) and he is at times insensitive about the suffering caused by war; he calls it a great game in which the gunners and bombardiers "could not ask for better sport" and "will be hunting the biggest game in the world" (74, 76). Obviously, the heavy bombers wreaked havoc not only upon military targets but upon the civilian population as well. Yet Steinbeck cannot be considered an accomplice in such later actions as the bombing of Dresden and of Hiroshima and Nagasaki.

In his introduction, Steinbeck portrays the nation as floundering without a direction during the Depression of the 1930s and finds that the war restores a sense of national purpose and draws together the nation's energy, ability, and vitality, directing them towards a common purpose. Thus the Axis powers, by attacking us, "destroyed their greatest ally, our sluggishness, our selfishness, and our disunity" (14). These are the weaknesses that must be overcome by the Allied survivors in *Lifeboat*. Steinbeck's account of the building of the American war machine sounds like a wartime newsreel. When it was written, *Bombs Away* was designed to inform and encourage the bomber crew trainees, but today its value is its vivid recreation of the atmosphere of the war years. It also contains some of Steinbeck's best narrative and descriptive prose, lean, precise, cinematic, and full of sensory detail as he dramatizes planes warming up, taking off, flying in formation, maneuvering, and returning from practice missions.

The book sold well and was purchased by Hollywood for the formidable figure of $250,000 (Lisca 184-85). (Margaret Mitchell got only $50,000 for *Gone with the Wind*.) When Steinbeck was not allowed to donate his royalties to the government, he gave them to the Air Forces Aid Society, a gift all the more generous because he had to pay income taxes on them (Benson 509). Despite paying an immense sum for film rights, Hollywood did not use Steinbeck or his material.

While waiting for the studio to make up its mind about filming *Bombs Away*, Steinbeck proposed another picture, reversing *The Moon Is Down* by having a Japanese invasion force parachute into a Middle Western town so that he could expose "the kind of greed and apathy of the country inside the mountains" that he had seen while crossing the country (Benson 507). Though Twentieth Century-Fox and Nunnally Johnson liked the concept, the head of the film division of the Office of War Intelligence vetoed it, asking Steinbeck instead to write about our defenses in Alaska but then procrastinating on giving him clearance to do so. A sequel to *Bombs Away* about bombers in combat failed to materialize. In December, 1942, Jack Wagner approached Steinbeck with an idea for a film and asked him to collaborate on the script. Together, they wrote in a few weekends the scenario for *A Medal for Benny*.

Steinbeck was expecting to be released from the O. W. I. and commissioned in the Air Force as an intelligence officer, but the plans bogged down in bureaucratic red tape. While he was waiting, Kenneth MacGowan of Twentieth Century-Fox informed him that the Maritime Commission had asked Alfred Hitchcock to make a picture about the merchant marine, and MacGowan invited Steinbeck to write the story. Steinbeck was receptive, saying that he had many ideas for such a story and that he would like to go East with Hitchcock and interview seamen who had been torpedoed. He would write it as a novella that he would be free to publish if he wished (*SLL* 249).

He never did publish the novella, which remains in the archives at Twentieth Century-Fox. Those who know *Lifeboat* only from the film that was released in 1944 as "Alfred Hitchcock's Production of *Lifeboat* by John Steinbeck" will be considerably misled as to what Steinbeck actually wrote, for the scenario is by Jo Swerling, who considerably distorted Steinbeck's treatment. Swerling was a competent screenwriter who had collaborated on Gary Cooper's *The Westerner* and *Pride of the Yan-*

kees for Samuel Goldwyn, but unfortunately, he altered Steinbeck's material, perhaps with Hitchcock's encouragement, to
make it more slick and melodramatic. Most of the dialogue and
many of the details of plot and characterizations are Swerling's
and Hitchcock's, not Steinbeck's. Hitchcock's own explanation is
as confusing as it is enlightening.

> I had assigned John Steinbeck to the screenplay, but his
> treatment was incomplete and so I brought in MacKin-
> lay Kantor, who worked on it for two weeks. I didn't
> care for what he had written at all . . . and hired an-
> other writer, Jo Swerling, who had worked on several
> films for Frank Capra. When the screenplay was com-
> pleted and I was ready to shoot, I discovered that the
> narrative was rather shapeless. So I went over it
> again, trying to give a dramatic form to each of the se-
> quences. (Truffaut 113)

The result is an uneven mixture of Hitchcock suspense,
Swerling situation and dialogue, and Steinbeck philosophy.
Enough of Steinbeck's ideas and structure survive that there is a
discernable resemblance to some of his novels. As in *The Wayward Bus*, Steinbeck isolates a group of representative individuals and then has them interact. In *Lifeboat*, we have adrift in the
ship's launch eight survivors of an American freighter that has
been sunk by a German submarine, plus the commander of the
U-boat, also sunk in the encounter. Except for the ending, when
an Allied destroyer sinks a German supply ship, all the action is
confined to the lifeboat, which becomes a microcosm.

In Swerling's scenario, the survivors are Connie Porter
(Tallulah Bankhead), a wealthy and bitchy reporter; Rittenhouse
(Henry Hull), a conservative millionaire; Gus (William Bendix),
a seaman with an injured leg; Kovac the oiler (John Hodiak), an
embittered leftist whom Connie considers a Communist or at
least a fellow traveller; Stanley Garrett (Hume Cronyn), a British
radio operator; Alice MacKenzie (Mary Anderson), an American
Red Cross nurse; Charcoal (Canada Lee), a Black steward; an
English woman with her dead baby; and the Nazi (Walter
Slezak).

In *Lifeboat*'s allegory, the representatives of democracy are
drifting aimlessly at sea, quarrelsome and ineffectual, while the
Nazi is dynamic, resourceful, and virtually assumes command.
He navigates, keeps the boat from capsizing, rows alone when
the others are too weak, maintains morale with his wit and

cheerfulness, amputates Gus's gangrenous leg, and displays such self-confidence that the others generally look to him for leadership. Overlooking the fact that he is also consistently treacherous, reviewers who had accused *The Moon Is Down* of being "soft" on Nazis now charged Steinbeck with perpetuating the myth of the Aryan superman. Bosley Crowther thought that though Hitchcock and Steinbeck "certainly had no intention of elevating the 'superman ideal,' . . . we have a sneaking suspicion that the Nazis, with some cutting here and there, could turn 'Lifeboat' into a whiplash against the 'decadent democracies'" ("Lifeboat" 17). Dorothy Thompson gave *Lifeboat* "ten days to get out of town," though what she would do after that deadline, she did not say, and the movie had a long and successful New York run (Lardner 65). According to a review in *Life*, most of the blame was put on Steinbeck, who "disclaimed any responsibility for Director Hitchcock's and Scenarist Jo Swerling's treatment of his material" (*Life* 16: 77). Apparently Steinbeck agreed with those critics who thought that the picture might encourage the Nazis, for he sent two protests to Twentieth Century-Fox, telegraphing in the second one: " . . . in view of the fact that my script for the picture Life Boat has been distorted in production so that its line and intention has been changed and because the picture seems to me to be dangerous to the American war effort I request my name be removed from any connection with any showing of this film" (*SLL* 267).

Certainly neither Steinbeck, Hitchcock, nor Swerling was pro-Nazi, but in any case the nearly superhuman Nazi is Swerling's and Hitchcock's portrait, not Steinbeck's. In the original novella, the Nazi nurses a broken arm, never rows the boat, is not a surgeon, is not an intellectual, cannot even speak English, and does not take command. But even in the film, he is sinister. While the others suffer from hunger and thirst, he has a secret supply of food tablets, energy pills, and water. With a hidden compass, he steers the boat towards a German supply ship, and when Gus discovers his deceit, the Nazi drowns him. Realizing his treachery, the others turn on the Nazi in a murderous hysteria, beat him, and drown him as he had drowned Gus. Hitchcock explained that *Lifeboat*'s allegory signified that "while the democracies were completely disorganized, all of the Germans were clearly headed in the same direction. So here was a statement telling the democracies to put their differences aside temporarily and to gather their forces to concentrate on the common enemy, whose strength was precisely derived from a spirit of unity and of determination" (Truffaut 1134). Lewis Jacobs agreed, finding that "*Lifeboat* was a grim reminder against underestimating the resourcefulness and power of the enemy" (Jacobs 38). *Time*'s reviewer concurred, calling *Lifeboat* "an adroit allegory of world shipwreck," paralleling e. e. cummings'

> King Christ this world is all aleak;
> and life preservers there are none . . .
> ("Cinema," *Time*, p. 94)

James Agee considered *Lifeboat* "more a Steinbeck picture than a Hitchcock" (Agee 108), but the reverse is the case. Steinbeck's novella is narrated in the first person by a seaman curiously named Bud Abbott at the time when Bud Abbott and Lou Costello were Hollywood's most popular comedy team. Abbot is a not-too-bright high school graduate whose language is realistically slack, run-on, and repetitive to the point where it becomes monotonous. He is not particularly interesting in himself, but he represents the ordinary man's commonsense attitudes towards politics and economics, and Steinbeck gives him extensive meditations on these subjects, all of which are missing from Swerling's screenplay. He complains of wartime propaganda and news commentators trying to stir up Americans to mindless hysteria by polarizing them into heroic allies and bestial enemies, manipulating them into losing their individuality.

> It seemed to me that most people were kind of comfortable with war, because they didn't have to think any more. We were all good and the enemy was all bad. And it made it kind of simple. When they bombed us they were murderers and when we bombed them, why we were winning for some good reason. And if they sunk our ships, they were stabbers in the back, and if we sunk their ships we were winning a war. You have to put a good name on a thing in a war, and I haven't seen any papers from Germany or heard any speeches, but I'd like to take a small bet that everything we say, they say, only it's the other way around . . . and I bet they believe it just as much as we do. (*Lifeboat* 75)

Perhaps this passage is Steinbeck's response to the critics who called him "soft on Nazis" when he portrayed the German sol-

diers as three-dimensional, occasionally sympathetic human beings instead of stereotypical Huns in *The Moon Is Down*. In any
case, his attack on self-righteously mindless propaganda resembles George Orwell's statement that "Actions are held to be good
or bad, not on their own merits but according to who does them,
and there is almost no kind of outrage . . . which does not change
its moral colour when it is committed by 'our' side . . . The na-
tionalist not only does not disapprove of atrocities by his own
side, but he has a remarkable capacity for not even hearing about
them" (Orwell 165-66).

Abbott goes on to observe that he doesn't know much
about the enemy, "But when they tell us we're all noble and
white, that's just a bunch of horse manure." He goes on to recall
crooked contractors and self-serving, flag-waving politicians at
home, but "Now you can't say it because you're interfering with
the war effort. Those chiselers are absolutely protected for the
duration of the war. I think that's bothering us as much as
anything else, but I think all of us know that's just part of the big
stick, just a part of the dirt of war. And we'll fight this war . . .
and we'll win it but we hate to be kidded all the time and we
hate to be yelled at and told what we ought to think and what we
ought to do." He especially objects to hate-mongering commentators who say how they'd love to be in combat so "they could
get in there with a bayonet and slaughter up a few Germans."
Abbot knows "that war is a dirty business . . . every part of it.
When you've got to clean out a cesspool you do it quick . . . You
don't have to get fighting mad to do it" (*Lifeboat* 75-79).

The film not only eliminates Abbott but cuts most of his
political consciousness. It makes some superficial attempts at
political controversy but fails to develop them. There is an initial conflict between Kovak, the leftist oiler (who in Steinbeck's
treatment is Albert Shienkowitz, a Pole from around Chicago,
who is not a fellow traveller and who falls in love with the
nurse rather than having a love-hate romance with Mrs. Porter)
versus the high-society Mrs. Porter and the right-wing Rittenhouse, but the film renders them as cartoon characters
(Rittenhouse even smokes cigars throughout the film, whereas
Steinbeck's character has salvaged nothing but the clothes on his
back) and turns them all into buddies, making a pitch for
wartime solidarity and suggesting that under the surface, all
Americans are pretty good guys. "We're all sort of fellow
travellers here, in a mighty small boat on a mighty big

ocean," says Rittenhouse (Swerling 45).

Steinbeck's novel makes the opposite point—that at home there is a lot of economic exploitation, profiteering, and corruption, and that when the GIs return, there must be radical reformation. In its attacks on propagandistic paranoia and in its comments on the less than utopian post-war world to which the veterans will return, Steinbeck's script resembles criticism of the Vietnamese War, its aftermath, and political and corporate crimes of the Watergate era. Abbott, the narrator, reflects,

> Albert, he says that some of the fellows that're yelling the loudest about protecting Democracy against Germany are the same guys that were using machine-guns on labor unions before the war. Albert, he says, well maybe the war changed those fellows and they aren't like that any more . . . We'll find out when the war is over. What I hope is that those commentators don't think that if we get good and fighting mad the way they want us to that we won't do any thinking any more, 'cause that's not the way it is (*Lifeboat* 79-80).

Reminiscing about the Depression, in which those who lost their jobs were accused of laziness, Abbott observes that there are 10 million men in the Armed Forces, and when they come home as veterans,

> they're going to be tough guys, and they'd better come back to something besides relief because they're not going to like that. I don't think anybody in the Army or out of it is so dumb to think that there is nothing wrong with this country. But it seems to me . . . they're all fighting because . . . the one thing that's best of all is that in this country if enough of you don't like a thing— you can go about and change it. Well, all those fellows are going to come back from the Army, and they're going to find a lot of people elected to office, that were elected by people who weren't in the Army, and they're not going to be the kind of people who'd . . . see that the Army didn't go back on relief. You see I remember when a bunch of Congressmen got up and said if they voted two billion dollars to feed starving people in this country it would bankrupt the nation and then a little later those same Congressmen they voted a hundred billion dollars for the war . . . Maybe all this kind of thing isn't a good thing to think about and talk about in a time of war, but I never could get the idea the best thing to do wasn't to tell people the truth. (*Lifeboat* 81-82)

Mrs. Porter, the spokesman for laissez-faire, tells Abbott "she wants to free the American workingman from a dictatorship of labor unions," but he reflects that "the people who were most anxious to free us laboring men from dictatorship and the unions were the same people that the unions made raise wages a little bit. Maybe what they wanted to free us from was good wages." He recalls a shipmate's saying that "we got one great right in the United States . . . poor people and rich people they got the right to starve to death. But he said rich people don't very often exercise that privilege" (*Lifeboat* 91-92). When Mrs. Porter talks "about how the unions were full of labor racketeers," Abbott thinks that "If there's one racketeer in a labor union why the whole country's all upset about it. But if a board member of a corporation goes west with the treasure, nobody thinks very much about it; they kind of expect it of him" (*Lifeboat* 93).

Steinbeck's novella makes a detailed case for the liberal position on economics and warfare. Unfortunately, most of his ideas, being part of Abbott's interior monologue, are not trans-latable to the screen. Swerling's dialogue fails to pick them up and turn them into conflict among the cast—probably sensibly so in cinematic terms, but a loss in terms of social consciousness.

One feature of the film that critics found particularly ob-jectionable is the racist stereotype of the Black steward. This characterization is entirely Swerling's, not Steinbeck's. Stein-beck protested to Twentieth Century-Fox against the film's "stock comedy Negro," pointing out that in his script, "instead of the usual colored travesty of the half comic and half pathetic Negro, there was a Negro of dignity, purpose and personality. Since this film occurs over my name, it is painful to me that these strange, sly obliquities should be ascribed to me" (*SLL* 266). In the film, the steward, called Charcoal, is a pickpocket and minstrel-show type; in Steinbeck's novella, where he is called Joe, he is a sensitive individual who plays the flute with a classi-cal chamber music group. In addition, he saves several people from drowning, and Abbott says, "I think Joe was about the bravest man I ever saw" (*Lifeboat* 243). Far from being racist, Steinbeck attacked racism, having Abbott observe "how hard it must be for him [Joe] to be in this boat, even harder than it was for the German. Nobody had anything against Joe except his color. We hated the German because he was an enemy" (203).

The movie ends on yet another racist note. When the German supply ship is sunk, the lifeboat survivors rescue a 17-

year-old boy, who proceeds to pull a pistol on them. Rittenhouse says, "You see? You can't treat them like human beings.
You've got to exterminate them" (Swerling 161-62). By contrast,
Steinbeck takes a broad humanitarian outlook that would not
have pleased the superpatriots any more than Swerling's
superNazi did. His original narrative argues against the insanity
of war, as the nurse says, "When you've helped take the arms
and legs off young men, you heard them raving in the night,
then maybe it wouldn't make any sense to you either." To her,
the German is "just a man with a broken arm" (*Lifeboat* 32).
When the German first comes aboard, Albert wants to throw
him overboard, but after he helps set the arm, he is ready to fight
to save him. "Albert said he could still hate Germans, but he
said once you laid your hand on a man why you couldn't hate
him the same anymore" (39-40). Nevertheless, Steinbeck has
Albert throw the Nazi overboard when the others discover that
he has been betraying them. Swerling's and Hitchcock's version
ends with what Swerling calls an "orgasm of murder," in which
the main attackers are the nurse and Mrs. Porter, who "are more
unbridled and primitive in their attack than the men" (Swerling
139-40). Audiences were apt to applaud, as they do the slaughter
in *Rambo* movies. Afterwards, Abbott feels "as though we
murdered that German, just murdered him in cold blood." The
nurse, who had not been involved, says, "I don't understand
about people hurting each other and killing each other . . . I'm
doing the only thing I can, trying to put them together again
when they get hurt . . . That's the only way I can keep from going
crazy, because the whole thing is crazy to me . . . " (*Lifeboat* 231).

But though it is far more commercialized and melodramatic than Steinbeck's treatment, the film is unusual, without
the customary Hollywood heroics of *Action in the North Atlantic*, the other wartime film about the Merchant Marine. It retains some of Steinbeck's ambiguity and his allegory about the
need for the confused and disorganized Allies to unite against a
common enemy, and its climax, in which the Allied survivors
turn upon the Nazi like a pack of savage animals and kill him in
an act of group hysteria, is startling; though altered by Swerling,
it recalls Steinbeck's story "The Vigilante" and the animal
imagery of *In Dubious Battle*, where "when the crowd saw the
blood they went nuts . . . it was just one big—animal" (*In Dubious Battle* 316-17).

Between the time that he finished his novella in February

1943 and the time that the film was released in January 1944, Steinbeck himself went to war. Fed up with waiting for the government to give him either a commission or an assignment, he decided to become a war correspondent for "a big reactionary paper like the Herald-Tribune because I think I could get places that way that I couldn't otherwise" (*SLL* 250). At the beginning of April 1943, he was accredited a war correspondent with the New York *Herald-Tribune* for the European theater (251). Early in June, he sailed for England aboard a troopship. In London, the only war was in the air, as German planes were still trying to keep up a blitz. Steinbeck found no hot war news to report; instead, he focused on the human factor among both the Americans and British, sending home dispatches that in their self-effacing way are more interesting than the first-person heroics in Hemingway's war correspondence. But Steinbeck too wanted to get where the action was, and in the second week of August, he got permission to go to North Africa. In Algeria, he observed the preparations for the invasion of Italy. At this point, he got himself assigned to a commando unit of Lord Louis Montbatten's Anglo-American Combined Operations department of strategic and tactical deception, for which Douglas Fairbanks, Jr. had organized amphibious operations nicknamed the "beach-jumpers." Steinbeck and Fairbanks were old acquaintances from Hollywood; Fairbanks recalls that they discussed Steinbeck's doing screenplays for prospective Fairbanks swashbucklers based on Scottish history—*The Armstrong* and *Bonnie Prince Charlie* —but as Fairbanks was unable to raise the money for them, neither materialized. Fairbanks suspects that Steinbeck may have asked to be attached to his unit, though how he knew about the highly secret operation remains a mystery.

   Fairbanks is one of the few actors who was an authentic war hero; for gallantry in combat, he was awarded the Silver Star, the Distinguished Service Cross, the *Croix de guerre*, membership in the *Légion d'honneur*, and a British knighthood. Though a civilian, Steinbeck conducted himself like one of the beach-jumpers, taking off his foreign correspondent identification and carrying a tommy gun when he climbed into a PT boat and went ashore on their hit-and-run night raids to create diversions, carry out rescue operations, or capture islands (Benson 532; phone conversation with Fairbanks). (Fairbanks does not recall that Steinbeck ever used the tommy gun.) Steinbeck joined the beachjumpers when they were trying to deceive the

Germans into thinking there would be an invasion in the north, while the actual invasion of Sicily was under way. In fact Fairbanks succeeded in tricking the Germans into holding an entire division north of Naples (Benson 529). When the Allies landed at Salerno, Steinbeck left Fairbanks' commandos and spent a week under fire at the front. Then he rejoined the beachjumpers for several more weeks and took part in capturing the island of Ventotene, when Fairbanks, with five fellow commandos and Steinbeck, went ashore under fire and took prisoner some 250 Italians and then, reinforced by 43 paratroopers, captured at least twice as many Germans as the landing party (87 according to Steinbeck; some 400 according to Fairbanks' biographer), entrenched on a hill, with machine guns and artillery. Steinbeck called it "A real Dick Tracy stunt. They had told us that there were no Germans on the island, so we landed with flashlights lit and yelling to one another and they thought we had an army with us. Hell, the captain and Douglas Fairbanks had nothing but tommy guns and, so help me, they took the whole island. Two very tough citizens they are" (Connell 164).

On September 24, Steinbeck was back in London. A few weeks later, he was in New York, where he sorted out his notes and turned them into further dispatches, so that the dates of the later ones do not correspond to the actual events. Though he had spent only three months in Europe and about six weeks in combat, the experience had been very intense, and the dispatches he collected in *Once There Was a War* (not published until 1958) remain fresh and vivid, perhaps his best work of nonfiction.

The first section of 34 dispatches, written between June 20 and August 12, 1943, is labeled "England," though in fact the first six take place aboard a troopship, from embarkation to docking. During the voyage, Steinbeck's account of rumors, fear, courage, anxiety, crap games and USO shows, with voices from a motley crew of representative and composite soldiers, resembles his treatment of migrant camps in *The Grapes of Wrath*, whose members are also journeying from the known to the unknown. There is prose poetry in his evocative descriptions of the ship casting off after midnight, being nudged out of the harbor past the darkened city and into a misty sea prowled by enemy submarines.

Once ashore in England, his first six dispatches, about a bomber station, are like a continuation of *Bombs Away*, with scraps of dialogue from crew members, remarks on the jivy names of aircraft, like *Bomb Boogie* or *Volga Virgin* rather than dignified ones like *St. Louis* or other cities that would injure the ship and damage morale, observations on the men's nerves on the night before a mission and a description of their careful and complicated dressing for a high altitude flight, and the suspense of waiting for the planes to return from their raid. Throughout the book, Steinbeck focuses on the human interest rather than dramatic news items. Many of the dispatches have a cinematic quality, with shifting angles of perspective and quick cuts from one person or scene to another.

Leaving the flying fortress base, Steinbeck moves in and out of London, not so much reporting as dramatizing episodes and people of interest. He contrasts the homesickness of GIs in London on the Fourth of July with images of the Fourth at home; imagines stories the veterans will tell after the war; admires the indomitable spirit of the common people of Dover under daily bombardment; tells how women operating a coastal battery work, live and play; and chronicles the comic transformation of a billy goat mascot to the alcoholic Wing Commander William Goat, DSO. His style is relaxed, conversational, often with the low-keyed humor of *Cannery Row*, though he can leave indelible images such as "St. Paul's against a lead-colored sky and the barrage balloons hanging over it. Waterloo Station, the sandbags piled high against the Wren churches . . ." (*Once There Was a War* 45). A chapter on the spreading popularity of the German song "Lili Marlene" has a folkloristic quality. Some dispatches are almost short stories, such as one about a soldier's disbelief that he saw a ghostly cottage, well-lit and comfortably inhabited, when it was in fact a bombed-out ruin, the apocryphal account of how Eddie's masterful crap-shooting on Sundays went haywire because he failed to account for the international date line; two dispatches on the artistry of Private Big Train Mulligan, an amiable and easygoing con man who would be at home in Tortilla Flat or Cannery Row; a wounded soldier beginning to regain the use of his crippled left hand. Steinbeck admires the English as well, with their victory gardens, and despite their shockingly bad cooking and brutality with vegetables, and shows how English and Americans have to overcome generalities about each other.

But his reporting is not all comic. Admiring Bob Hope's dedication and energy, he shows how difficult it was to be funny in a hospital, "the long aisles of pain" (90). He pictures a group of children laughing gleefully at a comic movie just before a bomb makes a direct hit on the theater, leaving the building "torn and shredded" and the children "broken," dead or "screaming . . . in pain and fear" (79). He portrays the Blitz with scraps of conversation, recalling the sound of "broken glass being swept up, the vicious flat tinkle," the sight of an evening slipper protruding from a pile of rubble, a pair of stockings hanging from the topmost fireplace of a bombed-out building, birds being killed by concussion, the curious things people save from the ruins, a blind man tapping to cross the street with everything in flames around him. He observes that "In all of the little stories it is the ordinary, the commonplace thing or incident . . . that leaves the indelible picture" (62), and it is these stories that he relates, so that his war correspondence consists of sketches rather than conventional dispatches.

Just as in *The Moon Is Down* and *Lifeboat* he objects to blind propagandized hatred, so he now observes that "civilian ferocity disappears from the soldier or the sailor close to action or in action" (65). And as in *Lifeboat* and *The Wayward Bus*, he is concerned about how the veterans will be treated after the war and their fear of the war's aftermath. Most of them, he thinks, are less afraid of the enemy than of returning home to unemployment and depression, of coming back to find "the cards stacked against them" by the same special interests that exploited them during the 1930s; for "They remember that every plan for general good life is dashed to pieces on the wall of necessary profits" (77). Steinbeck makes a passionate plea that the Four Freedoms be not just empty words but be practically extended to the veterans, who know they can win the war but are terrified of losing the peace.

Following the dispatches from England is a section of six from North Africa, mainly Algiers, "a mad, bright dreamlike place . . . a whorl of color and a polyglot babble" (125). The African dispatches are more fragmentary, though two of them make good short stories—one about the capture of a gang bootlegging GI watches and another about a kid from New York who succeeds in going home by drifting into a group of Italian prisoners of war about to be shipped to the States.

From North Africa, Steinbeck observed preparations for the invasion of Italy—the final training, the armada of ships and lighters, the night attacks by enemy planes, the tension, suspense and anxiety of untested men waiting to see how they will conduct themselves in combat. Always focusing on the human factor rather than the spectacle, he brings the actual invasion to life in one soldier's first-person account. From his own experience of battle, he recalls dust, shell bursts, slit trenches, ants crawling by his nose as he lay on his stomach under fire, groups of men "scuttling like crabs" under machine gun fire (157), dead and mangled mules, wrecked houses torn open with beds hanging out of holes in the walls, stretcher-bearers carrying bleeding casualties, the walking wounded "with shattered arms and bandaged heads," the smell of cordite and dust, the stench of dead men and animals and his own sweat, and the shocking sight of "a small Italian girl in the street with her stomach blown out" (158). Out at sea, bombed by German planes, the ships bombard enemy positions, while landing craft transport supplies to shore. Later, he recalls walking through the deserted streets of Palermo and being spooked by their dark emptiness.

Ordinarily, according to Douglas Fairbanks, Jr., Steinbeck was quite fearless, though horrified at the atrocities and mutilations on every hand. Attached to Fairbanks' commando Task Group 80.4, Steinbeck blended in with the group and became simply one of the beachjumpers. In his accounts of their activities, written later in London or New York, Steinbeck sometimes concealed identities, scrambled dates and combined details of different operations, both for artistic and security purposes. Fairbanks is never named, though he is the "commodore" at Ventotene and the captain of an MTB who goes ashore on a small island near Naples to rescue an Italian admiral and his wife. He may have been the commodore who indirectly orders an officer to rescue a worried bartender's pregnant daughter while supposedly forbidden to do so. Some of the episodes would make good films, especially Steinbeck's final six dispatches about the capture of Ventotene, which read like a Horatio Hornblower adventure, but Fairbanks does not know if Steinbeck contemplated any fiction or screenplays based upon their war experiences, though they did discuss the possibility of collaborating on a movie about the knights of the Round Table. (It was an introduction from Fairbanks that enabled Steinbeck and Eugène Vinaver to explore the Duke of Northumberland's Alnwick Castle, where they actually discovered a lost Arthurian manuscript of Sir Thomas Malory.) When Steinbeck and Fairbanks got together after the war, they mainly reminisced about times when and asked what happened to old so and so.

Back home, after writing the dispatches from his notes in Italy, Steinbeck wrote *Cannery Row* to enable both himself and his readers to escape from the war for a while. His final war movie dealt with the home front. *A Medal for Benny*, based on the story that Steinbeck and Jack Wagner had written at the end of 1942, was finally filmed by Paramount and released early in 1945. The original story has never been published, but Frank Butler's screenplay was included in *Best Film Plays*, 1945, edited by John Gassner and Dudley Nichols. Cut from the same cloth as *Tortilla Flat*, it returns to the paisanos, this time in a town called Pantera. Benny, who never appears in the film, is so legendary for his roistering and amours that he has been run out of town. During his absence, an amiable scamp named Joe Morales (Arturo de Cordova), who considers himself a better man than Benny any day, woos Benny's girl, Lolita Sierra (Dorothy Lamour). Benny has been (in the words of *Time*'s reviewer) "a five-star heel," and Lolita clearly prefers Joe but feels it her patriotic duty to be faithful to Benny because he is now in the Army. Joe's comic courtship is so irresistible that Lolita admits her real feelings. But when news arrives that Benny has been killed in action and is to be awarded a posthumous Congressional Medal of Honor, the community expects her to remain forever faithful to his memory.

Meanwhile, the mayor and chamber of commerce try to exploit for all it is worth the publicity that Benny's medal will bring. Like Abbott's reflections in *Lifeboat*, the film is sharply satirical of civic boosterism and wartime profiteering. The town's politicians and businessmen know so little of Benny that they think his name is Martin. When they discover that it is Martín and that he is a Chicano from the barrio, they try to move his grieving father (J. Carrol Naish) from the family shack to a new house, just long enough to make a good impression on the media and the military. When the father realizes what they are up to, he walks out in disgust, and the medal is awarded in the scruffy surroundings of the barrio. Benny may have been a heel, but he was also a hero, and the film defends the dignity of Chicanos against the snobbery, hypocrisy, and racism of the ruling class. In 1945, this was not a message that everyone wanted to hear, nor is it even today, but under Irving Pichel's direction, the film got rave reviews, and Steinbeck and Wagner were nominated for an Oscar for best original story.

In *The Wayward Bus*, his first full-length novel after the

war, Steinbeck touched again on the idea which Abbott discussed in *Lifeboat*, that the veterans would not want to return to business as usual and be thrown back on the economic slag heap by exploitative right-wing profiteers and politicians. Among the bus's passengers are Ernest Horton, a veteran who is now a traveling salesman, and Mr. Pritchard, a vacationing Babbitt-type businessman who has become a cold war warrior, fearing and hating as Red anything vaguely threatening his profits, even while he calls business "the most democratic thing in the world" (*The Wayward Bus* 147). When conversing with Horton, Pritchard says patronizingly that the veterans are "a fine bunch of boys . . . and I only hope we can put in an administration that will take care of them." "Like after the last war?" asks Horton cynically (154). Horton's father had believed in the puritan ethic of hard work and thrift only to see the corruption of the Harding administration and lose his shirt in the Depression. Now Pritchard says he worries that the returning soldiers "don't want to settle down and go to work. They think the government owes them a living for life and we can't afford it" (277). Horton looks sick at Pritchard's reactionary bias (Pritchard wants another president like Coolidge who will let business do whatever it wants) and protests that some of his friends, who would seem like bums to Pritchard, make more sense than members of the Cabinet, but he can't make a dent in Pritchard's right-wing ideology and finally says, in despair, that if there were another war, the most awful thing is that he would go fight again (278).

The war was not over when hostilities ended, for many of the survivors were maimed or mutilated, and all grieved for the dead. Bombed and shelled cities were in ruins. Steinbeck was acutely aware of the aftermath of the war. When in the summer of 1947, he and photographer Robert Capa went together to Russia, reminders of the war were everywhere, and Steinbeck noted them in *A Russian Journal*, their record of the trip. They found that the Russians were particularly reluctant to let Capa loose with his camera. Steinbeck's explanation was that the camera is especially frightening to people who have been bombed and shelled in war, "for at the back of a bombing run is invariably a photograph. In back of ruined towns, and cities, and factories, there is aerial mapping, or spy mapping, usually with a camera" (*A Russian Journal* 5). He found Helsinki "considerably shot up" but not too badly bombed. The planes in which they flew around Russia were C-47s left over from lend-lease. From the air, Steinbeck could see the scars of the siege of Leningrad—in addition to trenches and machine gun nests, "The burned farmhouses with black and standing walls littered the landscape. Some areas where strong fights had taken place were pitted and scabbed like the face of the moon" (12). Moscow, because of its formidable anti-aircraft defense, was less damaged, though there were some signs of the war. At the Lenin Museum, Steinbeck encountered a group of war orphans. Throughout the Ukraine, Steinbeck noted shell holes, trenches, roofless and burned buildings. He noted that the destruction was comparable to that "if the United States were completely destroyed from New York to Kansas" and if it lost fifteen percent of the population, for the Ukrainians lost six of their forty-five million civilians as well as military casualties (60). The destruction was particularly bad at Kiev, which was half in ruins, "Every public building, every library, every theater, even the permanent circus, destroyed, not with gunfire, not through fighting, but with fire and dynamite. Its university is burned and tumbled, its schools in ruins . . . this was the crazy destruction of every cultural facility the city had, and nearly every beautiful building that had been put up during a thousand years" (53). Steinbeck was incensed at this work of German "culture" and found a poetic justice in the fact that German prisoners were helping to clean up the debris. He did not register concern that the Russians still kept prisoners of war two years after the peace treaty. Instead, he reflected on "the stupid, calculated cruelties of the Germans" and understood why the Ukrainians would not look at the columns of prisoners, still in their uniforms (64). In the city park, he noted the graves of the city's defenders.

The Russians had been traumatized by the invasion and expressed fear and concern that the United States might attack them. Steinbeck tried to reassure them that the news stories about Americans calling for a preventive war reflected the views of the radical right, not of Americans as a whole. At the same time, Americans feared an attack from the Soviet Union, a mutual paranoia that grew during the Cold War. Steinbeck, on the spot, tried to allay the fears.

Meanwhile, the Ukrainians were trying to rebuild, but since the Germans had destroyed all the machinery, the reconstruction had to be done by hand until new machinery could be made. Steinbeck was impressed by the resilience of the Russian spirit, by the people's ability to live on hope. But many of the

Russians were the walking wounded—veterans with amputated limbs, a half-crazed woman lying in the ruins of a bombed chapel, children legless and missing an eye, a beautiful young girl living in a hole in the ground, scavenging for garbage, and snarling savagely, her eyes inhuman, at someone who offered her bread. Steinbeck noted that there were very few artificial limbs, that the survivors made do with the stump of an arm or leg. Veterans told him of the horrors of combat in the "dreadful cold," when one man warmed his hands in the blood of a friend just killed so that he could still pull his trigger. In the countryside, whole forests were ravaged by machine-gun fire, and everywhere were wrecked pieces of rusting military equipment. On some farms, the Germans killed all the animals, and if there was time, they detroyed the villages as well.

The worst devastation was at Stalingrad, around which the debris of war spread for miles. The city had been ravaged not so much by bombing as by shell and rocket fire, and its remaining walls were pocked by machine-gun bullets. Some of the survivors were living underground.

Back in Moscow, Steinbeck saw a display of war trophies near Gorki Park, with captured plans, tanks, artillery, and a variety of guns and vehicles, and observed the children looking with wonder as their fathers told what the equipment was and how they captured it.

Though Steinbeck and Capa spent much of their time in the Soviet Union being wined, dined, entertained with circuses, theatre, and ballet, the evidences of the war were unavoidable and unforgettable, and *A Russian Journal* is an eloquent *memento mori*, a fitting conclusion to Steinbeck's treatment of World War II and a warning against all future wars.

Works Cited

Agee, James. "Films." *The Nation* 158 (22 January 1944): 108.

Benson, Jackson J. *The True Adventures of John Steinbeck, Writer.* New York: Viking Press, 1984.

"Brighter Moon." *Newsweek* 21 (5 April 1943): 86.

"Cinema." *Time* 43 (31 January 1944): 94.

Connell, Brian. *Knight Errant: A Biography of Douglas Fairbanks, Jr.* Garden City, NY: Doubleday, 1955.

Crowther, Bosley. "Lifeboat." *New York Times* 13 January 1944: 17.

—. "The Moon Is Down." *New York Times* 27 March 1943: 8.

Dick, Bernard F. *The Star-Spangled Screen: The American World War II Film.* Lexington: University Press of Kentucky, 1985.

Fensch, Thomas. *Steinbeck and Covici: The Story of a Friendship.* Middlebury, VT: P. S. Eriksson, 1979.

Hartung, Philip T. "The Moon Is Down." *Commonweal* 27 (9 April 1943): 617.

Hyman, Stanley Edgar. *The New Leader* 10 December 1962: 10.

Isaacs, Hermine Rich. "The Films in Review." *Theater Arts* 27 (May, 1943): 289-90.

Jacobs, Lewis. "World War II and the American Film." *Film Culture* 47 (Summer 1969): 38.

Kazin, Alfred. "The Unhappy Man from Unhappy Valley." *The New York Times Book Review* 4 May 1958: 1.

Lardner, David. "The Current Cinema." *The New Yorker* 19 (4 February 1944): 65.

Life, 16 (31 January 1944): 77.

Lisca, Peter. *The Wide World of John Steinbeck.* New Brunswick, NJ: Rutgers University Press, 1958.

Mantle, Burns, ed. *The Best Plays of 1941-42 and the Year Book of the Drama in America.* New York: Dodd-Mead, 1942.

Orwell, George. "Notes on Nationalism." *Decline of the English Murder and Other Essays.* Harmondsworth: Penguin Books, 1965.

Swerling, Jo. *Lifeboat.* Revised Final Screenplay, July 29, 1943, Twentieth Century-Fox Film Corporation.

Steinbeck, Elaine, and Robert Wallsten, eds. *Steinbeck: A Life in Letters.* New York: Viking Press, 1975.

Steinbeck, John. *Bombs Away: The Story of a Bomber Team.* New York: Viking Press, 1942.

—. *In Dubious Battle.* New York: Random Modern Library, n.d.

—. *Lifeboat.* Unpublished manuscript, Twentieth Century-Fox Corporation, revised March 26, 1943.

—. *The Moon Is Down.* New York: Viking Press, 1942.

—. *Once There Was a War.* New York: Viking Press, 1958.

—. "Reflections on a Lunar Eclipse." *San Francisco Examiner* 6 October 1963: 3.

—. *A Russian Journal.* New York: Viking Press, 1948.

—. *The Wayward Bus.* New York: Viking Press, 1947.

Time 39 (18 May 1942): 84.

Time 41 (5 April 1943): 54.

Truffaut, François. *Hitchcock*, with the collaboration of Helen G. Scott. New York: Simon & Schuster, 1967.

Tuttleton, James W. "Steinbeck in Russia: The Rhetoric of Praise and Blame." *Modern Fiction Studies* 11 (Spring 1965): 82.

From Artist to Craftsman:
Steinbeck's *Bombs Away*

Alan Brown

By most accounts, the outbreak of World War II marks the beginning of John Steinbeck's decline as a writer. Robert Murray Davis claims that Steinbeck's first two really bad books—*Bombs Away* and *The Moon is Down*—were direct contributions to the war effort (3). Speaking of these same books, Richard Astro declared, "Steinbeck's capitulation to the pressure of political expediency had disastrous consequences on his art" ("Travels with Steinbeck" 40). Steinbeck himself supported this assessment of the work that he did during this period in the preface to *Once There Was a War*: "Yes, we only wrote about part of the war, but at the time, we believed, we fervently believed, that it was the best thing to do" (XII). Although Steinbeck was forced by the rules of censorship, self-imposed or otherwise, to write about a different war than the one that he really wanted to write about, one gets the impression that the flaws in such books as *Bombs Away* cannot be attributed solely to a lack of artistic freedom. Indeed, in 1975, Warren French traced the source of Steinbeck's failing artistic powers to the expertise that he had acquired from his commissioned works: "[Steinbeck learned] that art and craft are not easily distinguishable, that his awesome talent could be channeled into the production of propaganda as well as into the embodiment of his own vision" (110). French went on to say that in works like *Bombs Away*, Steinbeck "turned craftsman in order to do quickly and without fresh imagining what he already knew he could do well" (111). Despite the outright attacks and critical neglect that have plagued *Bombs Away* since its publication in 1942, the book is an important key to understanding how Steinbeck's willingness to manipulate themes and characters from his previous novels to suit the needs of the armed services eventually caused him to lose track of the artistic vision that had guided him to greatness in such works as *Of Mice and Men* and *The Grapes of Wrath*.

Steinbeck's willingness to compromise his artistic principles has its roots in the patriotic fervor that he, along with many other Americans at that time, succumbed to. His fervent belief that Hitler and Mussolini endangered the liberty of freedom-loving people all over the world prompted him to offer his services to the U. S. Government. In a letter dated June 24, 1940, Steinbeck proposed to President Roosevelt that propaganda directed at the Axis powers be disseminated through a special radio and film organization (*SLL* 207). When the Office of War Information (OWI) was established two years later, Steinbeck offered his services and soon became involved in various propaganda projects. In an unpublished letter to Webster F. Street, Steinbeck described these projects as "speeches, essays, stories, plays, broadcasts, a whole volume about the training of bomber crews, everything I could devise or that was suggested to me . . ." (Simmonds 16).

During his service as foreign news editor of the OWI, Steinbeck was approached in April, 1942 by General "Hap" Arnold of the Army Air Force who suggested that Steinbeck write a book detailing the training of a bomber crew from induction to efficient flying team. Steinbeck was initially attracted to the idea because the proposal offered him a chance to return to the west coast to assist in the making of the film version of the book. However, the project also supported his views regarding the role played by young people in the political process: "Communist, Fascist, Democrat may find that the real origin of the future lies on the microscope plates of obscure young men, who, puzzled with order and disorder in quantum and neutron, build gradually a picture which will seep down until it is the fibre of the future" (*SLL* 194). Accompanied by photographer John Swope, Steinbeck visited Air Force training bases across the country to collect material in May and June. By the end of June, 1942, he had immersed himself in his work, churning out words at the rate of four thousand a day (Simmonds 19).

Although Steinbeck's unswerving faith that God was on the side of the United States in 1942 prevented him from admitting, either publicly or privately, that he was prostituting his art, he did seem to be aware during the writing of *Bombs Away* that his war work was having a corrosive influence on his writing ability.   Writing once again to Webster F. Street in July 1942, Steinbeck complained that the war effort was requiring him to do "things" in his writing that made him uncomfortable, but "as long as there is a war, I must do them and they aren't natural things for me to do so they won't be well done" (19).   To keep from losing complete control of the creative muse that he felt was gradually slipping away from him that year, Steinbeck began writing a five-hundred-word short story each day (20).   A month later, the frustration produced by putting his artistic imperatives on hold, combined with the pressures of having to appease the military bureaucracy, caused him to declare to Webster F. Street, "You know, I often wonder whether given the leisure again, I could write slowly and with the old joy.   If it is ever peacetime again, I am certainly going to try" (20).   When Steinbeck finally did get to California to work on the movie, he had become convinced that "there isn't much you can do with an air force except fly planes" (20).

The source of Steinbeck's despondency in this period can be traced to the techniques that he employed in this commissioned work.   Essentially, his transformation from the slow-working, meticulous novelist to the deadline-motivated, assembly-line propagandist required that he transfer the characters and themes that he was already familiar and comfortable with from a rural to a military setting.   While a shift in locale did not by itself force Steinbeck to abandon his artistic principles, the Air Force's need to project a certain image did.   The faces and ideas from Steinbeck's novels may be present in *Bombs Away*, but the comprehensive vision of man that gave them life and power in works like *In Dubious Battle* and *The Grapes of Wrath* is not.

Although *Bombs Away* is purportedly a reportorial account of the training of a bombing crew, the book is actually shaped more by the requirements of fiction than by hard fact. *Bombs Away*, like *The Grapes of Wrath*, has a plot, and the excerpts from the government publications parallel the interchapters from *Grapes*.   In both books, the main characters show their mettle by surviving and learning from their initiatory experiences (French 108).   If Steinbeck's bout of depression that occurred in 1942 can be directly traced to this book, as his letters seem to indicate, then it is possible that it was precipitated by his decision to write in the fiction format that he was familiar with instead of using the techniques of the journalist.

It is fitting that the theme that branded him as a propagandist in the eyes of some readers in *The Grapes of Wrath*—his concept of group-man—is the focus of *Bombs Away*. This concept springs from Steinbeck's conviction, voiced by Jim Casy in *The Grapes of Wrath*, that all men and women are "a little piece of a great big soul" (24). While this theme attracted quite a bit of attention in *The Grapes of Wrath*, it actually permeates many of his works. Rama in *To a God Unknown* declares that a man "is not a man, unless he is all men" (66). The term "group-man" was first used by Doc in *In Dubious Battle*, who tells Mac, "You might be an expression of group-man, a cell endowed with a special function, like an eye-cell, drawing your force from group-man" (131). In *The Red Pony*, Grandfather describes the westward movement of the pioneers as "a whole bunch of people made into one big crawling beast" (91).

Of course, the idea of group-man is also fundamental to the military, which attempts to play down individualism so that men can learn to function as a unit. In *Bombs Away*, Steinbeck describes the process by which a group of unruly boys is transformed into a unit of fighting men. Although this process is a complicated one, consisting of a plethora of examinations and drills, Steinbeck insists that Americans take easily to this kind of indoctrination because teamwork is a hallowed American tradition: "From the time of their being able to walk, our boys and girls take part in team playing. From one ol' cat to basketball, sand-lot baseball, to football, American boys learn instinctively to react as members of a team" (30). By the end of bombing school, the inductee has learned to enjoy conformity: "At first he had disliked the formations, but as he became precise in his step and carriage he grew to like them . . . He discovered something he had not learned, which the directionless depression had not permitted him to learn—the simple truth that concerted action of a group of men produces a good feeling in all of them" (49). In *The Grapes of Wrath*, Steinbeck tried to protect himself from charges of being a communist by presenting the problems he was concerned with in terms of the way they affected the Joads, thereby forcing his readers to consider the effects of these social injustices on an individual family (French 96). In *Bombs Away*, however, Steinbeck showcases the theme of a common interest at the expense of the individual personalities of the inductees, who soon blur into a bland, generic flight crew.

Even though Steinbeck's theme of group-man is just as strongly felt in *Bombs Away* as it is in some of Steinbeck's novels, his attitude toward organized groups of men does a complete "about face" in *Bombs Away*. In *The Grapes of Wrath*, Steinbeck criticized the four organized methods of solving problems: "organized charity, organized religion, organized government, and organized private enterprise" (108). While it is true that the Okies do organize themselves into a small group under the leadership of Jim Casy, this group is actually closer to what Kennedy refers to as a kind of "primal collectivism" consisting of a gathering of ragged men who have voluntarily come together and who do not require a rigid chain of command or fixed rules to regulate themselves. In *Bombs Away*, Steinbeck's disdain for organizations surfaces to a slight extent in his assertion that the Air Force is "different" from other military organizations: "It must delegate its authority to the ground crew mechanic who is as responsible for the flight of a plane as the pilot" (34). Despite the flight crew's veneer of democracy, the fact remains that the Air Force is basically a type of superimposed collectivism, the likes of which Steinbeck rejected whole-heartedly in *The Grapes of Wrath*. Moreover, the purpose of the "organization" in *Bombs Away* has changed. Instead of fostering life as the informal groups of men in *The Grapes of Wrath* do, the primary mission of the Air Force is to crush life (Kennedy 164). The absence aboard the bomber of a "Ma" figure, who is the very epitome of love in *The Grapes of Wrath*, is a very telling omission.

What sets *The Grapes of Wrath* apart from *Bombs Away* is Steinbeck's love of people, not doctrine: "He has been interested in people from the beginning, from long before he had any theory to account for their ways" (Warren 250). Unlike the socialistic Upton Sinclair, who started with a theory and then created characters who proved the theory, Steinbeck created characters in *The Grapes of Wrath* who seem to be alive because they are not secondary to a political message: "They have something in them that is more than stoical endurance. It is the will to live, and the faith in life." *The Grapes of Wrath* is populated with a legion of characters who can be described as colorful, pitiful, farcical, disorderly, well-meaning, shrewd, brave, ignorant, loyal, anxious, obstinate, insuppressible mortals (264). Like real people, these characters also grow; their survival depends upon their adaptability to new conditions. As a result of this life force that keeps them from despair, the Joads take the various calamities that beset them, such as the loss of the grandparents and their farm, in stride. In doing so, they triumph over the adversity that seems bent upon destroying them.

In *Bombs Away*, on the other hand, the characters are flat and lifeless. They are heavily documented types, not living, breathing people. This lack of credibility in these characters can be attributed in part to the emphasis he places on the group: "The Air Force is much more a collaboration than a command" (33). In other words, the sum total of the "parts" of the crew is much more important than the individual "parts." In *The Grapes of Wrath*, the Joad family bears a strong resemblance to the flight team in that some members have specific functions that they perform. For example, Pa is the titular head of the family, Ma is the spiritual head of the family, and Al is the mechanic. In addition, Ma periodically reminds her loved ones that the unity of the family is of supreme importance to her, just as the unity of the flight crew is of supreme importance to the squad commander. To Steinbeck the artist, however, the individual personalities of the members of the unit are much more important than they are to Steinbeck the propagandist. For example, Al, the sixteen-year-old son who keeps the Joads' old jalopy in working order, is like many other adolescent boys his age who are preoccupied with girls and cars. Although he takes a boastful pride in his mechanical ability in the beginning of the trip to California, the humbling burden of responsibility hits home in the guilt he feels when an oversight on his part causes the truck to break down. On the other hand, Al's counterpart in *Bombs Away*—Abner, the flight mechanic—is nothing more than a stereotype of what Steinbeck calls "almost uniquely an American kind of man. Nearly every town has its Abner. The children know him, and the boys with their old cars ask his advice" (146). Devoid of the human desire for love, money, or position, Abner is so far removed from the world of human beings that he views the airplane engines "as his babies" (147). Such an uncomplicated character, who is blindly in love with his designated duty, may not be well-suited for a novel, but he is certainly "tailor-made" for propaganda. The fact that Steinbeck replaces the farmers of his previous novels with the fliers in *Bombs Away* also suggests that World War II had convinced him of the inefficacy of agrarianism as a solution to social and economic problems (Astro, "Steinbeck's Post-War Trilogy" 109).

Steinbeck's admiration for the common people, who are showcased in such novels as *Of Mice and Men*, *In Dubious Battle*, *Tortilla Flat* and *The Grapes of Wrath*, is also apparent in *Bombs Away*, but to a lesser extent. His faith in the persistence of the plain people received its most eloquent expression in *The Grapes of Wrath*. Voicing the philosophy of the proletariat, Ma proclaims, "It ain't kin we? It's will we? . . . As far as 'kin,' we can't do nothin', not go to California or nothin'; but as far as 'will,' why, we'll do what we will" (111). Even though the Joads are endowed with extraordinary qualities, Steinbeck makes it very clear that they share these qualities with all poor, oppressed people who must draw from their love of and faith in life. In *Bombs Away*, Steinbeck also populates his crew with young men from common backgrounds: "Suppose a young farmer from South Carolina and a young graduate from a small college looking for a job and an Idaho trumpet player all have made applications for the Air Force [and] have been accepted for induction . . . so that they end up at last with two hundred and fifty others at a railroad station near an induction center" (36). This conglommeration of soda jerks, garage mechanics, and ham radio operators who eventually become Army Air Force cadets certainly seem to represent the common man, but Steinbeck insists that they "were drawn from a cross-section background of America but they are the top part of the cross-section" (30). Needless to say, the "commonness" of these cadets is no more than an illusion; in fact, Steinbeck seems to be so intent upon stressing their superior qualities that he even stoops to elitism: "The Army Air Force is recruiting thousands of young men, and they must be a very special kind of young men. They must, in fact be the best physical and mental specimens the country produces" (32).

Closely connected to elitism is Steinbeck's concept of the ideal man, who appears in various forms in several of his novels as well as *Bombs Away*. Billy Buck in *The Red Pony* and Doc Burton in *In Dubious Battle* certainly exhibit noble qualities, but it is Ed R. Ricketts who comes closest to the naturalistic basis of Steinbeck's image of man. He is, in fact, a god-like man who finds opportunities for kindness and compassion in the natural order (Lisca 6). The god-like man can also be found in *Bombs Away*, but in a much different incarnation. Al, who is presented as the typical air gunner, had traded in Doc's compassion for the killer instinct, a trait which Steinbeck seems to admire in this book: "Like a hunter he wanted to see live game in his sight, and when his work was done he wanted to see the smoke of a destroyed enemy trailing behind a falling ship. He was the hunter of the air, the stinger in the tail of the long range bomber, and he wanted to join his group." His eagerness to "hunt" people, along with the fact that he is described as an amateur boxer who is five feet five inches tall, likens Al to another Steinbeck character who is also a short young man endowed with boxing ability. Unlike Al, though, Curley in *Of Mice and Men* is a villain, a diminutive tyrant who lords his boxing skills and authority over the helpless denizens of his father's ranch, especially Lenny, whom he "hunts" in the end of the novel. One gets the impression that Curley might have been an outsider in peacetime but that his counterpart found a home in the war.

It stands to reason that if there exist people whom society has elevated above all others because of their superior qualities, then there must also exist people whom society has ostracized because of characteristics that society has deemed to be inferior. Although Steinbeck features victims of discrimination in many of his works, his attitudes toward them in his novels and in *Bombs Away* are quite different. In novels like *Of Mice and Men*, Steinbeck is clearly the literary champion of the rights of victims of racial hatred, which was very much alive in the 1930s. Crooks, the stable buck who has been exiled to a one-room apartment next to a manure pile, tries to explain his status on the ranch to Lenny in the hope that the retarded giant, himself a victim of discrimination, might understand: "If I say something, why it's just a nigger talking" (43). In "Junius Maltby" from *The Pastures of Heaven*, Steinbeck satirizes the racial overtones that characterized America's war with Japan. Robbie, Junius's son, tries to prevent his little Japanese friend, Takashi, from joining his club but reluctantly lets him in when Takashi agrees to spy on his own father. In *The Moon is Down*, Steinbeck refused to succumb to the wartime tendency to stereotype the enemy as inhuman monsters and, as a result, was severely criticized: "I had written of Germans as men, not supermen, and this was considered a very weak view to take ("My Short Novels" 147). The sincerity of Steinbeck's artistic stand against racial and ethnic hatred is at least partially borne out in a letter he wrote to Twentieth Century Fox concerning certain unauthorized changes in the script that he had written for Alfred Hitchcock's *Lifeboat*: "While it is certainly true that I wrote a script for *Lifeboat*, it is not true that in that script as in the film there were any slurs against organized labor nor was there a stock comedy Negro. On the contrary, there was an intelligent and thoughtful seaman who knew realistically what he was about and instead of the colored travesty of the half comic and half pathetic Negro there was a Negro of dignity, purpose and personality" (*SLL* 266).

In his commissioned work, however, Steinbeck's private view toward the enemy, which he had previously expressed only in letters, became public. Defending himself in a letter to Reverend L. M. Birkhead against charges that "Steinbeck" was a Jewish name and that *The Grapes of Wrath* was Jewish propaganda, Steinbeck retorted, "On both sides and for many generations we are blond and blue-eyed to a degree to arouse the admiration and perhaps envy of the dark-complexioned Hitler" (204). Whereas Steinbeck had previously suppressed his personal views toward race and certain ethnic groups for the sake of his art, he found it advantageous in 1942 from the point of view of the propagandist to voice these views. In *Bombs Away*, Steinbeck the Biologist brands the enemy as a vicious subspecies: "Germany and the dark Aryans of Italy and the yellow Aryans of Japan developed air forces. The purpose was to blast and maim and kill" (20). He goes on to stereotype the Italian soldiers as "young Mussolinis" (20) who employed bombs and machine guns against the hapless Ethiopian horsemen. He also includes the account of Harris, a ham radio operator, whose contacts in Germany "told horrible things before their sets went dead" (150). Evidently, Steinbeck felt that the humanistic stance that he had taken toward the Nazis earlier that same year in *The Moon is Down*—that the Nazis were people who had been hypnotized into committing atrocities (Slochower 305)—no longer suited his purposes as a spokesman for the military.

Ironically enough, most of the critics who have searched for evidence substantiating their claims that John Steinbeck was essentially a writer of propaganda have concentrated on *The Grapes of Wrath* and have totally disregarded his one blatant venture into propaganda writing—*Bombs Away*—which they dismiss as having very little artistic significance. Actually, one should not judge Steinbeck too harshly, since he was only one of many writers who subordinated their talents to the war effort, omitting certain truths in order to foster certain popular American illusions. Admittedly, this branch of integrity did not finish Steinbeck as a writer, but *Bombs Away* may have caused him to stagnate creatively by showing him that he could write quickly and effortlessly if he simply recycled certain tried-and-true themes and characters. How sad it is that the echoes of Steinbeck's great themes and characters that resonate in diluted form throughout *Bombs Away* emanate from the works of the past, not the future.

Works Cited

Astro, Richard. "Steinbeck's Post-War Trilogy: A Return to Nature and the Natural Man." *Twentieth Century Literature* 16 (1969): 109-22.
—. "Travels with Steinbeck: The Laws of Thought and the Laws of Things." *Steinbeck Quarterly* 8 (1975): 40-47.
Davis, Robert Murray. "Introduction." *Twentieth Century Views: Steinbeck*. Ed. Robert Murray Davis. Englewood Cliffs, NJ: Prentice-Hall, 1972.
French, Warren. *John Steinbeck*. Boston: Twayne Publishers, 1975.
Kennedy, John S. "John Steinbeck: Life Affirmed and Dissolved." *Steinbeck and His Critics: A Record of Twenty-Five Years*. Ed. E. W. Tedlock, Jr. and C. V. Wicker. Albuquerque: University of New Mexico Press, 1957. 119-34.
Lisca, Peter. "Steinbeck's Image of Man and His Decline as a Writer." *Modern Fiction Studies* Spring 1968: 3-10.
Simmonds, Roy S. "Steinbeck and World War II: The Moon Goes Down." *Steinbeck Quarterly* 17 (1984): 14-34.
Slowchower, Harry. *Literature and Philosophy: Between Two World Wars*. New York: Citadel Press, 1964.
Steinbeck, Elaine, and Robert Wallsten, eds. *Steinbeck: A Life in Letters*. New York: Viking Press, 1975.
Steinbeck, John. *Bombs Away: The Story of a Bomber Team*. New York: Viking Press, 1942.
—. *In Dubious Battle*. New York: Viking Press, 1963.
—. *The Grapes of Wrath*. New York: Penguin Books, 1976.
—. "My Short Novels." *English Journal* March 1954: 147.
—. *Of Mice and Men*. New York: Bantam Books, 1979.
—. *The Red Pony*. New York: Bantam Books, 1972.
Warren, Joseph. "John Steinbeck: Art and Propaganda." *Steinbeck and His Critics: A Record of Twenty-Five Years*. Ed. E. W. Tedlock, Jr. and C. V. Wicker. Albuquerque: University of New Mexico Press, 1957. 250-65.

"I Know It When I Hear It On Stage": Theatre and Language in Steinbeck's *Burning Bright*

John Ditsky

John Steinbeck's 1950 "play-novelette" *Burning Bright* has surely established itself as his least popular work of fiction among both critics and the general reading public. Not particularly successful in its initial stage production, it caused its author to waffle between passionate defense of its supposed merits and resigned acceptance of its apparent defects. As is well known, moreover, it was not included in Steinbeck's collected *Short Novels* (1953). And if even the early *Cup of Gold* can be assayed for glimmerings of the mature Steinbeckian style, and though *To a God Unknown* can be endlessly subjected to psychological analysis, *Burning Bright* has failed to make it into either the classroom or the scholar's study. What routine attention the work has received to date in the course of chronological surveys of Steinbeck's canon has been both grudging and confined to issues of theme and language.[1] In terms of the play-novelette genre, *Burning Bright* is usually viewed as the final stage in the decline of a form that began brilliantly with *Of Mice and Men* and began to fall apart with *The Moon Is Down*. And yet that form—that attempt, at least in the latter two instances, to write simultaneously for the reader and for the stage audience—has hardly ever been considered in its own right, however truly innovative it may actually have been. So that whether or not one rescues *Burning Bright* from critical oblivion in the process, one at least owes it and every production by a major artist the obligation to judge it *in its own terms*, that is, as a work of fiction that is structured and delivered to its audience according to the special needs and requirements inherent in stage performance. Let us begin that process here and now.

I

Almost five years ago, I made a first attempt at a transitional discussion of the ways in which language arises out of situation in Steinbeck's work as a whole. Entitled "Steinbeck as Dramatist," this preliminary account, as I subtitled it, was an attempt to direct attention to the dramatist in John Steinbeck—the artist whose sense of *scene* was responsible for the irruption into *language* of differing levels and qualities of expression. As a writer known to have tried out his dialogue aloud, against empty air, Steinbeck's ear is usually so fine that the nature of his achievement can easily be taken for granted, that is, be neglected or ignored. But in the case of *Burning Bright*, where the language that is made to arise out of situation is so palpably nonnaturalistic that it seems to have been written by someone scarcely literate or deaf or both, it is all too tempting to dismiss the entire piece as an outstanding example of what English critic Roy S. Simmonds has frequently referred to as the failure of language of the later works. My paper was written for the Second International John Steinbeck Congress in Salinas, and it has been published fairly obscurely only in Japan; thus at peril of self-quotation, I will include at this point the pages from it that are specifically relevant to *Burning Bright*, so that these beginning remarks might serve as both an encapsulation and, after five years, a point of departure:

> In *Burning Bright*, John Steinbeck's least successful venture into the theater and into scriptwriting generally, unreal dialogue is spoken by unreal characters in unreal settings. Something in *The Moon Is Down* must have struck a body of judges enough to use it as a pretext to give John Steinbeck the Nobel Prize. Nothing in *Burning Bright* has thus far struck anyone enough to use it as a reason to say or do anything in the writer's behalf. But is this wholly Steinbeck's fault? What if his play has never received the production it demands? What if his play-novel has never had the appropriate readership it re-

quires? Considering that Steinbeck was both involved with questions of his own familial heritage and the Arthurian legend as a literary subject while he was creating *Burning Bright*, the resulting texture of his play is not surprising. Rightly or wrongly, he deliberately changed the setting from Circus to Farm to Sea. In establishing the universality of his story, Steinbeck undercut its human singularity by emphasizing Life in almost a laboratory sense. While Hemingway was obsessed with the writing of a Land, Sea, and Air trilogy, John Steinbeck was attempting to demonstrate the oneness of all three. The circus ("Air," for him) was trapeze and magic and wonder. But his play ends in the environment of an amniotic sea where Joe Saul becomes the Joseph-like father of a baby not descended from his single seed. If by this time Steinbeck's audience has not begun to think in terms appropriate to *Everyman*, or to respond to his triple changes of setting by having the three of them melt imaginatively into one, then the play in production must inevitably fail. The key dramatic dialogue comes in the final scene of this "failure" of Steinbeck's, when Joe Saul enters the hospital room in which his wife is resting after having delivered a child deliberately conceived by another man. The scene begins with Joe Saul pulling the covers away from the son Mordeen has just given birth to:

> "Mordeen!" he said softly.
> As though she heard him, she took a great gasp of air into her lungs and her head twisted from side to side. "Dead," she whispered. "Dead—the whole world—dead—Victor dead."
> He said, "No, Mordeen, not dead—here and alive, always."
> She threshed her head violently and she whimpered, "Friend Ed, I wanted—I wanted him to have his child. I wanted—but it's dead. Everything is dead."
> Joe Saul said, "Listen to me, Mordeen. He is here— and resting. He's had a great effort and now he's sleeping—a little wrinkled and very tired—and the soft hair—" He looked down. "And his mouth—the sweet mouth—like your mouth, Mordeen." . . .
> He wiped her forehead until her throat relaxed. "Rest," he said. "I do know and I know more. I know that what seemed the whole tight pattern is not important. Mordeen, I thought, I felt, I knew that my par-

ticular seed had importance over other seed. I thought
that was what I had to give. It is not so. I know it
now."

She said, "You are Joe Saul? Faceless—only a voice
and a white facelessness."

"I thought my blood must survive—my line—but
it's not so. My knowledge, yes—the long knowledge remembered, repeated, the pride, yes, the pride and
warmth, Mordeen, warmth and companionship and
love so that the loneliness we wear like icy clothes is
not always here. These I can give."

"Where is your face?" she asked. "What's happened to your face, Joe Saul?"

"It's not important. Just a face. The eyes, the nose,
the shape of chin—I thought they were worth preserv-
ing because they were mine. It is not so."

"It is the race, the species that must go staggering
on. Mordeen, our ugly little species, weak and ugly, torn
with insanities, violent and quarrelsome, sensing evil—
the only species that knows evil and practices it—the
only one that senses cleanness and is dirty, that knows
about cruelty and is unbearably cruel." (154-57)

Joe Saul concludes that there is such a thing as "*a
shining*" among humans, the moment when humans
create beauty; and that the child he now adopts as his own
is "*the Child*" because "every man is father to all children
and every child must have all men as father" (158).
Whatever private reason John Steinbeck had for writing
these passages as he did, should they be judged by the old
rules, the old naturalism and its simplicities?

This business about shinings and "the Child" and
the universal fatherhood of men is such patent dogma,
however, that the superficial implausibility of the lines
which express such an idea as purported to be coming
from the mouth of a recognizable human being is hardly
worth noting. But on the stage the opportunity always
exists for a human visage to utter whatever language we
impute to it, whether that language be the speech of the
marketplace or the imagined voices of angels passing. Of
course *Burning Bright*, with its expedient murder, is not
Steinbeck's most endearing statement of the human condition. If Steinbeck made a central error in the conception
of *Burning Bright*, it is that novice poet's mistake of stating grand ideas in universal terms, instead of grounding

them in recognizable human experience. In *Burning Bright*, people who never existed utter language no one has ever spoken in a setting that does not hold still long enough to be plausible on any level. Ironically, the play is most successful in terms of these negative achievements, for its stated purpose is to deny the singularity of any human life. With its cosmic perspective, *Burning Bright* is a play written for an audience of gods (Ditsky, "Steinbeck as Dramatist" 20-22).

That passage, with its lengthy sustained quotation, is itself the index of the difficulties of dealing with *Burning Bright* critically: shorter excerpts merely heighten the impression that Steinbeck's dialogue is ludicrous and nothing more. Quotations of single lines foster devolution into hilarity. Yet the material I have just put forward serves to spotlight the paradox *Burning Bright* seems to represent for the critic interested in the process by which language arises out of situation in Steinbeck.

II

Very recently, a graduate student of mine[2] prepared a presentation for our Steinbeck seminar in which she pursued a clue that had been provided by a prior class discussion. She argued that Steinbeck had, on his own, come up with a theory of drama that in many respects paralleled Brechtian Epic Theatre; and she thereupon worked up a model production of *Burning Bright* in Epic Theatre terms, showing how the play might be seen to "work" if only the producer and director, instead of embarrassedly attempting to hide the seeming infelicities of the text out of view of the audience, were to accept them for what they are and try to exploit, to heighten them as deliberate dramatic devices. I have no intention of stealing my student's ideas, however. Her sample production is a work of the imagination, for one thing; and the paralleling of Brecht's essays on the theatre and Steinbeck's letters and the contents of *Burning Bright* are, by nature, the stuff of graduate-student exercises that comparatists are welcome to further, to their fascination. Yet I mention her accomplishment as an example of the direction which I wish to take in reading *Burning Bright*, almost as though it were the only way—

because finally, I think it may indeed be Steinbeck's way, whether or not his intentions can be made to come to the rescue of his achievement.

Without intending to vary much from my announced plan to stick with the *dramatic* aspects of *Burning Bright,* I draw attention to its title's obvious source in William Blake's enormously famous poem, which is itself partially quoted in the opening pages of the published text. Blake's "Tyger" is a ferocious and devouring and irresistible force of nature, the very opposite of the cuddly, helpless (and sacrificial) "Lamb." In its own poem, the Lamb seems ignorant of its Maker; but the Tyger is a cosmic force so immense that the poet seems unable to reconcile its creation with that of the Lamb as the work of the same Maker. (Not incidentally, though *Burning Bright* has its evident share of Christian biblical referents, the divinity of the "Tyger" is just as evidently something that operates by its own rules, and without the system of Mercy; it may be useful, therefore, to remember that the sky-god Zeus bears a name that translates as either of *Burning Bright*'s sky metaphors: "bright" and "shining.") In *Burning Bright,* the Lamb can be said to be the helpless baby Mordeen gives birth to at the ending of the play-novelette; but this Lamb, if that image is an accurate one, arrives as the result of a process so implacable and ineluctable that a murder is casually committed in its name. In other words, *Burning Bright* is a text about harsh truths whose nativity within our consciousnesses can only be acknowledged with awe. And it is also a play with the world for its stage.

While it is tempting to rely upon Steinbeck's letters from the period of *Burning Bright*'s creation and first production, letters which—as mentioned above—alternatively become defensive about the work and then confess its defects—the risk of the "intentional fallacy" may outweigh the benefits of such a distraction from the main purpose. The text either does or does not speak adequately for itself in this respect. Suffice it for now to note that the author, in the "Foreword" which precedes the published text, first draws attention to the "terse description" (10) of the normal playscript, minimal language that "gives the director and the set designer greater leeway in exercising their own imagination in production," and then goes on to argue the merits for the fleshing-out that his hybrid genre makes possible for the many who do not and cannot "read" plays imaginatively. Seeking to establish the best of both possible literary worlds in his play-novelette, John Steinbeck is running the risk of confusing both his potential audiences.

On the other hand, Steinbeck sees that the concision demanded of dramatic presentations, colored by the possibilities of description which are taken for granted among writers of fiction, makes the hybrid form worth the extra effort: "It gives a play a wide chance of being read and a piece of fiction a chance of being played without the usual revision" (13). The true artistic and critical worth of either of these possibilities may be moot, in fact, and of course "the usual revision" is highly likely to prove necessary when a text intended to work in two genres at once betrays a lack of sufficient purity in dramatic production. The key to success, Steinbeck argues near the end of his Foreword, is in the artist's "*seeing* his story before his eyes" (13). Steinbeck's emphasis on seeing is interesting, especially coming from a writer generally associated with accurately *heard* speech. If there is a way of reconciling these often-conflicting demands, perhaps it lies with *accepting* the clash between the seemingly naturalistic and visual elements, rather than by attempting to gloss them over—and this clash may seem the greater when we employ, as is the case here (for reasons of general availability), the text of the play-novelette instead of the somewhat different playscript with which few readers or theatregoers are acquainted.

To return to Roy S. Simmonds's phrase "failure of language," which he would apply to just about everything Steinbeck wrote after *The Grapes of Wrath*, I am arguing that the dialogue in *Burning Bright*, and ultimately the work as a whole, can be seen most constructively as a *deliberate* failure of language. While only the most neurotic of us deliberately fail at what we attempt, of course, I am suggesting that to hold its determinedly non-naturalistic quality against the dialogue in *Burning Bright* is critically no more profound than objecting to opera on the grounds that we do not actually sing our ways through life. Confining myself—as promised earlier—to only a few brief snippets from the letters of the period, one sees that Steinbeck—concerned with "revision" as opening night approached as any playwright would be, predictably professed faith in what he had wrought until the big event, whereupon he admitted to Eugene Solow, "The critics murdered us" (not wholly true but generally accurate) even though "it is a good play" (*SLL* 412). The fault lay with the critics, of course; yet by the time a month had passed, he could assure Jack and Max Wagner that "the critics . . . were not at fault"; "It was not a good play." (By this time, it was almost as if the blame should be imputed to those who had praised the play earlier on.) "The thing read wonderfully but it just did not play," he went on; the piece lacked something he could not give it now—"I don't know what that quality is but I know it when I hear it on stage."[3] Now, the man's two views of how "good" the play may have been can be readily explained away by the differing stresses of the two occasions; but what remains of interest is Steinbeck's faith in his instinctive grasp of what makes a drama "play," that that quality is something you "hear," and that the text (the play-novelette was already in print) still "read wonderfully."

Does *Burning Bright* in any sense "read wonderfully"? Few have thought so, and those who have expressed themselves on paper have fairly universally made sport of Steinbeck's dialogue. In doing so, it is as though his critics pretend for the moment of condemning the play-novelette that Steinbeck had never or seldom before departed from the carefully "heard" naturalistic American vernacular of his more popular "proletarian" works. Consider the fictions animated by the study of myth and Romance—*Cup of Gold, To a God Unknown, The Acts of King Arthur and His Noble Knights*—or the paisano translationese of *Tortilla Flat*, not to mention the "universal" idiom of the prior play-novelette, *The Moon Is Down*. Consider too the self-conscious philosophizing of *East of Eden* or of any work in which a "Doc" figure appears, plus the self-aware Christness of Casy in *The Grapes of Wrath* and the antiChristness of Ethan in *The Winter of Our Discontent*. Perhaps it is truly primarily in narrated passages and in the non-fiction that a masterful example of "real" speech can be heard in Steinbeck. As a play-novelette, *Burning Bright* quite simply *depends* upon the kind of language which consistently appears in Steinbeck's work, but which elsewhere we have found the means to take more or less in our strides, still insisting as the early critics did that he was a realist, even a naturalist, writer.

III

Burning Bright may be said to work best when its artifices are not glossed over, but emphasized instead. Even in its play-novelette form, the work proclaims its theatricality; Act 1 begins with a paragraph of what is evidently set-description of a clearly limited, non-detailed, and non-naturalistic sort: a dressing tent for "The Circus" has stained walls; the floor is earthen and barley-stubbled; a well-worn trunk stands open, a mirror across its lid. "Prickles of sun glittering" come through the tent material, less a light cue than a visual effect. With that, the stage is set (17); leave it at that, moreover, and the audience still knows where it is, and that it is watching a play where what is unsupplied must come from its imagination, or from the implications of dialogue. The next paragraph (17-18) introduces a main character, Joe Saul, who is dabbing makeup onto his face; stage directions are thus being combined in this and the next two paragraphs (18-19) with a character's initial description, and the audience—theatrically—begins to come to conclusions about Joe Saul. He is showing signs of age but, though "rough," is still fit—with eyes that, at least with the help of makeup, look "large and dark and glittering"—a thematic linkup with the "glittering" sun outside, no casual usage in a play with a title like *Burning Bright* and whose major image is light. We are even made to notice Joe Saul's "spatulate" fingers and the fact that the musculature of his arms is that of someone who clings and hangs with them instead of lifting. We're poised on the edge of drama, we realize, and we haven't needed the conversations of naturalistic Ibsenian servants to bring it about; this isn't fourth-wall drama at all, in fact, and if the theatre audience couldn't actually recognize the points about fingers and muscles from its distance—or if actors' casting couldn't oblige with the right sort of body—well then, so much the better—we are left with the image of a man putting on makeup: getting ready to act in a "play" of sorts.

(Incidentally, the matter of characters' names can be used to show how one can differentiate between traditional thematic interpretation of the play-novelette and what is being attempted here. In this latter view, it matters less that Joe Saul bears his creator's initials, and that Steinbeck had fatherhood on his mind when he dedicated his piece "To, for, and because of Elaine"— the new wife who had brought marital happiness back into his life—and that a figure who was a surrogate father in the playscript [a "Joseph"] is also converted [a "Saul"] by a great shining at its close—less, I say, in the thematic sense than that by giving his protagonist this stagy sort of name [one not wholly unalike a number of those in earlier fictions, however] he is drawing attention to him as a person of the drama, as a shell fairly fleshed forth by nothing more than the fact that an actor plays him. Even more so is this true of "Friend Ed," for though John Steinbeck's best friend was an Ed—Ricketts, recently dead when the play was being written—and though this other had also had a fairly expedient, science-based, sense of morality, it interests me more that he has been given such an unsubtly Brechtian—and thus audience-distancing—title which denotes his explicit dramatic *function* more than anything else.)

The last paragraph of text before the actual beginning of the play is an assemblage of offstage sounds. These are included not *seriatim*, as they might be in nature, but in so tight a piece of prose that they suggest a collage of nearly inseparable sounds: the barker's call, the calliope's "skirl," a merry-go-round's waltz and the "chutter of gathering people." And then animal sounds— lions, elephants, pigs, and horses—"against the brass wail of a circus trombone" (19). This is immediately followed by Joe Saul's looking down at his hands, upon which cue three whistles are heard from outside, and as instructed Friend Ed enters and the play proper begins. Admittedly, in a stage production these sounds can be made the stuff of many minutes of speechless time, but for the reader they will only consume as long as it takes to read about them, and they can be staged that way as well—as an atmospheric and contrived tape of concrete music whose volume is abruptly lowered so that those three ritual whistles can be heard. Thus far, we might well be watching the start of a Beckett play.

The ensuing dialogue may be said to begin naturalistically enough, but fairly quickly it begins to reflect the situation's underlying tensions by means of artificial expression. Steinbeck has Joe Saul refer to a minor and offstage character in a way that almost parodies conventional dramatic exposition: "I'm sure, Friend Ed, I don't tell you for the first time that Mrs. Malloy has got a son Tom that's in college and only nineteen. Did you hear about that, Friend Ed? Did you hear about it twenty thousand times?" (20). The artificiality is quickly heightened as the theme of genetic continuity is introduced; by the time Joe Saul mentions his new partner Victor, who "has no ancestry" in the trapeze trade (Joe Saul and his late cousin Will were the "end products" of "a thousand years"), we are being treated to such Anglo-Saxon hyphenizations as "wife-loss" and "friend-right"

(22-23). They lead us into a world of language in which Joe Saul's ancient ancestors are described as having been "nature spirits once," which makes Friend Ed reply, suddenly turned Old Celt, "It's a strange telling for children" (26-27). And with this, the themes of the play are taken—by language—out of a particular time and place.

Indeed, very shortly thereafter Joe Saul confesses that as a result of his inability to sire a child, he has been "digging like a mole into my own darkness," though he understands that "it is a thing that can happen to anyone in any place and time—a farmer or a sailor, or a lineless, faceless Everyone!" (30). Note that this line encapsules the theme of the play, as well as the basic approach taken by the dramatist—not only the universalization of character but also that of situation; moreover, simultaneous with the lifting of language onto a new plane, we are given the adumbration of the remainder of the play, as action moves through three nominally different settings from "darkness" to "*a shining*." This is the way a dramatist employs an image and makes poetic theatre thereby, and it is one of the evidences for concluding that Steinbeck's dramatic instincts were as sound as he felt them to be. My "Steinbeck as Dramatist" essay argued that Steinbeck generally proceeded as a dramatist would, and not merely in the play-novelettes; because he observes character and situation essentially from without, and objectively (or seemingly so), he relies on language that—under situational and psychological pressure—soars.

This rising of language under dramatically justified circumstances is a movement upward from the ordinary to the special, not necessarily a boost in qualitative terms that all readers or audience members might appreciate. But it is a consistent index of how Steinbeck thinks as a dramatist would. In *Of Mice and Men*, the "rising" can be said to be towards the poetic and quasi-religious; in *The Moon Is Down*, towards the theatrical and "stagy"; and in *Burning Bright*, towards the mythic and universal. In each instance, there is a deliberate eschewal of the mundane and familiar, but in the latter case the playwright goes even further: he is constantly reminding his audience, through theatricality including language, that it is watching a morality play unfold, and that the theme of sterility is being used to key humanity into what Steinbeck customarily referred to as a "breaking through" still not achieved in actuality.

As this Act continues, moreover, Steinbeck's grasp of the

playwright's need for economy of measures shows forth. No sooner has Friend Ed finished his conversation with Joe Saul than he is called to perform, and just as he exits, Mordeen returns, reporting that her friend's baby is so wonderful that "He grabbed at a shaft of sunshine with his hand" (32). All of this serves to remind Joe Saul that he can't quite make the sun shine himself, but the scene leads towards an ardent display of mutual love between Mordeen and Joe Saul, at the exact peaking of which Victor enters. Victor is "large and powerful, dark and young. His mouth was full and arrogant, his eyes sullen." His skin blooming with youth, he wears a "gold medallion on a golden chain" (35). Steinbeck seems to have created the stereotype of the stud male years before this type became a familiar fixture of resort life and television fare. As a stereotype, however, Victor is disposable; and that is what—shockingly in terms of naturalistic expectations—eventually happens to him once he has impregnated Mordeen. Victor is, remember, a "stud animal" (103), a source of semen in a play about blood-lines and their real importance; in the backwash of an era of Nazified eugenics, Steinbeck is deliberately challenging conventional notions about the preciousness of individual DNA—which of course had not been discovered as yet.

Joe Saul is just about the age of John Steinbeck at the time of the writing of *Burning Bright*, nearly fifty (45); yet this is, like many a modern drama, a play within an individual consciousness in which characters represent aspects of a single psyche: the philosophical and detached Friend Ed resembles not only Steinbeck's Doc figures but also *East of Eden*'s Lee; Mordeen echoes Cal's discovery in that novel when she affirms, "If I am wrong about anything it will be *my* wrongness . . . " (61); and with the rutting Victor resembling the pre-Elaine Steinbeck, there is little reason to suppose that the play is "about" any single individual. Indeed, it is ultimately "about" the futurity represented by the baby born at the play's ending and accepted at last by Joe Saul as his own. But this is to theorize about meanings. The point essential to our present purposes has to do with practices that are consistent throughout the play and, as they have been examined using Act 1 as the main example, the practices of a self-taught dramatist with some clear notion of what playwrights *do*. When Friend Ed disposes of Victor and then moves on himself, we are left with a curious variation on a comic ending; half of the Freudian quartet has vanished, and only Joe Saul and Mordeen are left. And the child.

This is of course a very special child, the final symbol on which the play's statements rest. Joe Saul says at the end of the play that he had to walk "into the black . . . to know that every man is father to all children and every child must have all men as father . . . This is *the Child*" (158). It should be noted that such a statement would be absurd in a naturalistic play, or even in a naturalistically conceived production; people simply don't make such statements. But by focusing the short second scene of his Act III on the small hospital room in which Joe Saul formally accepts Mordeen's baby as his own, John Steinbeck makes it possible to use lighting to focus in on a small part of his stage where something very Bethlehemlike is going on. It takes little imagination to realize that Mordeen parallels Mary, and of course we have already compared Joe Saul to Joseph. But that does not make the baby a Christ symbol in the usual sense. As I have argued elsewhere, Steinbeck uses religious narrative to inform his fiction, but not as a literary crutch or to elicit a sigh of recognition from his audience; rather, he is retelling the religious story to make it *happen* once more, and *more truly*. When Joe Saul ritualistically says the final lines of the play—"Mordeen, . . . I love the child . . . I love our child . . . *I love my son*," we are told that "his face was shining and his eyes were shining" (159). Yet this is no ordinary literary "Christ figure" that Joe Saul accepts "in triumph"; it is, in the play's terms, a second Christ come to save the world from its past obsession with blood-ties; in that sense, this is an evolutionary step upward as radical as the one that ends *The Grapes of Wrath*. In Joe Saul, the human race comes to accept responsibility for the futurity of itself as a whole for the first time; in this action, when and if it occurs, its true redemption lies—in Steinbeck's view.

The adoptive and basic familial unit seen by the audience at the curtain—or blackout—is a deliberately emblematic final tableau. Joe Saul leans in so that Mordeen can see his face, as she has asked; it shines with light. From where? Theatrically, it might just as well be illuminated from close at hand—from the ostensible "baby" lying next to Mordeen. The play has little to lose from having the "baby" glow as a source of the light of Joe Saul's illumination; after all, *Burning Bright* is a kind of science fiction. And that this is a very special baby has already been conveyed by such language as Mordeen's description of her initial reactions to an X-ray of the infant as "like the nave of a cathedral with a vaulted roof and one great column—that was ribs and spine" (115). (Microcosm is also macrocosm, as in Albee's *Tiny Alice*.) In this view, all the puzzling machinations of the plot can be viewed as simply that: means by which to achieve the final moment of epiphany. In other words, it would almost be surprising if in a production of this play the "baby" did not in fact *glow*.

A few years ago, I undertook a brief survey of a fascinating aspect of modern drama I had noticed. It is this: children being troublesome presences onstage, dramatists tend to avoid them except when they are thematically necessary, generally as embodiments of the drama of their parents. This being the case, in serious drama children tend to be created only to be destroyed, as the tensions inherent in their makeup finally prove too great for them.[4] The interesting thing about *Burning Bright* is that it accepts this convention, one which is by no means prominent in "straight" fiction, and succeeds in turning it around for its special purposes. By all the rules of theatrical logic, Victor's and Mordeen's baby ought to be born dead; Mordeen is even shown as sure that this must be so—in the long quotation with which I began. Yet the child—"*the Child*"—lives—precisely because Joe Saul accepts it as his own. Dramatically, his adoptive act changes what would have been tragedy to cosmic comedy, and there is no way of writing precisely that except by the route of expressionist dialogue complemented by expressionist format. Putting things another way, this baby is a "Christ" who redeems without the necessity of being sacrificed; and in a play whose characters are in "reality" the whole human species, there is no justification for evading or even diminishing the tendency towards stylization of language and action. Alone among contemporary playwrights, oddly enough, Brecht and Steinbeck seem to share the theme of suprareligious redemption of the past through the future: we are not victims of some Original Sin. *Burning Bright* may fly apart when read as a "play-novelette"; there may finally exist no such thing. But the instincts of its creator were those of a dramatist, surely; and given a production in which all the theatrical elements worked complementarily, *Burning Bright* might get a fair hearing at last.

Notes

[1] For example, I made one such attempt in my "Steinbeck's *Burning*

Bright: Homage to Astarte," *Steinbeck Quarterly*, 7, 3-4 (Summer-Fall 1974): 79-84, and another in "Ritual Murder in Steinbeck's Dramas," *Steinbeck Quarterly*, 11, 3-4 (Summer-Fall 1978): 72-76. But all such endeavors are doomed to fail at least partially if they do not consider the nature of the sub-genre Steinbeck was trying to create.

   [2] Ms. Friedel Liptay.

   [3] Letter of 28 November 1950, in *Steinbeck: A Life in Letters*, 414. The classic and eloquent defense of the play-novelette is of course John Steinbeck's own "Critics, Critics, Burning Bright," collected in E. W. Tedlock, Jr., and C. V. Wicker, eds., *Steinbeck and His Critics* (Albuquerque: University of New Mexico Press, 1957) 43-47. Neither petulant nor overly defensive from this writer's point of view, Steinbeck naturally feels that the majority of critics do not seem to have understood what they so vehemently attacked. But in doing so he makes observations about his approach to drama which seem both straightforward and sound, and I have merely attempted to pursue his points even further.

   [4] "Child-Sacrifice in Modern Drama: A Survey," *Ariel*, 15.3 (July 1984): 3-15. John Steinbeck is, moreover, not above "sacrificing" a child when it suits his literary purposes; it happens in *The Grapes of Wrath* and *The Pearl*, for instance, and almost happens in *East of Eden* and *The Winter of Our Discontent*.

   Robert DeMott's *Steinbeck's Reading: A Catalogue of Books Owned and Borrowed* (New York: Garland, 1984) confirms Steinbeck's awareness of at least the *poetry* of Federico Garcia Lorca, but there is no evidence I am aware of that the fictionist/playwright knew the *plays* of the dramatist/poet. This is a pity, but it does not prevent me from wondering aloud if John Steinbeck might have known the Spaniard's *Yerma*, a tragedy built around childlessness. The title character is so anxious to bear a son that she eventually strangles her husband, Juan, who is content with having *her*; by the play's ending, Yerma (whose name refers to her "barrenness") knows that she has now "killed" her "Child," though she might have borne one had she not been such a dutiful wife that she resisted the temptation to mate with her longtime love, the temporary third in this triangle. Steinbeck's Mordeen manages to override such conventional considerations, and thus turn tragedy to thoughtful comedy. "Mordeen" as a name has a suggestive impact similar to "Yerma," but I have long wondered why Steinbeck chose the name "Victor" for his play-novelette's sperm donor. But in *Yerma*, the putative parent—who departs in mid-play—is named Victor.

Works Cited

Demott, Robert. *Steinbeck's Reading: A Catalogue of Books Owned and Borrowed*. New York: Garland Publishing, 1984.

Ditsky, John. "Ritual Murder in Steinbeck's Dramas." *Steinbeck Quarterly* 11. 3-4 (Summer-Fall 1978): 72-76.

—. "Steinbeck's *Burning Bright*: Homage to Astarte." *Steinbeck Quarterly* 7. 3-4 (Summer-Fall 1974): 79-84.

—. "Steinbeck as Dramatist: A Preliminary Account." *John Steinbeck: From Salinas to the World*.   Ed. Shigeharu Yano, Tetsumaro Hayashi, Richard F. Peterson, and Yasuo Hashiguchi. Tokyo: Gaku Shobu, 1986.

20-22.

Steinbeck, Elaine, and Robert Wallsten, eds. *Steinbeck: A Life in Letters.* New York: Viking Press, 1975.

Steinbeck, John. *Burning Bright.* New York: Viking Press, 1950.

—. "Critics, Critics, Burning Bright." *Steinbeck and His Critics.* Ed. E. W. Tedlock, Jr., and C. V. Wicker. Albuquerque: University of New Mexico Press, 1957. 43-47.

Viva Zapata!:
HUAC and the Mexican Revolution

Jeremy G. Butler

> To be a member of the Communist Party is to
> have a taste of the police state. It is a diluted
> taste but it is bitter and unforgettable.[1]
> —Elia Kazan (1952)

> My true feeling personally is that in one
> guise or another, all revolution is permanent
> and always will be permanent. I think there
> always has to be some struggle within a society
> to keep it moving forward, and attack the
> tendency in people to become crooked, to become
> bastards.[2]   —Elia Kazan (1974)

Viva Zapata! marks the intersection of two historical
epochs, of two significant ideological moments in the twentieth
century: Mexico, 1910-1920 and Hollywood, 1947-1953. It is a film
about the Mexican Revolution and the importance of revolutionary ideals but, in apparent contradiction, it is also a film in-
scribed with the reactionary ideology of Hollywood at a time
when the House Un-American Activities Committee (HUAC)
had provoked a blacklist. The Mexican revolutionary Emiliano
Zapata would thus seem to be an odd choice for a film industry
fearful of being associated with radical ideology. And it seems a
particularly strange project for director Elia Kazan, one of
HUAC's "friendly witnesses" who informed on his former colleagues in the Communist Party, U. S. A. (CPUSA) while the
film was in production. How does *Viva Zapata!* accommodate
these seemingly contradictory factors? Is the title's exclamation

point undercut with right-wing irony or does this cold war film actually applaud a quasi-socialist hero? Finally, are these seeming ambivalences evident in the film's narrative structure and visual style?

The Historical Contexts

Emiliano Zapata (1879-1919) and his *Zapatistas* were agrarian rebels, disputing the hegemony of wealthy landowners. This landed gentry dominated the policies of the corrupt President Porfirio Diaz, who had paternalistically ruled Mexico for decades. Zapata and other revolutionary forces were held together, loosely, by the leadership of the exiled Francisco Madero, who galvanized them with his Plan of San Luis Potosi (1910). In challenging Diaz, Madero and Zapata did not call for a total, socialist redistribution of the land, but rather maintained that the peasants' small parcels of land had been stolen by the large estates and that they should thus be returned to their original owners. Their demands for land reform escalated into a stop-and-go revolution that lasted from 1910 to approximately 1920—concurrent with the Russian Revolution (1917) and the European/U. S. World War (I). Although there would be eventual success for the revolutionaries and Diaz would indeed be deposed, Zapata himself would not survive the revolutionary process. On April 10, 1919, his troops reduced to small guerrilla bands, Zapata was ambushed and shot to death by the government forces of Venustrano Carranza. The following year, General Alvaro Obregon would overthrow Carranza, accede to the presidency himself and make peace with the *Zapatistas*.

Less than three decades later, Elia Kazan convinced John Steinbeck to create a screenplay based on Edgcumb Pinchon's *Zapata, the Unconquerable*. Steinbeck's work had enjoyed substantial popularity in its 1940s film versions (e.g., *The Grapes of Wrath* [1940], *Of Mice and Men* [1940] and *Tortilla Flat* [1942], among others) and Kazan's star also appeared to be rising on the strength of his earnestly liberal social problem films, *Gentleman's Agreement* (1947) and *Pinky* (1949).[3] With their credentials as the literary and cinematic consciences of liberal America secured, Steinbeck and Kazan appeared to be the logical choices to tell Zapata's story. Historical events, however, were to overtake Kazan before *Viva Zapata!* could be released in February 1952.

The post-War decade saw many ideological re-alignments. Principal among these were the repudiation of America's recent ally, the Soviet Union, and the denial of pre-War, New Deal liberalism and left-wing radicalism. Many U. S. citizens were embarrassed by the liberal—or perhaps even socialist—ideals of the 1930s. After all, they had just won a world war; probably the only new deal they wanted was a VA mortgage on a home in suburbia. Prosperity beckoned to white, middle-class society. The left-wing, share-the-wealth notions of the 1930s seemed increasingly threatening to that image of prosperity. The growing antipathy toward socialism was further fueled by the fear of Russian and Chinese imperialism, as the Berlin airlift was quickly followed by the Korean War (1950-1953). In the eyes of many Americans, the "iron curtain" that Winston Churchill described in 1946 seemed to be perilously close to wrapping itself around the U. S. perimeter. The House of Representatives would eventually prove to be the shock troops of America's ideological chilling—especially in filmmaking circles. At the same time that Steinbeck began work on the *Viva Zapata!* script, the House Un-American Activities Committee initiated its first investigation into supposedly subversive filmmaking in Hollywood.

HUAC's initial foray (1947) into the film capital was met by strong resistance from the accused screen professionals, as well as Hollywood's liberal community. Soon, however, this resistance crumbled in the face of the film producers' blacklist of past and present CPUSA members (if they did not recant their membership), a brush that also tarred moderate liberals if their allegiances were suspect. By 1952, when Kazan appeared before the Committee, the battle lines had been drawn. Serving voluntarily as a "friendly witness," Kazan renounced his mid-1930s membership in the CPUSA during a closed session of the Committee that was held January 14, 1952, one month before the release of *Viva Zapata!* At the time, however, he declined to "name names," to identify other members of the CPUSA. But soon after the film was released, Kazan reconsidered. Reappearing before HUAC, he struck out at his former colleagues in the Group Theatre and marked ten of them—including Clifford Odets—as communists.[4] He also purchased a large advertisement in the *New York Times* in order to present his rationale for informing (Kazan 7). Curiously, at the same time Kazan was undermining the civil liberties of his former friends by labeling them communists, he still labored to maintain his liberal reputation. To the accusation that he was now joining with those who sought to curtail these rights, Kazan retorted: "I have thought soberly about this. It is, simply, a lie. Secrecy serves the Communists . . . Liberals must speak out" (7).

Kazan's true motives for informing cannot be known, but his publicly available statements about the incident foreground an ambivalence that belonged more generally to the liberal ideology of the time—perhaps also to Steinbeck—and may be found in *Viva Zapata!* itself. In an interview published in 1974, Kazan said,

> . . . it's ambivalent. Since then [the time of the HUAC hearings], I've had two feelings: one feeling is that what I did was repulsive, and the opposite feeling, when I see what the Soviet Union has done to its writers, and their death camps, and the Nazi pact and the Polish and Czech repression—well, Krushchev says in his book what we all knew at the time was going on. (Ciment 83)

Kazan maintains now that his anti-communism of the 1950s was specifically anti-*Stalinism*, not anti-socialism. He defends his filmwork as "Left and progressive" (Ciment 88). His informing was meant to confront the "dictatorship and thought control" of the CPUSA, not the general principles of socialism (Kazan 7). Indeed, in the 1970s—a safe distance from the debilitating power of the blacklist—he took pleasure in the interest in *Viva Zapata!* expressed by student radicals and the so-called "New-Left," who, he claimed, compared it favorably to *The Battle of Algiers* (1966), a film sympathetic to the Algerian fight for independence (Ciment 94). The sincerity of Kazan's leftist sentiments and reasons for informing has been questioned elsewhere.[5] I don't intend to continue that ultimately futile discussion here, but I would like to offer some thought on the ways in which Kazan's ambivalences surface in the narrative structure and cinematic style of *Viva Zapata!*

Zapata in Hollywood

Viva Zapata! bears the marks of the aforementioned personal and social histories in its narrative/thematic structure. Central to this, obviously, is how Zapata is represented as a revolutionary, for the film traces his rise, fall and spiritual resurrection. Most U. S. viewers would have but a vague understanding of Zapata's position in the Mexican Revolution. Kazan and Steinbeck were consequently at liberty to inflect Zapata's actions in a fashion that would suit their ambivalently liberal discourse.

As the film begins, Zapata (Marlon Brando) is but one of a group of peasants petitioning President Diaz (Fay Roope) for land reform. Our protagonist quickly emerges from these nameless faces, however, as the boldest one among the nascent revolutionaries. He draws the President's ire and, in extreme close-up, his name is circled on the list of peasants. Narratively, this scene serves several purposes—some of them seemingly contradictory.

Most importantly, this exposition identifies a single individual as the embodiment of the revolutionary spirit. This approach to revolution owes much to the ideology of individualism, of history as a series of "Great Men." Even though the Mexican Revolution was a rebellion of the people, they do not serve as the film's protagonist. Indeed, most revolutionary stories are also ensnared within this individualist discourse. Only the Russian silent filmmakers—e.g., Eisenstein in *Strike* (1925) and *Battleship Potemkin* (1925)—and a very few others have attempted to break the stranglehold of narrative convention and feature an entire class of people as protagonist. Perhaps it is an obvious point to make, but *Viva Zapata!* is concerned less with the Mexican Revolution than it is with the struggles of a single man. However, even though *Viva Zapata!* shares the individualist prejudices of many films that have come before and since, Kazan struggles to downplay the significance of the individual and make Zapata a self-effacing leader. Zapata tells his patron Don Nacio (Arnold Moss) that he does not want to be the "conscience of the world," that he is content to court Josefa (Jean Peters) and retreat from history into the comforts of monogamy. More to the point, when his heroic brother Eufemio (Anthony Quinn) descends into greed and lustfulness after early revolutionary success, Zapata chastises his followers for placing their faith in inevitably flawed individuals: "There are no leaders but yourselves. A strong people is the only lasting strength."

The notion of a leaderless revolution might be read as democratic populism (Frank Capra's *Mr. Smith Goes to Wash-*

ington in bandoliers), but in the context of the peasant-based Mexican Revolution it approaches a socialist discourse. "Strong people," says Zapata to his wife just before his death, "Don't need a strong man [to lead them]." The corrupting prepotency of power and the disrepute of authoritarian leaders are crystallized in a scene which recalls the first name-circling incident. By now, Zapata's collaboration with Pancho Villa (Alan Reed) has placed him in authority and he rules Mexico from President Diaz's former office.[6] Zapata's ascension to power seems complete. His aide even calls him "president," though Zapata corrects him and insists on "general." The parallel with Diaz is completed, nonetheless, when Zapata meets with a group of peasants from his home state asking him to discipline his brother. One peasant is particularly contentious and Zapata demands to know his name, which he writes down and begins to circle. Suddenly he stops. The camera pulls in to a tight close-up; the lighting focuses on his face and highlights his shifting eyes; and the music swells. Zapata's epiphany seems inevitable. Recognizing how close he has come to despotism, Zapata casts aside the presidency and leaves with the peasants, but not before castigating Fernando (Joseph Wiseman), the professional revolutionary: "No fields, no home, no wife, no woman, no friends. You only destroy, that is your love." Zapata exits the halls of power, predicting Fernando's betrayal of him and anticipating his (Zapata's) martyrdom. In Kazan's revolution, the idealistic revolutionary cannot triumph without sliding into corruption.

As a cold war parable of the morally corrosive influence of power upon revolutionaries, it is difficult not to see *Viva Zapata!* as a direct commentary on Stalin's domination of the Soviet Union. Stalin, Kazan seems to be suggesting, is what Zapata would have become, had he remained within the power structure. First would come the circling of names and then the repression of entire peoples—as in the Stalinist purges. But Zapata escapes from this fate into death and legend—leaving to the treacherous Fernando, Zapata's former comrade, the function of Stalinist allegory. Like Stalin, Fernando is a professional ideologue of revolution, a "ritualistic Leftist," in Kazan's words (Ciment 94). He fights solely for power and ideology. Zapata, in contrast, fights for fields, home, wife, and friends. Not long after their confrontation and Zapata's departure, Fernando arranges for his former friend's murder. The parallel to Stalin suggests itself once again. Stalin also betrayed his revolutionary comrades—as in the case of the more progressive Trotsky, who he presumably had assassinated (in Mexico). Fernando is the only true villain in *Viva Zapata!* Zapata's military adversaries are necessary antagonists, of course, but in Fernando we find cruelty, deceit and treachery in service to nothing more than hunger for power: "No fields, no home [etc.]" Fernando is the revolutionary as dictator.

In some respects, then, *Viva Zapata!* is a reactionary film. Revolutionary leaders are endemically flawed. When successful they become boorish gluttons (Eufemio) or Machiavellian traitors (Fernando). Ideologically, the best revolutionary leader is the martyr, the legendary figure who, in *Viva Zapata!*, is said to be wandering the hills in preparation for the next revolution. But does the next one ever arrive? The end credits of *Viva Zapata!* roll over a shot of Zapata's horse in the hills. Throughout the film the horse has served as a blunt symbol of the "revolutionary spirit": wild, free, untamable, and so on. (Kazan possibly saw his repudiation of the Stalinist CPUSA in these terms.) But the film offers no route through which the revolution-as-wild-stallion transforms into the revolution-as-permanent-government. In short, he presents the short-term evils of revolution without allowing for long-term possibilities. One wonders how Kazan (and Steinbeck) might have handled biographies of revolutionaries who *survived* their revolutions and yet did not sink into a quagmire of corruption and/or authoritarianism.

Pictures of a Revolution

Kazan and cinematographer Joe MacDonald developed a visual realization of Zapata's life that may well be the most enduringly revolutionary element of *Viva Zapata!* The film's visual style valorizes Zapata, his forces and the land for which they fought in a way that transcends narrative ambiguities. This is achieved partially through the use of location shooting, although, ironically, they were not permitted to shoot in Mexico itself.[7] Gabriel Figueroa, the head of the Mexican syndicate of film technicians, read the script and objected to the use of an Anglo in the role of a Mexican hero. Kazan tells the story this way:

> He [Figueroa] said an amusing thing: "Suppose a Mexi-
> can company came up to Illinois to make a picture about
> Abraham Lincoln's life with a Mexican actor playing
> the lead, what would you think of that?" And I said to
> him, "I think it would be great, I'd love to see that."
> We left Mexico the next morning. (Ciment 90)

As a result, *Viva Zapata!* was shot in Texas, but very close to the
Mexican border. The harsh, arid land is emphasized in shot after
shot and is especially notable in the scene in which Fernando
first meets Zapata. The small band of *Zapatistas* is camped on a
rocky outcropping that both mirrors the arduousness of their
struggle and represents the central issue of this revolution: the
land and its ownership. Fernando climbs to their camp but is ill
at ease in these surroundings. The *Zapatistas*, in contrast, are
connected to the land in a primal, almost mystical way. After all,
these are basically guerrilla fighters and, as in any guerrilla war,
their knowledge of the land is one of their few, perhaps only,
superior capabilities over conventional forces.

Kazan's use of location shooting was not limited to exterior scenes. He also staged many interior scenes in houses at the
Texas location. Moreover, several interior scenes make the
viewer aware of the exterior locations through the use of deep
focus. When Zapata courts Josefa in her parlor, we see through
the window, across the street and into the window of a bar in
which Eufemio jokes about this courtship. All three planes—
parlor, street, bar interior—are sharply in focus, permitting the
interplay of Zapata, Eufemio and Josefa, and stressing the harsh
environment. Thus, through deep focus the viewer is constantly made aware of the significance of the characters' surroundings.

Three photographic/cinematic antecedents add to the vi-
sual resonance of *Viva Zapata!*: (1) the *Historia Grafica de la
Revolucion* (Archiva Casa Sola), a photographic history of the
Mexican revolution (2) the Russian silent filmmakers (especially
Eisenstein), and (3) John Ford's Westerns and his direction of
Steinbeck's *The Grapes of Wrath*.

The most direct connection between these three visual
precursors and *Viva Zapata!* is that of *Historia Grafica de la Revolucion*. The film derives much of its mise-en-scene from this
photographic account of the Revolution. Costuming and set design were copied directly from these period photographs. In one
extreme instance of this, Kazan duplicated the costumes, figures

and positions of a photograph of Pancho Villa, Zapata and their men—commemorating their triumphant entry into Mexico City. The scene in the film accurately copies the historical original, down to the sombrero in Zapata's lap. Of course, such detailed replication verges on gimmickry and is not as significant as the general similarity between Kazan/MacDonald's images and those of *Historia Grafica de la Revolucion*. This similarity is meant to denote verisimilitude and authenticity, but, more accurately, by emulating the style of documentary photographs it signifies "documentary-ness"—just as the handheld camerawork at the start of each *Hill Street Blues* episode connotes *cinema verite*. The overall effect on the viewer is that he/she is witnessing a "realistic" film, one that tells the "truth" about Zapata—even though, as indicated above, this truth is Kazan/Steinbeck/20th Century-Fox's truth, a polysemic truth.

Some writers have presumed that a second direct source for the visual style of *Viva Zapata!* is Eisenstein's unfinished *Que Viva Mexico*.[8] Indeed, Eisenstein himself had planned to explore Zapata's story, but through the perspective of *la soldatera*, the women-soldiers, in Zapata's army. This episode of *Que Viva Mexico*, "La Soldatera," was never filmed, but over 100,000 feet of film of fiestas, the Day of the Dead, and other Mexican activities were shot, all bearing Eisenstein's unique style. This footage found its way into several films released during the 1930s, none of which were edited or authorized by Eisenstein.[9] Kazan could conceivably have seen some of this footage, but he himself denies the influence of this specific film or its bastard progeny—acknowledging, however, that he absorbed many techniques from the silent films of directors such as Eisenstein and Dovshenko. This is most evident in the nearly dialogueless scene in which Zapata is arrested and led down the road by a rope around his neck. In silence, his supporters slowly gather around him until the soldiers are surrounded and subsequently set him free. Reminiscent of the funeral in Eisenstein's *Battleship Potemkin*, this scene is one of the few in which the power of the people is rendered *visually*, where Zapata's rebellion begins to look like a *people's* revolution. Elsewhere, Zapata's words may be undercut by his ambiguous actions, but in this simple scene the film communicates the strength of a populist revolution.

The final significant antecedent to the visual style of *Viva Zapata!* is the work of John Ford. The Steinbeck texts (screenplay or novel) underpinning *Viva Zapata!* and *The Grapes of Wrath* are enough to suggest a certain intertexuality between the two films, but beyond literary comparisons between Zapata and Tom Joad one can observe certain visual correspondences. Ford's predilection for static, low angle shots and back lighting—as techniques for ennobling humble, simple "folks"—works as well on the *Zapatistas* as it does on the Joad family. Ford himself worked with the Mexican people in *The Fugitive* (1947), his most visually "poetic," allegorical film since *The Informer* (1935).[10] One needs only look to the scenes of Zapata's death and the subsequent mourning in the village square to see the influence of Ford's representation of Mexican figures.

Kazan's visualization of the Mexican landscape also owes much to Ford's visual style. Whether the Oklahoma dustbowl or Morelos' rocky crags, the land's harsh beauty is rendered through long shots which dwarf the human form. An even more significant antecedent than *The Grapes of Wrath* in this respect would be Ford's Westerns of the late 1930s-1940s. *Stagecoach* (1939), *My Darling Clementine* (1946), *Fort Apache* (1948), *Three Godfathers* (1948), *She Wore a Yellow Ribbon* (1949) redefined Western iconography in the cinema. The jutting buttes and rocky plateaux of Ford's Monument Valley came to identify the U. S. West. Kazan incorporates this view of the American West's brutal beauty and successfully translates it into Mexican terms. The dry, thorny desert becomes an objective correlative for the tough men and women who call it their home.

Memories of the striking visual style of *Viva Zapata!* may well be the most concrete element viewers take away from a screening of the film. The power of the Mexican people and the sainted martyrdom of Zapata are unequivocally expressed through the film's imagery. The narrative structure, however, cannot be said to be so unequivocal, for it bears the ambivalences of a liberal ideology fissured under the stresses of virulent and undiscriminating anti-communism. *Viva Zapata!* emphasizes the ultimate failure of an individualistic revolutionary leader and thus would not offend the sensibilities of an increasingly conservative U. S. It does leave one wondering, however, how the historical Zapata—not Kazan's version of him—might have handled the House Un-American Activities Committee. Would he have taken out an ad in the *Times*?

Notes

[1] Elia Kazan. "A Statement." *New York Times* 12 April 1952: 7 (a paid advertisement).

[2] Michel Ciment. *Kazan on Kazan*. New York: Viking Press, 1974. 94.

[3] *Gentlemen's Agreement* deals with anti-Semitism and *Pinky* addresses racial injustice.

[4] The others named on April 10, 1952 were Lewis Leverett, J. Edward Bromberg, Phoebe Brand, Morris Carnovsky, Tony Kraber, Paula Miller, V. J. Jerome, Andrew Overgaard, and Ted Wellman (AKA, Sid Benson). C. P. Trussell, "Elia Kazan Admits He Was Red in '30's," *New York Times* 12 April 1952: 8.

[5] "The reality which informed informing was this: four dozen witnesses so feared losing their careers and their income that they cooperated. Sterling Hayden and Elia Kazan eventually stepped out from behind the shrubbery that every other informer was beating around and forthrightly conceded that they had exposed their comrades in order to save their own careers." Larry Ceplair, Steven Englund., *The Inquisition in Hollywood*, (Berkeley: University of California Press, 1983), 377.

[6] The office is a recurring motif. Madero (Harold Gordon) uses the same room during his brief reign.

[7] Kazan established his significant use of location shooting with the New Orleans locations in *Panic in the Streets*—just two years before *Viva Zapata!*—and would continue to use this technique in films such as *On the Waterfront* (1954) and *Wild River* (1960).

[8] In the early 1930s, Eisenstein journeyed to Mexico after an unsuccessful attempt to direct films in Hollywood. Shooting began on the six-episode *Que Viva Mexico*, with funding arranged by novelist Upton Sinclair. With just the "*La Soldadera*" episode remaining to be shot, Sinclair withdrew his support and the project collapsed. Eisenstein returned to Russia where, in his absence, Stalin had consolidated his rule. Eisenstein would direct again, but only after recanting his earlier "formalist excesses"—a twisted analogue of Kazan's performance before HUAC.

[9] Jay Leyda's assemblage of this material in the 255 minute *Eisenstein's Mexican Film: Episodes for Study* (1958) is the most comprehensive account of Eisenstein's Mexican work.

[10] For a more comprehensive discussion of Ford's visual style see: J. A. Place, *The Non-Western Films of John Ford* (Secaucus, NJ: Citadel Press, 1979); and J. A. Place, *The Western Films of John Ford* (Secaucus, NJ: Citadel Press, 1974).

Works Cited

Ceplair, Larry, and Steven Englund. *The Inquisition in Hollywood*. Berkeley: University of California Press, 1983.

Ciment, Michel. *Kazan on Kazan*. New York: Viking Press, 1974.

Kazan, Elia. "A Statement." *New York Times* 12 April 1952: 7 (a paid advertisement).

Trussell, C. P. "Elia Kazan Admits He Was Red in '30's." *New York Times* 12 April 1952: 8.

Changing Attitudes Toward Steinbeck's Naturalism and the Changing Reputation of *East of Eden*: a Survey of Criticism Since 1974

Charles L. Etheridge, Jr.

Until a few years ago, John Steinbeck's literary reputation depended upon how critics perceived his naturalism. As long as he wrote in what was perceived as a naturalistic vein, he received high praise. When his work became less overtly naturalistic, his reputation declined drastically. During the past fifteen years this pattern of criticism has changed as critics have begun to question whether or not Steinbeck was a naturalist.

No novel is a better barometer of how Steinbeck's reputation is faring than *East of Eden*. Upon its initial publication, it was considered a disaster; now some scholars call it Steinbeck's finest work. The purpose of this study is to survey how the perception of Steinbeck's naturalism has changed since the early 1970s, when scholars began to reevaluate Steinbeck's post-World War II fiction, and to speculate on how these changes have affected the reevaluation of *East of Eden*.

The Steinbeck Society Session at the 1974 Modern Language Association Convention marks the beginning of the reevaluation of Steinbeck's Naturalism. These papers were collected and published in a special issue of the *Steinbeck Quarterly* in 1976. In his "Introduction," Warren French divides Steinbeck's work into two distinctive categories: the "Naturalistic" works and the "Dramas of Consciousness," placing both *The Grapes of Wrath* and *East of Eden* in the latter category. That he grouped these two novels into the same category marks a departure from previously held views such as the one Leo Gurko stated in his 1952 review of *East of Eden*: "The Steinbeck who was as much the genius of the 30's as Sinclair Lewis was of the 20's is scarcely in evidence" (235).

French continued to explore what he felt was a change on the part of Steinbeck from naturalistic to other forms of writing in "John Steinbeck: A Usable Concept of Naturalism," originally published in 1975. French finds three distinctive stages in the novelist's naturalism. Steinbeck's first two works exhibited no naturalism, the works from *Pastures of Heaven* to Chapter 14 of *The Grapes of Wrath* are decidedly naturalistic, and everything from that chapter on is neither naturalistic nor post-naturalistic. French concludes that in 1938 Steinbeck "was shaken out of the pessimistic viewpoint undergirding [his naturalistic novels]" (78) and points to Lee's speech explaining the significance of the "thou mayest" translation of *timshel* to show that "Steinbeck's post-World War II novels . . . are not naturalistic."

Although it was probably not apparent in 1975, the concluding sentence of French's essay marks an important step forward both in Steinbeck criticism and in the reevaluation of *East of Eden*:

> Apparently from his observation during and after World War II, he reached the conclusion that man must take responsibility for his actions and that man is capable—however reluctantly—of taking this responsibility. (78)

Unlike critics who had previously written on *East of Eden*, French was not holding Steinbeck to a preconceived standard of what his work should have been like. By concluding that Steinbeck's apparent departure from naturalism was a result of a conscious artistic and philosophical choice, French anticipates a generation of critics who will begin to examine and appraise the artistic choices Steinbeck made and the changes he underwent, rather than making the *a priori* assumptions that the later works were different from the earlier and are therefore inferior.

One of the most damning comments made about *East of Eden* was that in it Steinbeck virtually abandoned naturalism. Yet in papers such as Peter Copek's "Steinbeck's 'Naturalism?,'" critics began to question an assumption which a critic writing two decades earlier would have thought self-evident and unquestionable: that John Steinbeck was a naturalist. While Copek does find strong evidence of naturalistic elements in Steinbeck's fiction, he concludes that such elements do not necessarily a

naturalist make; he does not find the author of *East of Eden* or
The Grapes of Wrath a naturalist "in that this does not lead to a
pessimistic vision, a cynical vision, or even one which I could
comfortably describe as a fiction whose characters are 'at the
mercy of' omnipotent determining forces" (10).

Copek then points to a passage from Steinbeck's own
work which apparently refutes a conventionally naturalistic
reading of his work: "whoever employs this type of [non-teleo-
logical] thinking with other than few close friends will be referred to as detached, hard hearted, or even cruel. Quite the
opposite seems to be true. Non-teleological methods more than
any other seem capable of great tenderness, of an all-embracing-
ness which is rare otherwise" (*Log* 147). Copek continues, "such
thinking-without-blaming becomes 'living into'" (11). Rather
than seeing Nature as something which places people "at the
mercy of omnipotent determining forces," Steinbeck finds an
"almost spiritual" quality in nature. What critics call Steinbeck's
naturalism should instead be referred to as "ecology" or "a spirit
of ecstasy" (12). Copek affirms the label Woodburn Ross placed
on Steinbeck in 1949: "Naturalism's High Priest" (206). But
Copek is careful to emphasize a less often-quoted passage from
Ross in which he notes that Steinbeck was "the first . . . to build a
mystical religion upon a naturalistic base" (Ross 214). Copek
stresses over and over that when the term "naturalism" is used
in conjunction with the work of John Steinbeck, it should not be
confused with the naturalism of a Stephen Crane or a Frank
Norris or an Ernest Hemingway.

Donald Pizer, author of a number of books on naturalism,
reinforces Copek's thesis when he says, "I am uncertain that calling John Steinbeck a naturalist offers a useful insight into the
distinctive nature of his work or of his literary imagination"
(12). Like Copek, Pizer believes that "the term is too encrusted
with the clichés and polemics of past literary wars to serve as a
guide to the complex individuality of either a major Steinbeck
novel or Steinbeck's work as a whole." Clearly, both critics felt
in 1974 that the term "naturalism" as it had come to be understood was "not particularly useful" when applied to Steinbeck.

Such comments show the beginning of a movement toward a reevaluation of Steinbeck's work, and they question
previously held views. And it is not unreasonable that such a
critical reexamination may ultimately rejuvenate Steinbeck's
literary reputation. Pizer implies that perhaps Steinbeck's work

has been read in a less than advantageous light when he says, "it would probably be disastrous to attempt a complete explication of a Steinbeck novel as a reflection of naturalistic themes and techniques" (12). Ultimately, Pizer concludes that the naturalistic elements in Steinbeck's writing bear stronger affinity to the naturalists of the nineteenth century than of the twentieth.

Although in their discussion of Steinbeck's naturalism critics such as Pizer, Copek, and French do not always consider *East of Eden*, the issue of Steinbeck's naturalism is nevertheless central to an understanding of how critics perceive the book. One of the most bitter criticisms leveled against the novel by its earliest reviewers was that in it Steinbeck "abandoned" his naturalism. It would be inaccurate to say that the naturalism they found missing had never been there, but it would not be incorrect to look at the comments of a Pizer or of a French and conclude that the naturalism Steinbeck displayed in *East of Eden* is not the naturalism the book's reviewers expected to see. Whatever the critics ultimately conclude about it, the issue of what form of naturalism is present in Steinbeck's writing will appear again and again in criticism which seeks to reevaluate the work.

John Ditsky sought to explain the apparent change in Steinbeck's style in the first chapter of his 1977 book *Essays on East of Eden*. Entitled "Toward a Narrational Self," Ditsky's essay deals mainly with biographical elements, showing passages from Steinbeck's works and letters in the 30s and 50s and using them as examples of how Steinbeck's work changed. For the Steinbeck of the 1930s, the role of the artist is to become "merely a recording consciousness, judging nothing, simply putting down the thing" (1); as a result the author "developed the device of the objective and dispassionate narrational voice."

Later, as Steinbeck's interests changed, he became less concerned with the idea of "group-man," a semi-deterministic theory about the biological nature of man which is central to what is probably the most naturalistic of Steinbeck's novels, *In Dubious Battle*, and informs the earlier chapters of *The Grapes of Wrath*.

In a letter which bears a strong resemblance to Chapter 13 of *East of Eden*, Steinbeck recants much of his previous belief in group man:

> I think I believe one thing powerfully—that the only creative thing our species has is the individual, lonely mind. Two people can create a child but I know of no other thing created by a group. The group ungoverned

by individual thinking is a horrible destructive principle. (Ditsky 4)

At this point, says Ditsky, "John Steinbeck has finally resolved
the issue of the group-man by returning to something like the
Christian idea of moral responsibility—and is ready to incorpo-
rate the changes in his attitudes, and in himself as a person, into
the novel" (4).

Ditsky maintains, as does French in "A Usable Concept of
Naturalism," that the break from naturalism apparent in *East of
Eden* is a stage in Steinbeck's development as artist. Ditsky takes
his case farther than do either French or Copek, and provides for
the first time in print an overt denial of Steinbeck's naturalism,
saying, "Throughout a lifetime of writing third-person fiction,
John Steinbeck had resisted the temptation to moralize, but he
had done so at the cost of sundering spirit and substance. The
price of his apparent objectivity was a *mistaken reputation as a
naturalist, however impressive the achievement*" (13, emphasis
added). Ditsky's position is clear; he is dissatisfied with prevail-
ing wisdom about Steinbeck and about *East of Eden* and, like
French and other critics who question Steinbeck's naturalism,
feels that aspects of Steinbeck's art are as yet unexplored. It is
Ditsky who labels much Steinbeck criticism "cookie cutter" (ix).

The question of naturalism and other strong disagree-
ments with previous Steinbeck criticism figure prominently in
Karen J. Hopkins' "Steinbeck's *East of Eden*: A Defense." Hopkins echoes Ditsky's commentary about "cookie cutter criticism"
when she notes "that most critics who read *East of Eden* expect it
to live up to some standard they've set, either for the novel as a
genre, or for Steinbeck in particular, especially the Steinbeck of
The Grapes of Wrath" (63). Furthermore, "both points of view
respond to conventions rather than to the individual work."
Like Ditsky, Hopkins feels that commentary about *East of Eden*
has been prescriptive rather than descriptive. Steinbeck irritated
a generation of critics by violating these conventions, or, as
Hopkins puts it, "there are certain things which can't be done in
a novel, and Steinbeck does them, QED" (63).

Borrowing from Charles Child Walcutt's *American Literary Naturalism: A Divided Stream*, Hopkins notes that "American naturalism has refused to accept" that "the mind is merely
a chemical reaction" (65). In other words, American literary
naturalism has tended to be idealistic. In *East of Eden*, Steinbeck

articulated this tension between naturalism and idealism by incorporating elements of both.

Many critics have considered this novel anti-naturalistic because of the Old Testament elements and the discussion of *timshel*. However, says Hopkins, "The problem with this . . . is that the universe of the novel is as fiercely deterministic as even the most determined naturalist could want, more deterministic and much less pleasant, in fact, than exterior nature in some of Steinbeck's other novels" (67).

Hopkins also says that the essential element in *East of Eden* is the way characters react to their universe; she divides the characters in the novel into two categories: "those who tend to fictionalize and those who tend to analyze" (68). Characters who hold too closely to their fictions—Cyrus, Aaron, Cathy—are often destroyed. Put another way, "Man, enjoying a narrow and therefore false security in his ability to decipher and understand his surroundings, is suddenly destroyed or nearly destroyed by the intrusion of facts that imagination has refused to ack-nowledge" (68). The world of this novel is naturalistic.

Hopkins' study is instructive for a variety of reasons. Ob-viously, this work is a landmark in that it is the first article in a critical collection or journal which openly praises *East of Eden*. Also, it is instructive to note the way in which Hopkins summa-rizes and appraises earlier criticism of the work; to her it is a book whose reputation has sunk low enough (and in her opin-ion, unfairly so) that she feels it needs defense. Her reasoning anticipates Steinbeck criticism in the 1980s which seeks to reevaluate Steinbeck's naturalism.

During the 80s, the view that Steinbeck never was a naturalist gathered momentum. Robert DeMott's view, which he himself labels "extremely revisionary," stems from the proposition that "we have misread Steinbeck" who is "primarily a Romantic ironist, who experimented tirelessly with varying formal and technical elements in his fiction, and maintained an intense lifelong interest in psychology, myth, and the shaping processes of the creative imagination" ("The Interior Distances of John Steinbeck" 87-88). DeMott, who bases his case solely on Steinbeck's post-1945 fiction, notes that "in his later years, from 1945 on, he consciously moved toward fabulation . . . in order to explore the implication inherent in the structural and epistemo-logical tradition of the Romantic expressive fictional line" (88). Most of DeMott's premise hinges upon his discussion of the "interior life" of certain characters in *East of Eden* and *Winter of Our Discontent* (a more detailed analysis of this argument follows here in discussion of changing critical reactions toward Steinbeck's characters such as Kate/Cathy). DeMott concludes his discussion of Steinbeck's "Romanticism" with a quote from *Travels With Charley*: "I am happy to report that in the war between reality and romance, reality is not the stronger" (136). DeMott is not the first to find Romantic tendencies in Steinbeck, but he is among the first to view these tendencies positively.

DeMott backs away from his somewhat radical suggestion in the last sentence of his essay by saying, "It is time, I suggest, to recognize Steinbeck's adherence not only to the tradition of mimetic or empirical writing, but to the larger and infinitely more exciting tradition of Romantic fictionalizing" (99); apparently Steinbeck used not only naturalistic elements but other elements as well.

DeMott is not alone in suggesting that Steinbeck should be read as a Romantic rather than a Naturalist. In 1979, Daniel Buerger writes that "the hero of *East of Eden* is the Romantic 'I' narrator" (12). By 1980, Paul McCarthy can write of "Steinbeck's Realism" as a "necessary realignment" to aid in the reading of Steinbeck's post-World War II fiction: "romance provides . . . [the] influence and mode in *East of Eden*" (118) and "something romantic is perceptible in the general patterns of *East of Eden*" (119).

Although it is risky to use a term such as "consensus" in connection with any Steinbeck novel, one might say that two of the most recent and influential works concerning Steinbeck have reached some sort of consensus in Steinbeck's naturalism. The first is Jackson J. Benson's *The True Adventures of John Steinbeck, Writer*, a book which has rapidly become the "standard" biography of the writer. Benson contends that Steinbeck was a naturalist, but differed from other American writers of this tradition: "he would become, to use a term more familiar to those involved in literature, the most thoroughgoing naturalist among modern writers" (236). What distinguishes Steinbeck's particular brand of naturalism was that "he was the only major writer within the American tradition of naturalism who reacted to science in a positive way, embraced a scientific perception of the universe with enthusiasm, and who knew something about science" (244). Furthermore, "Steinbeck's own lack of ego made it easier for him to accept the relative unimportance of man and turn instead to a calm and even joyful realization of man's interdependence with the whole of nature." The works of other naturalistic writers constitute something of a lament; Steinbeck accepted this view of the universe.

Benson does not view *East of Eden* as a "departure" or an "abandonment" of naturalism. Rather, he feels that it was an "outgrowth" of Steinbeck's naturalism, a further formulation or refinement of an idea he had worked out in his previous novels:

> Basic to his philosophy and carried over into *East of Eden* are the beliefs that man is but a small part of a large whole that is nature and that this whole is only imperfectly understood by man and does not conform to his schemes or wishes. Furthermore, as a part of nature, man often obscures his place and function and the true nature of his environment by putting on various kinds of blinders—whereas it is essential to both his happiness and his survival that he learn to see himself and his surroundings . . . In *East of Eden*, Steinbeck adds a further element, prompted by his own recent struggle to survive and his concern for the future of his sons: in this materialistic, mechanistic universe, is there any chance for the individual to affect his own destiny? (236-37)

Benson's view gains strength because he is the "authoritative" biographer of Steinbeck. His opinion, as well, anticipates the increasingly accepted stance that *East of Eden* is philosophically consistent with Steinbeck's previous fiction. This is as "revisionary" as DeMott's thesis that Steinbeck was never a naturalist. And although Benson does not suggest that *East of Eden* is Steinbeck's best novel (in fact, he finds it seriously flawed), neither does he suggest that the work is without merit or reflects a "decline" in the novelist's powers.

John Timmerman's view, put forth in his 1986 *John Steinbeck's Fiction: The Aesthetics of the Road Taken*, takes a synthetic view, somewhere between that of Benson, who called Steinbeck "the most thoroughgoing naturalist" in American letters, and DeMott, who denies that Steinbeck ever was a naturalist. Instead, Timmerman finds in Steinbeck a "supernatural naturalism" and "a world which God has departed, like the dissipation of other ancient myths" (15). Timmerman places this aspect of Steinbeck's naturalism "solidly within the framework of his literary precursors" such as Crane, Hart, or Dreiser (26).

However, Steinbeck is also outside the naturalist tradition; "the term 'naturalistic' simply will not do as a final description of Steinbeck's view of humankind" (29). Instead, he "finds a supernatural power and presence observable *in* the natural, in the flora and the fauna and earth itself, and in humankind" (29). Where Crane would find the cosmos indifferent or perhaps even hostile, Steinbeck would find something which is nurturing and generative. He "probes the supernatural with typology and symbolism" (30).

In *East of Eden*, says Timmerman, Steinbeck's conception was basically naturalistic:

> Furthermore, its vastness was compelling to him. Instead of being a small slice of life like *Tortilla Flat*, *Cannery Row*, or *Sweet Thursday*, this work took on the whole life. It contained in practice the theory of *The Log from the Sea of Cortez*—that all life must be seen whole in its whole environment, in relation to the all. It would bring all the threads together for him. It is no accident that over and over in *Journal of a Novel* he concludes a letter to Covici with this phrase: "I will get to my knitting." (211)

Although Timmerman's view is unique, it presents a plausible synthesis of other views.

The various attitudes towards Steinbeck's naturalism, particularly its relationship to the novel under discussion, indicate recent changes in critical perception. Certain assumptions are simply no longer held or clung to. The issue of whether or not Steinbeck "declined" is no longer argued and, while the question has never been resolved, it has been replaced by new and perhaps more productive studies which examine the wealth of the Steinbeck canon. Perhaps the clearest indication that *East of Eden* is finally being given a close reading and judged on its own merits is that many studies of the novel make no mention of *The Grapes of Wrath*. Perhaps Steinbeck critics have abandoned the "cookie cutter" John Ditsky complained of more than a decade ago.

Works Cited

Benson, Jackson J. *The True Adventures of John Steinbeck, Writer*. New York: Viking Press, 1984.

Bloom, Harold. *Modern Critical Views: John Steinbeck*. New York: Chelsea House, 1987.

Buerger, Daniel. "'History' and Fiction in *East of Eden* Criticism." *Steinbeck Quarterly* 14 (1981): 6-14.

Copek, Peter. "Steinbeck's 'Naturalism'?" *Steinbeck Quarterly* 9 (1976): 9-12.

DeMott, Robert. "The Interior Distances of John Steinbeck." *Steinbeck Quarterly* 12 (1979): 86-99.

—. "Mapping *East of Eden*: Introduction to the 1979 MLA/Steinbeck Society Meeting Papers." *Steinbeck Quarterly* 14 (1981): 4-5.

Ditsky, John. *Essays on East of Eden*. Steinbeck Monograph Series, 7, 1977.

French, Warren. "Introduction." *Steinbeck Quarterly* 9 (1976): 8-9.

—. "John Steinbeck: A Usable Concept of Naturalism." In Bloom. 63-78.

Gurko, Leo. "Steinbeck's Later Fiction." *The Nation* 175 (22 September 1952): 235-36.

Hopkins, Karen J. "Steinbeck's *East of Eden*: A Defense." *Essays on California Writers*. Ed. Charles L. Crow. Bowling Green: Bowling Green State University Press, 1978. 63-78.

Pizer, Donald. "John Steinbeck and American Naturalism." *Steinbeck Quarterly* 9 (1976): 12-15.

Ross, Woodburn. "John Steinbeck: Naturalism's Priest." Eds. E. W. Tedlock and C. V. Wicker *Steinbeck and His Critics: A Record of Twenty-Five Years*. Albuquerque: University of New Mexico Press, 1957. 206-15.

Steinbeck, John. *East of Eden*. New York: Penguin Books, 1952, 1984.

—. *The Log from the Sea of Cortez*. New York: Penguin Books, 1941, 1952, 1983.

—. *Travels with Charley in Search of America*. New York: Penguin Books, 1961, 1984.

Tedlock, E. W. and C. V. Wicker. *Steinbeck and His Critics: A Record of Twenty-Five Years*. Albuquerque: University of New Mexico Press, 1957.

Timmerman, John. *John Steinbeck's Fiction: The Aesthetics of the Road Taken*. Norman: University of Oklahoma Press, 1986.

The Shameless Magpie:
John Steinbeck, Plagiarism,
and the Ear of the Artist

John H. Timmerman

In 1962 John Steinbeck wrote Louis Paul, "Let's face it. In 60 years I've left a lot of tracks" (*SLL* 751). Indeed he did, but were they all his own? Steinbeck possessed an inquisitive and intellectually acquisitive mind, relentlessly pursuing arcane trails of interest and freely collecting souvenirs of his interests along those trails.

East of Eden demonstrates well the extent of Steinbeck's borrowing and influences. Steinbeck considered the novel to be one of his major works, so much so that he often referred to all his earlier work as practice for it. The novel had been in his mind as early as the 1930s; actual preparation began in the mid-1940s; a start on it occurred in 1948; its writing was finished in July 1952.[1] *East of Eden* may have been of such importance for Steinback because it was, in part, his story, his family, set in his home place. Yet the influences upon this uniquely personal novel are huge. Scholars have observed echoes and borrowings from the Bible, from Milton's *Paradise Lost*, from Lewis Carroll's *Alice's Adventures in Wonderland*, from Raoul Faure's *Lady Godiva and Master Tom*, from Erich Fromm's *Psychoanalysis and Religion*, from *Dr. Gunn's Family Medicine*, from Nathaniel Hawthorne, Marcus Aurelius, Herodotus, Plutarch, Malory, and Henry James.[2] One begins to wonder what belonged to Steinbeck himself.

Questions about Steinbeck's borrowing, ranging from innuendos whispered here and there to blatant vilification, have been around for a long time. My intention is to investigate and respond to those charges against Steinbeck, and to provide an accounting for the artist's use of sources by examining Steinbeck's short story, "Johnny Bear."

To do so, however, several distinctions should be made. For example, we should recognize, first of all, that the general area of influence, slippery and uncertain as it is, does not constitute plagiarism. An author who goes through life unaffected by the ideas of others probably writes popular romances or farming manuals rather than imaginative literature. Steinbeck's eclectic, probing mind soaked up ideas, whether they were Ed Ricketts' speculations on marine biology or Carl Jung's speculations on the subconscious. He listened avidly to stories by Beth Ingels and his Aunt Molly about the Corral de Tierra and used them freely in *The Pastures of Heaven*. Susan Gregory's stories about paisanos slipped into *Tortilla Flat*. He listened to Cicil McKiddy, Caroline Decker, and Francis Whitaker and wrote *In Dubious Battle*. He milked Tom Collins for everything he could get on the migrants and used the information in *The Grapes of Wrath*. He read the Bible in several different versions and incorporated both biblical themes and symbolism in *The Grapes of Wrath* and *East of Eden*. *The Winter of Our Discontent* is a tapestry of influences ranging from the Bible to Carl Jung, and perhaps, as Donna Gerstenberger suggests, to T. S. Eliot. Such influences bear the mark of an active mind wrestling with great ideas and allowing them to seep into the shaping of the artwork. Every artist does this. Ernest Hemingway pointed out that "If a writer stops observing he is finished. But he does not have to observe consciously nor think how it will be useful . . . Everything he sees goes into the great reserve of things he knows or has seen" (Plimpton 198). Marianne Moore observed that "If you are charmed by an author, I think it's a very strange and invalid imagination that doesn't long to share it" (Plimpton 65).

Steinbeck's life, thinking, and work have rewarded critical investigation into literary borrowings, for his was a life cast in reading, his was a thinking shaped by stimulating ideas, and his was a work that bears echoes ranging across the course of literary history. Yet he has rightly been hailed as one of the most original of American authors, doggedly pursuing his own way, telling his own stories, marked by his own style. Robert DeMott notes Steinbeck's abhorrence of plagiarism, yet acknowledges that here was an author deeply influenced by his reading. In *Steinbeck's Reading*, Robert DeMott argues that

> Beginning in the early 1920s . . . Steinbeck's reading in-
> formed his art. It was informed, that is, in the widest
> sense, ranging from oblique suggestions and resonant
> echoes to direct influences and even some shameless bor-
> rowings. This is not to accuse him of plagiarism, which
> he consciously avoided to the best of his knowledge and
> characteristically abhorred. (DeMott xx)

DeMott points out that while "Steinbeck was not above pilfering from the library of available material," it should be clear that "he asserted imaginative dominion over those appropriated elements by transmuting them in such a way that they became his own fictive property" (DeMott xx).

Though all writers draw from the literature of the past, a bit more serious in relation to charges of plagiarism is the issue of imitation. Whatever the motivating factors—to master admired techniques, to break into print on the heels of one who has already done so—imitation often forms the apprenticeship of a young writer and is frequently an uncontrollable response to works admired. Imitation is not necessarily a bad thing for a young writer finding his or her way in the forest of publication. The woods are deep and threatening, and one needs a path to follow.

In his early stages of writing, Steinbeck was driven by several forces: the urge to tell a story was primary among them, but he also desperately wanted to publish his work and to earn some money by it. Steinbeck's most original works during the 1920s were his fiery satires, including parts of "Fingers of Cloud," and "Adventures in Arcademy," both of which were first published in the *Stanford Spectator*, and "Saint Katy the Virgin," which was first drafted in poetic form while he was a student in Stanford Professor Edward Hulme's class in European thought and culture, but was not published until late 1936 when Pascal Covici brought it out in a Christmas edition of 199 signed and numbered copies. Satire, however, is a luxury only of very great writers and students. But localized satire serves poorly to pave a way into a larger literary market. And Steinbeck desperately wanted to crack that market.

His first effort was *Cup of Gold*, a frank imitation of swashbuckling romances that were the rage at the time, particularly Rafael Sabatini's *Captain Blood*. Also a popular writer of romances in the 1920s was James Branch Cabell. In *John Steinbeck: The Good Companion*, Carlton Sheffield remarks: "A stronger literary influence on John's developing style was the work of James Branch Cabell, whose delicate ironies and stylistic arabesques for a time hypnotized many of the would-be writers of the 1920s. We read and admired *Jurgen* together and in our letters and literary experiments, we strove to emulate its polished frivolities."[3] R. S. Hughes has observed in *Beyond the Red Pony* that "The setting and characters of 'The Gifts of Iban' are nearly identical to those in chapters three and four of Cabell's *Jurgen*" (Hughes 26). Steinbeck himself was well aware of this influence. To A. Grove Day, he wrote in 1929: "the book [*Cup of Gold*] accomplished its purgative purpose . . . I think I have swept all the Cabellyo-Byrneish preciousness out for good" (*SLL* 17).

The highly imitative *Cup of Gold* bears another different significance for this study, however, in that it was one of two cases of possible plagiarism of Steinbeck's work by others. In 1939 Berton Braley published an epic poem called *Morgan Sails the Caribbean*, using characters and events from Steinbeck's novel. Harry Thornton Moore recounts the situation:

> Braley explains this by saying that "In the course of reading for background to the Morgan story Mr. Steinbeck's work was consulted as historical material, and the author of this ballad absorbed, as historical facts, incidents that were actually fictional inventions of Mr. Steinbeck." Steinbeck didn't object, and wrote "this troubador" (as Braley calls himself) a note which was printed in the foreword to *Morgan Sails the Caribbean*. This said in part: "It is far from unpleasant for a writer to find that some of his building or design has been found valid. Literatures are built in exactly this way. Please feel free to use what you wish of my work, subconsciously or consciously. (Moore 17)

Perhaps Steinbeck acknowledged in part his own practice.

The second instance in which the issue of plagiarism of Steinbeck's work arose reveals his sensitivity to the issue. Steinbeck wrote *The Red Pony* stories from May, 1933, to Winter, 1934, a period during which he also drafted *Tortilla Flat*, "The Murder," and "The Chrysanthemums." Marjorie Kinnan Rawlings began work on *The Yearling* in March, 1936, over two years after "The Gift" had been published in the *North American Review*. Rawlings worked on the book for well over a year, at one point throwing out the manuscript altogether, restarting, and

finally completing it in December, 1937. When it did appear in
the spring of 1938, *The Yearling* became an immediate best seller,
winning the Pulitzer Prize for that year.[4] The potential conflict
arose from the fact that both *The Red Pony* and *The Yearling* featured young protagonists named Jody who have unusually close
relationships with animals. Steinbeck was aware of the similarity, for in February, 1941, with plans underway to film *The Red
Pony*, he wrote to Elizabeth Otis: "I wish you would read The
Yearling again. Just a little boy named Jody has affection for a
deer. Now I know there is no plagiarism on The Red Pony. But
we are going to make The Red Pony, and two stories about a little boy in relation to animals is too much, particularly if in both
cases the little boy's name is Jody. Will you see if we can't stop
them from using the name and as much of the story as seems
possible? If we don't want money we might easily get a court
order" (*SLL* 255). While Steinbeck himself recognized the im-
probability of any plagiarism, the similarities between the two
works did make him mindful of how fine the line between coincidence and plagiarism could be.

While *Cup of Gold* was his first imitative effort to wrest a
pot of green from the publishing world, his second was the ill-
fated *Murder at Full Moon by Peter Pym*, an unpublished
manuscript held by the University of Texas at Austin. The
manuscript has been best described by Jackson J. Benson as
"Jungian-flavored mumbo jumbo" (Benson 207). Probably the
less one says about this wild, burlesque detective story set in
Cone City the better, but to the point here it must be said that
Steinbeck did deliberately set out to imitate the popular detective
story of the time.

The detective story, of which Steinbeck generally held a
low view, was to have repercussions years later. It is clear that
the major influence behind *Murder at Full Moon* was Edgar
Allan Poe, whose works Steinbeck had read as a teenager. In
May, 1954, Steinbeck wrote the Poe-esque narrative "The Affair
at 7, Rue de M—" for the French periodical *Figaro*, which published it in the August 28, 1954, issue. The French appetite for
Poe had always been large, and perhaps Steinbeck capitalized on
that shared affection.

"The Affair" may be built on the foundation of a mystery,
modeled as it is in tone and incidents upon Poe's "The Murders
in Rue Morgue," but it grows quickly into farce. Appropriately
for the Poe-esque ratiocinative detective, the narrator is at first

detached from the events: "I had hoped to withhold from public scrutiny those rather curious events which have given me some concern for the past month" (*Portable* 619). With the dispassionate calm of the empiricist, the narrator states that "I shall set down the events as they happened without comment, thereby allowing the public to judge of the situation" (619).

This detached, rational tone changes dramatically several paragraphs into the story. The sentence describing the narrator's son John is pure Steinbeck, both in the character of the boy (John IV was born on June 12, 1946, and like the character was eight years old), and the language used to describe him: "If one must have an agency in this matter, I can find no alternative to placing not the blame but rather the authorship, albeit innocent, on my younger son John who has only recently attained his eighth year, a lively child of singular beauty and buck teeth" (620). From this point on pretenses are set aside for the most part, and a slapstick plot abetted by puns and asides develops. The narrator happens to be a scholar working on an essay titled "Sartre Resartus." When father and son examine a blob of bubble gum which is now chewing the boy, the narrator observes, "I regarded it with popping eyes."

Had Steinbeck lived in the Renaissance, his early ability to imitate quality would be regarded as a noble thing. The effort of the apprentice writer then was to stylize, improve upon, and complicate what had been appropriated from established masters. Not until the cult of originality arose with Romanticism did literary types begin to cast a demeaning glance upon the practice. The cult of originality still reigns, especially where there is a drought of ideas. It took the genius of an Andy Warhol, a brilliant copyist hailed as an originator because he copied with such audacity, to show us just how deeply common experiences affect artistic making.

In much the same way that Warhol drew attention to the commonplace items that are a part of all our experience, so too the fiction writer makes us mindful of shared experience. One extension of this, when we consider it in the context of plagiarism, is the retelling of a story that is part of a people's tradition.

In 1948 Steinbeck published "The Miracle of Tepayac" in the Christmas issue of *Collier's*. The story of Our Lady of Guadalupe is so well known that Steinbeck undoubtedly heard it often while in Mexico. It is likely that he would have seen the famous shrine at the old basilica (the new one was built in 1976) during his visits to Mexico City. But his attention could also have been drawn to the legend by his reading of Willa Cather's *Death Comes for the Archbishop*, one of several of Cather's books that Steinbeck had in his library. He considered Cather one of the best American authors, and may very likely have read Cather's account of the legend in Chapter Four of the novel.

According to the earliest testimonies, preserved in native Aztec language, Juan Diego and his family were among the first converts to Christianity among the Aztecs. Steinbeck is faithful to the historical circumstance in the opening paragraphs of his story, as he recounts the death of Juan Diego's wife Maria Lucia. Bowed with grief, Juan Diego sets out on Saturday, December 9, 1531, to hear Mass celebrated in Santiago. While walking past the hill, Diego hears his name called out of a bright light emanating from the top of the hill, a pattern in keeping with biblical theophanies in which God reveals himself in a vision of light and by calling the recipient's name.

Juan Diego is told by the Virgin that a temple should be erected at the hill of Tepayac. The implication is that religion belongs among the common people and is not the exclusive province of city officials. Juan Diego's beseeching of the bishop to build a temple is rebuffed twice. On the third time he brings a sign of the Virgin's will by carrying to the bishop a bouquet of roses of Castille (growing out of season) that he picked from the hill of Tepayac and carried in his cloak. When he unfurls the cloak, the roses are still fresh and the Virgin's image appears in the weave of the cloth.

Although Steinbeck adds the fiction-writer's touch to the legend by relaying the troubled emotions and the adamant persistence of Juan Diego in pursuing the Virgin's request, his rendition is completely loyal to the original. He refuses to pursue larger implications, ending the story with the character, Juan Diego, rather than the historical and religious significance of the event, the fact that the revelation was instrumental to the missionizing of Mexico.[5]

We recognize, then, that in his very early work especially there was an imitative quality in Steinbeck. While trying to shoulder his way into recognition, he tried techniques that had proven successful for others. Second, we recognize that Steinbeck was influenced in his reading by a host of authors, but that he channeled such influences in an artmaking inimitably his own. And, third, we recognize that in at least one instance he was so enamored of a tale that he retold it in almost slavish fidelity to the original. Are there, however, more specific instances that thrust us closer to the charge of plagiarism? Three possibilities appear in which charges of plagiarism have been or might be levied. In their order of composition, these are: "How Edith McGillcuddy Met R. L. Stevenson," "The Raid," and *Of Mice and Men*.

One of Steinbeck's closest boyhood friends was Max Wagner. Steinbeck particularly liked to visit the Wagner kitchen where Mrs. Wagner would spin stories of her youth in Salinas, a delight to Steinbeck who already felt the impulse to story-telling in himself. One such story was of how Mrs. Wagner, as a child, had traveled to Monterey by train and there met Robert Louis Stevenson. According to Jackson J. Benson, "In late 1933, she had written to [Steinbeck] to tell him that she liked *To A God Unknown*. Her letter triggered the memory of the story she had told him many years before, and he started writing it shortly thereafter" (Benson 280). Mrs. Wagner had herself written a story of the meeting, and submitted it unsuccessfully to *Reader's Digest* for publication.

Steinbeck wrote Mrs. Wagner in February, 1934, that "I have been doing some short stories about the people of the country. Some of them I think you yourself told me" (*SLL* 94). It may have taken her some time to respond, for not until June 4, 1934, did Steinbeck write again. Apparently this marks the first time that Steinbeck knew that Mrs. Wagner had drafted a copy of the story she had told him some years prior:

> Your letter came this morning. I didn't know you had done a version of the story and I sent mine off with a lot of other stuff. I will do whatever you wish about the affair, divide in case of publication or recall the manuscript. Please let me know...
>
> I'm terribly sorry if I filched one of your stories. I'm a shameless magpie anyway, picking up anything shiny that comes my way—incident, situation or personality. But if I had had any idea, I shouldn't have taken it. I'll do anything you like about it. (*SLL* 95)

Nine days later, he again wrote Mrs. Wagner:

> I am writing to my agents today, asking them to hold up the story. It is awkward for this reason—

> they've had the story for at least two weeks and since
> they are very active, it has undoubtedly gone out.
> However, it can be stopped. I hope you will let me
> know how yours comes out, as soon as you hear. If it
> should happen to have been bought by the time my
> letter reaches New York, it can be held up. Mine, I
> mean . . . Well, I hope nothing untoward happens about
> this story. In sending it away I enclosed a note saying it
> had been told me by you. Plagiarism is not one of my
> sins. I'll write you when I hear any outcome. (*SLL* 96)

During the years that followed, Steinbeck withheld the story. When, a half-dozen years later, Mrs. Wagner had been unable to publish her version, Steinbeck requested permission from her to publish the story. He sold it to *Harper's Magazine* where it was published in August, 1941, and forwarded the payment, $225.00, to Mrs. Wagner. Steinbeck's sensitivity toward Mrs. Wagner in withholding his story, and his magnanimity toward her in forwarding the payment (she was elderly and in very poor health in 1941) are all the more remarkable in that the Edith McGillcuddy story must have had a personal attraction for him, based as it is upon one of his favorite authors and with its close tie to Salinas and Monterey.

While in "Edith McGillcuddy" Steinbeck recast Mrs. Wagner's story in his own telling, in the case of "The Raid" a series of literary echoes suggests a more direct borrowing. The story relates the initiation of a young warrior, Root, into battle at the side of the labor-leader Dick. As the confrontation draws near Root fears that he will run, and that the surge of emotion in the face of the unknown will blot out his conviction in the cause. The story of Root's fear bears striking similarities to that of Henry Fleming in Stephen Crane's *The Red Badge of Courage*. Pieces of conversation are nearly identical. When Henry Fleming questions Jim Conklin about the battle, he asks: "Think any of the boys'll run?" Jim responds: "Oh, there may be a few of 'em run, but there's them kind in every regiment, 'specially when they first goes under fire (Crane 12). When Root first expresses his fear, his comrade Dick warns him that he has to endure the trial:

> "Do you think you'd try to get away, Dick?" Root
> asked.
> "No, by God! It's against orders. If anything hap-
> pens we got to stick. You're just a kid. I guess you'd run

if I let you!"

Root blustered, "You think you're hell on wheels just because you been out a few times. You'd think you was a hundred to hear you talk."

"I'm dry behind the ears, anyway," said Dick.

Root walked with his head down. He said softly, "Dick, are you sure you wouldn't run? Are you sure you could just stand there and take it?" (*Valley* 94)

While Root's fear is very much like Henry Fleming's, Dick is far less tolerant than Jim Conklin in *The Red Badge of Courage*. Nonetheless, he functions in much the same way, as a foil for the younger man's fears. After Jim's discourse in the opening passage of the novel, the "loud soldier" starts to say:

"Oh you think you know—" began the loud soldier with scorn. The other turned savagely upon him. They had a rapid altercation, in which they fastened upon each other various strange epithets. The youth at last interrupted them. "Did you ever think you might run yourself, Jim?" he asked. (13)

In *The Red Badge of Courage*, Henry Fleming gives voice to his fears a second time. It is the night before battle. Everything about him is a confusion in darkness: "From far off in the darkness came the trampling of feet. The youth could occasionally see dark shadows that moved like monsters. The regiment stood at rest for what seemed a long time. The youth grew impatient. It was unendurable the way these affairs were managed. He wondered how long they were to be kept waiting" (15). Similarly, in "The Raid" Root seems to hear footsteps and voices in the night. He wonders how long they will be kept waiting at the deserted store as his anxiety grows:

Root leaned back against the wall again. "I wish they'd come. What time is it, Dick?"

"Five after eight."

"Well, what's keeping them? What are they waiting for? Did you tell them eight o'clock?" (96)

Both Henry and Root undergo the savage rite of battle, are stripped of cowardice and hesitation, and achieve manhood. Both receive their red badges of courage by head wounds. For Henry Fleming it happens like this: "'Well then!' bawled the man in a lurid rage. He adroitly and fiercely swung his rifle. It crushed upon the youth's head" (59). For Root, "A piece of two-by-four lashed out and struck him on the side of the head with a fleshy thump" (103). The result for Henry Fleming is a certain hardening of vision, as he forsakes his religious past: "And at last his eyes seemed to be opened to some new ways. He found that he could look back upon the brass and bombast of his earlier gospels and see them truly. He was gleeful when he discovered that he now despised them" (109). Root is told by Dick to "Lay off that religious stuff," and Root replies, "there wasn't no religion to it. It was just—I felt like saying that. It was just kind of the way I felt" (105).

A third charge of plagiarism came from F. Scott Fitzgerald, who may himself have been influenced by Hemingway's well-known jealousy of Steinbeck's early success. Fitzgerald, who was overseeing a dramatization of "The Diamond as Big as the Ritz" by an amateur group in Pasadena, and who was hoping to have a play produced from *Tender is the Night* in New York, remarked in 1937 that "Mice + Men has been praised all out of proportion to its merits" (Bruccoli and Duggan 483). It was fairly typical of Fitzgerald to denigrate the work of contemporaries who had not publicly supported him. But he overstepped his own precarious boundaries of taste when he wrote Edmund Wilson in 1940:

> I'd like to put you on to something about Steinbeck. He is a rather cagey cribber. Most of us begin as imitators but it is something else for a man of his years and reputation to steal a whole scene as he did in "Mice and Men." I'm sending you a marked copy of Norris' "McTeague" to show you what I mean. His debt to "The Octupus" [sic] is also enormous and his balls, when he uses them, are usually clipped from Lawrence's "Kangaroo." I've always encouraged young writers—I put Max Perkins on to Caldwell, Callaghan, and God knows how many others but Steinbeck bothers me. I suppose he cribs for the glory of the party.[6]

Fitzgerald fires three shots at Steinbeck in close order. Do any of them strike home? The comparison to D. H. Lawrence is one that Fitzgerald suggested several times in his letters, and a similarity between the two does exist in their concepts of nature and religion. If one were pressed to find an artistic tie, it would extend between *The Rainbow* by Lawrence and *To A God Unknown* by Steinbeck, a relationship carefully analyzed by Reloy Garcia in *Steinbeck and D. H. Lawrence: Fictive Voices and the*

Ethical Imperative. The primary relation, according to Garcia, lies in the authors' "clear conceptions of the nature of art and the function of the artist, conceptions often so strikingly similar that one might suppose a kinship or at least an extended correspondence; for this conviction impelled them both: art was moral (Garcia 4). Garcia is careful to present his analysis in terms of observed similarities rather than in terms of direct influence. While several other critics have speculated upon a Lawrence-Steinbeck link, it is difficult to specify particular instances.[7]

Fitzgerald's second and third shots aim at Steinbeck's alleged plagiarism of Frank Norris' *The Octopus* and *McTeague*. In regard to *The Octopus*, the relationship has to be judged as one of historic coincidence, nothing more. Norris' panorama of the San Joaquin valley, with its clashes of workers and ranchers, happens to be a locale similar to that of *In Dubious Battle* and *The Grapes of Wrath*, but a charge of an "enormous debt" of Steinbeck to Norris is untenable.[8]

Several passages from *McTeague*, however, may support Fitzgerald's charge. The first occurs in a sequence of dialogues between Maria Macapa and the junk-dealer Zerkow in chapters three through five. Like Lennie from *Of Mice and Men*, Maria has a dream of great riches which represents her escape from impoverishment. Rather than showing the tenderness that George demonstrates toward Lennie, however, Zerkow en-courages Maria's dream to titillate himself. As he listens to her tale of the golden plates, "He was breathing short, his limbs trembled a little. It was as if some hungry beast of prey had scented a quarry" (Norris 39). Zerkow's encouragement of the dream is almost a kind of masochism as he urges Maria on, tor-turing himself with the vision of wealth: "'Now, just once more, Maria,' he was saying. 'Tell it to us just once more.'" As Maria swings into the familiar litany, Zerkow becomes obsessed by the vision:

> "And it rang like bells, didn't it?" prompted Zerkow.
> "Sweeter'n church bells, and clearer."
> "Ah, sweeter'n bells. Wasn't that punch bowl awful heavy?"
> "All you could do to lift it."
> "I know. Oh, I know," answered Zerkow, clawing at his lips. (54)

While one might observe some echoes in the revelation of the impossible dream, and the pacing of the dialogue, it is clear that Zerkow is utterly bereft of any of the tenderness George shows toward Lennie.

A second possibility appears in the fight between Marcus and McTeague in chapter eleven. When Marcus bites through McTeague's ear, "The brute that in McTeague lay so close to the surface leaped instantly to life, monstrous, not to be resisted" (182). McTeague catches Marcus' wrists in his huge hands— "Gripping his enemy in his enormous hands, hard and knotted and covered with a stiff fell of yellow hair"—and breaks Marcus' arm. Only with Heise crying for McTeague to stop, in the same way George cries out to Lennie as Lennie crushes Curley's hand, does McTeague relent.[9]

We are left with the question of how to assess critically the issue of plagiarism in Steinbeck's work. In the light of his vast achievement, we must admit that the issue is of negligible significance, evident primarily in his apprenticeship years when he was finding his own way as a writer. But the issue may have a critical significance more important than a simple adjudication of moral right or wrong, and more than simply an exoneration of the artist's huge originality. This larger significance, the very reason why it is necessary to explore the subject at all, has to do with the artist's view of artmaking itself. Finally, the significance is not only ethical but also aesthetic.

Viewed in that way, how the mind of the artist functions in the crafting of his art, we are helped considerably by a relatively overlooked short story, "Johnny Bear," one of the most important fictional works in gaining an understanding of Steinbeck's view of the task of the artist. Critical attention toward Steinbeck has turned in recent years from simple evaluation and analysis to studies of the method and philosophy of composition. The unpublished ledger notebooks held by Stanford University, San Jose State University, and the University of Texas at Austin, as well as the published and unpublished letters, have been rich resources for such study. Such study is well-rewarded for, as Tetsumaro Hayashi demonstrates in *John Steinbeck on Writing*, "Steinbeck, as a conscious artist sensitively aware of the process of creative writing, extensively and frequently discussed the concept of writing" (Hayashi 37). His letters and ledgers provide a remarkable and reliable record of that concept of writing.

Other fictional works surely provide valuable clues. "The Chrysanthemums" probes Elisa Allen's gift for planting, likened by Steinbeck to the gift of the fiction writer for nurturing stories. Tularecito's misunderstood gift is like the artist misunderstood by society. Henri, the excessively private artist of *Cannery Row*, and Joe Elegant, the mystic symbolist of *Sweet Thursday*, show us a way that Steinbeck would not go, a kind of aesthetic *via negativa*. But "Johnny Bear" deserves the central place in such works that reveal the mind of the artist. If Steinbeck said of "The Chrysanthemums" that it "is designed to strike without the reader's knowledge" (*SLL* 91), then "Johnny Bear" strikes with the jarring force of whiplash. Steinbeck often spoke of his works having several layers of meaning. Few of them so successfully weave those layers into one whole tapestry as "Johnny Bear." Yet the story is also a masterpiece of veiled disclosure, so that one is hardly aware of those layers of meaning until one steps back a moment to assimilate the whole. The several layers of meaning in the story may be arranged around three narrative focal points: the first-person narrator, the subject Johnny Bear, and the story of the Hawkings sisters.

"Johnny Bear" is one of only two works in *The Long Valley*, and one of very few in Steinbeck's canon, to be narrated in the first person. It is a fairly dangerous point of view, subject to reader distrust and a narrower focus than the third-person narrator that Steinbeck customarily used. The eyes of this narrator are remarkably objective, however, and lend credibility and unity to the diffuse string of events.

A crew foreman on a dredging barge assigned the task of draining the black tule swamps north of Salinas, the narrator is from the working class. As such, he is realistic about his own life—the hard labor of dredging, the fearful accidents that occur—and also about life in the small town of Loma. Disliking the mosquito-choked bunkhouse in the swamp, he takes a room in town with Mrs. Ratz, which room, he observes with acid humor, befits her name.

He is similarly realistic about Loma itself, a weary little town of 200 people, the prominent buildings of which he can list in a very brief sentence. Among those is the Buffalo Bar. Presided over by the dour Fat Carl, the Buffalo is the town newsroom, social life, and shelter. The Buffalo Bar is also a nexus between the narrator and townsmen. The narrator is recognized there, and there also he meets Johnny Bear. The relationship between the narrator and Johnny Bear, however, has to do with a lot more than plot structure; it has a great deal to do with the writer's task.

Though Steinbeck alternated between two titles for his story while drafting it—"Johnny Bear" or "The Sisters"—it was first published in *Esquire* under the title "The Ears of Johnny Bear." The title is applicable, for Johnny Bear, the eavesdropper, is also very much like the ears of the artist listening in on the secret murmurings of life and revealing them to the public. Afflicted with a huge thirst for Fat Carl's whiskey, Johnny Bear reveals an inimitable ability to replay, not just to act out but to replay like a tape-recorder, conversations he has heard. For a whiskey, he turns on the tape of his memory and becomes the person he plays. Johnny Bear is the *idiot savant*, retarded mentally, like Tularecito, but with one great gift. The narrator's friend Alex Hartnell comments that, "'He can photograph words and voices. He [a university expert] tested Johnny with a long passage in Greek and Johnny did it exactly. He doesn't know the words he's saying, he just says them" (*Valley* 149). The narrator, however, asks the hard question: "'But why does he do it? Why is he interested in listening if he doesn't understand?'" (149). Alex's response is that Johnny Bear loves whiskey, but there is more to the answer than this.

When attention turns to the Hawkins sisters, Alex, who has known them best and longest of anyone in Loma, reveals his fears about Johnny Bear's revelations. He realizes that Miss Emalin is "fighting something terrible," and has considered shooting Johnny Bear in order to protect her secret. The narrator responds, "It's not his fault. He's just a kind of recording and reproducing device, only you use a glass of whiskey instead of a nickel" (162). Is this also the task of the artist? To be simply a recording and reproducing device, supplying words without fully understanding their meaning or contexts?

Any answer discerned solely from the character Johnny Bear in the story is insufficient. Also functioning in the story is the narrator, who provides the context of meaning for Johnny Bear's tape-recording of life. As the narrator walks back to Loma after talking with Alex, he reflects, "I smiled as I walked along at the way a man's thought can rearrange nature and experience to fit his thoughts" (162). The artist also rearranges nature and experience to fit his thoughts.

This was to be a view Steinbeck held for the rest of his career. A work grows from the inside out; the experience is arranged by the artist to suggest rather than declare. When Steinbeck wrote of *The Grapes of Wrath* having "five layers" of meaning (*SLL* 178), those layers were the work of a conscious, artistic design, not a tape recording. To Peter Benchley in 1956, Steinbeck wrote:

> A writer out of loneliness is trying to communicate like a distant star sending signals. He isn't telling or teaching or ordering. Rather he seeks to establish a relationship of meaning, of feeling, of observing . . .
>
> Of course a writer rearranges life, shortens time intervals, sharpens events, and devises beginnings, middles and ends, and this is arbitrary because there are no beginnings nor any ends. (*SLL* 523)

During the composition of "Johnny Bear" in 1934, however, Steinbeck had only begun to sense this aesthetic attitude that would later emerge as a creed. "Johnny Bear" is the crucial work in his developing understanding that an artist rearranges observed experience to "establish a relationship of meaning."

Metaphorically, the small rise of Loma is somewhat like the narrator himself, rising above the fogs of recorded experience to arrange experience into a meaningful pattern. It is not an accident that the narrator is by profession the crew foreman of a dredger, draining the swamp, beating back the fog. So, too, the narrator functions for the story.

"Johnny Bear" functions as both a powerful story in its own right and also as an important document in Steinbeck's artistic development. The pairing of the mimetic gift of Johnny Bear and the arranging task of the narrator, however, should not be seen as mutually exclusive polarities, as two different kinds of artistic telling. Rather, they are synchronously merged by the mind of the artist—the one who faithfully represents "what is," then arranges it in such a way that the full life is revealed and that the reader can also "live into" the event.

The story also pertains to the issue of plagiarism. In a sense, the influences, echoes, and imitation we find in Steinbeck's early work are like the ears of Johnny Bear absorbing and relating his experience of an event. But Steinbeck the artist is like the narrator of the story, rising above the given materials to make sense out of them. Steinbeck's success at that task finally lays charges of plagiarism to rest. Even in the few questionable cases, the questions are answered by the unique genius of the artist arranging the given materials in his own way.

"Edith McGillcuddy" is no longer Mrs. Wagner's story, but Steinbeck's creation of the wonder of Edith before the pale, sickly Robert Louis Stevenson. "The Raid" is not *The Red Badge of Courage* rehashed, but is a powerful story of Root's effort to test his political idealism and physical realism. And Lennie is not Zerkow in *McTeague*, but remains the figure of tragic dreams, crazy for one small plot of land he can call his own. We may observe, then, certain influences, echoes, and imitations of other artists in Steinbeck's early work. In fact, we welcome such observations insofar as they reveal the developing mind of the artist. Finally, however, we also observe the domination the mind of that artist exercised over such materials. That recognition lays to rest the charges of plagiarism and establishes the individuality of Steinbeck's work.

Notes

[1] In 1933, Steinbeck wrote George Albee:
> I think I would like to write the story of this whole valley, of all the little towns and all the farms and the ranches in the wilder hills. I can see how I would like to do it so that it would be the valley of the world. But that will have to be sometime in the future. I would take so very long. (*SLL* 73)

The germ of *East of Eden* lies in the idea of writing a history of the valley, having it represent a larger world, and spending a long time writing it. In 1944, Steinbeck announced his intention to begin working on this same novel: "Within a year or so I want to get to work on a very large book I've been thinking about for at least two years and a half. Everything else is kind of marking time" (*SLL* 273).

[2] Robert DeMott has examined many of the sources influencing *East of Eden*. See the "Introduction" to *Steinbeck's Reading: A Catalogue of Books Owned and Borrowed* (New York: Garland Publishing, 1984), xxxii-xliii, and the essays "'Culling All Books': Steinbeck's Reading and *East of Eden*," *Steinbeck Quarterly* 14 (Winter-Spring, 1981): 40-51; "'A Great Black Book': *East of Eden* and *Dr. Gunn's Family Medicine*," *American Studies* 22 (Fall, 1981): 41-57; and "Lady Godiva and Cathy Ames: A Contribution to *East of Eden*'s Background," *Steinbeck Quarterly* 14 (Summer-Fall, 1981): 72-83. Agnes McNeill Donohue has discussed the relationship between Hawthorne and Steinbeck in "'The Endless Journey to No End': Journey and Eden Symbolism in Hawthorne and Steinbeck," *A Casebook on "The Grapes of Wrath"* (New York: T. Y. Crowell, 1968). 257-66.

[3] Carlton Sheffield, *John Steinbeck: The Good Companion* (Portola Valley, CA: American Lives Endowment, 1983). 80. Robert De Mott points out that the character of Henry Morgan was probably influenced by Maxwell Anderson and Lawrence Stallings, *The Buccaneer*, in *Three American Plays* (New York: Harcourt, Brace, Jovanovich, 1926). See *Steinbeck's Reading*, p. 131.

[4] For details of Rawlings' composition of *The Yearling*, see A. Scott Berg, *Max Perkins: Editor of Genius* (New York: E. P. Dutton, 1978).

[5] In his definitive study of the Image of Guadalupe legend in *The Image of Guadalupe: Myth or Miracle?* (Garden City, NJ: Doubleday, 1983), Jody Brant Smith points out that

> News of the miraculous appearance of the Virgin's image on a peasant's cloak spread quickly throughout New Spain. Indians by the thousands, learning that the mother of the Christian God had appeared before one of their own and spoken to him in his native tongue, came from hundreds of miles away to see the image hung above the altar of the new church.
>
> The miraculous picture played a major role in advancing the Church's mission in Mexico. In just seven years, from 1532 to 1538, eight million Indians were converted to Christianity. In one day alone, one thousand couples were married in the sacrament of matrimony.

[6] F. Scott Fitzgerald, *Correspondence of F. Scott Fitzgerald*, ed. Matthew J. Bruccoli and Margaret M. Duggan (New York: Random House, 1980). 612. The letter influenced Wilson's judgments in *The Boys in the Back Room: Notes on California Novelists* (San Francisco: Colt Press, 1941). 41-53.

[7] For other views on the Lawrence-Steinbeck relationship see Richard Peterson, "Steinbeck and D. H. Lawrence," *Steinbeck's Literary Dimension: A Guide to Comparative Studies*, ed. Tetsumaro Hayashi (Metuchen, NJ: Scarecrow Press, 1973), 67-82, and Marilyn Mitchell, "Steinbeck's Strong Women: Feminine Identity in the Short Stories," *Southwest Review* 61 (Summer, 1976): 304-15.

[8] Leonard Lutwack has argued in *Heroic Fiction: The Epic Tradition and American Novels of the Twentieth Century* (Carbondale, IL: Southern Illinois University Press, 1971), that "the line of descent from *The Octopus* to *The Grapes of Wrath* is as direct as any that can be found in American literature" (47). This is true, perhaps, in terms of general locale and theme, but there is little evidence of a direct influence. Steinbeck's style in the novel is distinct, and his subject matter, influenced by first-hand experience and Tom Collins' journals, is quite different.

[9] In "Struggle for Survival: Parallel Theme and Techniques in Steinbeck's 'Flight' and Norris's *McTeague*," *Steinbeck Quarterly* 21 (Summer-Fall, 1988), Elaine Ware demonstrates "that the plot of Steinbeck's 'Flight' clearly parallels the action of the last two chapters in *McTeague*" (97). Her extensive comparisons justify her conclusion that "This knowledge about Steinbeck's reading as well as the internal evidence—that is, the parallel theme and techniques between Norris and Steinbeck outlines here—convince me that Norris was an influence on Steinbeck in 'Flight'" (102-03).

Works Cited

Benson, Jackson J. *The True Adventures of John Steinbeck, Writer*. New York: Viking Press, 1984.

Bruccoli, Matthew J., and Margaret M. Duggan, eds. *Correspondence of F. Scott Fitzgerald*. New York: Random House, 1980.

Crane, Stephen. *The Red Badge of Courage*. Ed. Sculley Bradley, et al. New York: Norton/Critical Edition, 1976.

DeMott, Robert. "Introduction." *Steinbeck's Reading: A Catalogue of Books Owned and Borrowed*. New York: Garland Publishing, 1984.

Garcia, Reloy. *Steinbeck and D. H. Lawrence: Fictive Voices and the Ethical Imperative*. Steinbeck Monograph Series, No. 2. Muncie, IN: Ball State University Press, 1972.

Gerstenberger, Donna. "Steinbeck's American Waste Land." *Modern Fiction Studies* 11 (Spring 1965).

Hayashi, Tetsumaro, ed. *John Steinbeck on Writing*. Steinbeck Essay Series, No. 2. Muncie, IN: Ball State University Press, 1988.

Hughes, R. S., Jr. *Beyond "The Red Pony": A Reader's Companion to Steinbeck's Complete Short Stories*. Metuchen, NJ: Scarecrow Press, 1987.

Moore, Harry Thornton. *The Novels of John Steinbeck: A First Critical Study*. Chicago: Normandie House, 1939.

Norris, Frank. *McTeague*. New York: New American Library, 1964.

Plimpton, George, ed. *Writers at Work: The "Paris Review" Interviews, Second Series*. London: Secker and Warburg, 1963.

Sheffield, Carlton. *John Steinbeck: The Good Companion*. Portola Valley, CA: American Lives Endowment, 1983.

Steinbeck, Elaine, and Robert Wallsten, eds. *Steinbeck: A Life in Letters*. New York: Viking Press, 1975.

Steinbeck, John. *The Long Valley*. New York: Penguin Books, 1986.

—. *The Portable Steinbeck*. Ed. Pascal Covici, Jr. New York: Penguin Books, 1976.